FORT MEADE & THE BLACK HILLS

FORT MEADE
&
THE BLACK HILLS

Robert Lee

University of Nebraska Press

Lincoln & London

Copyright © 1991 by
the University of Nebraska Press
All rights reserved
Manufactured in the
United States of America
The paper in this book meets
the minimum requirements of
American National Standard for
Information Sciences—Permanence of
Paper for Printed Library Materials,
ANSI Z39.48–1984.
Library of Congress Cataloging-in-Publication Data
Lee, Bob, 1920–
Fort Meade and the Black Hills / Robert Lee.
p. cm.
Includes bibliographical references and index.
ISBN 0-8032-2896-1
1. Fort Meade Region (S.D.)—History. 2. Frontier and pioneer
life—South Dakota—Fort Meade Region. 3. Indians of North America—
South Dakota—Fort Meade Region—History. 4. Black Hills (S.D. and
Wyo.)—History. 5. Frontier and pioneer life—Black Hills (S.D. and
Wyo.) 6. Indians of North America—Black Hills (S.D. and Wyo.)—
History. I. Title.
F659.F675L43 1991
978.3'44—dc20 91-4362
CIP

CONTENTS

Illustrations

ACKNOWLEDGMENTS

A work of this magnitude and length of research naturally required considerable assistance and cooperation from a great number of people. Especially helpful over the years of research and writing were the following friends: Erwin and Kip Putnam of Falls Church, Virginia, who housed me while I did research at the National Archives; Major David Super, a former newspaper colleague whose tour of duty with the National Guard Bureau in Washington enabled him to ferret out information on the all-Indian cavalry unit and company of loyalty suspects that served at Fort Meade, as well as on the German POW camp there; David Laudenschlager, who loaned me his microfilm reader for longer than even friendship warrants; Marilyn Bates, who read each chapter as it evolved and offered criticism that greatly improved the manuscript; and my son and daughter-in-law, Mark and Jeanette Lee, who educated me on computer usage and guided me through numerous technical crises.

South Dakota State Historical Society employees who were also of considerable assistance were State Historian Dayton Canaday, Bonnie Graham, John Borst, Ann Jenks, and Nancy Tystad Koupal. The staff of the research division of the North Dakota State Historical Society in Bismarck was helpful too. Local librarians who provided invaluable cooperation and services were Marjorie Pontius of the Deadwood Library and Carol Davis, Arlon Wipf, Rita Schwartz, and most especially, Julie Moore of the Sturgis Public Library. Much help and encouragement was received from Ralph Hackert, Marilyn Bender, Jean Trumpe, and the late Arthur Piehl of the Old Fort Meade Museum Association, as well as from the Sturgis historians Phyllis Egge and Terri Howell. In addition to Piehl, former Fourth Cavalry soldiers who gave me firsthand accounts of Fort Meade's last years were Merton Glover, Paul Ross, Henry Putnam, William Rudebeck, Harold J. Kelley, and Vernon Allison. Francis Langin, also of Sturgis, gave me much useful information about the Civilian Conservation Corps camp at Fort Meade.

Members of the South Dakota congressional delegation helped by cutting through the red tape of the federal bureaucracy in pursuit of research information for me over the years. I am grateful to the late U.S. Senator Karl Mundt, former Senators George McGovern, James Abourezk, and James Abdnor, and Senators Larry Pressler and Tom Daschle for their efforts on my behalf. My wife, Dode, was a constant encouragement to me and inspired me to continue the struggle when the volume of research material threatened to overwhelm me. Lastly, I am grateful to my many history-buff friends who showed their interest in this project by asking, "When are you going to finish that Fort Meade history?" Their persistent prodding was a definite factor in its completion! I am pleased to be able to respond, at long last, "Here it is."

FORT MEADE & THE BLACK HILLS

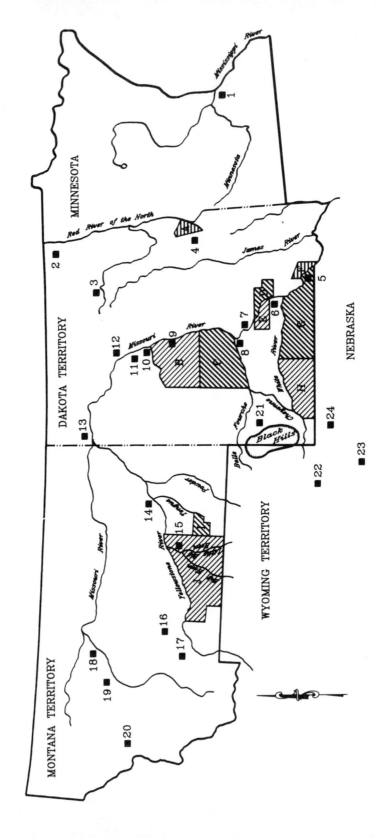

POSTS IN THE DEPARTMENT OF DAKOTA IN 1878, THE YEAR OF FORT MEADE'S
ESTABLISHMENT

MAP LEGEND

1. Fort Snelling (1820–1946)
2. Fort Pembina (1870–95)
3. Fort Totten (1867–90)
4. Fort Sisseton (1864–89)
5. Fort Randall (1856–92)
6. Fort Hale (1870–84)
7. Fort Sully (1863–94)
8. Fort Bennett (1870–91)
9. Fort Yates (1874–1903)
10. Fort Rice (1864–78)
11. Fort Abraham Lincoln (1872–91)
12. Fort Stevenson (1867–83)
13. Fort Buford (1866–95)
14. Fort Keogh (1876–1908)
15. Fort Custer (1877–98)
16. Camp Baker (1869–80)
17. Fort Ellis (1867–86)
18. Fort Benton (1869–81)
19. Fort Shaw (1867–91)
20. Fort Missoula (1877–98)
21. Fort Meade (1878–1944)
22. Fort Fetterman, Wyo. (1867–82)*
23. Fort Laramie, Wyo. (1849–90)*
24. Fort Robinson, Neb. (1874–1948)*

These forts were in the Department of the Platte, commanded in 1878 by General George Crook.

WESTERN INDIAN RESERVATIONS IN THE DEPARTMENT OF DAKOTA

A—Sisseton Indian Reservation
B—Standing Rock Indian Reservation
C—Cheyenne River Indian Reservation
D—Crow Creek Indian Reservation
E—Lower Brulé Indian Reservation
F—Yankton Indian Reservation
G—Rosebud Indian Reservation
H—Pine Ridge Indian Reservation
I —Northern Cheyenne Indian Reservation
J —Crow Indian Reservation

Map drawn by Donald Egge.

xi

THE PLACE FOR A POST

The establishment of a permanent military post in the Black Hills of what was to become Dakota Territory was first proposed in 1857. The post did not come into existence, however, until twenty-one years later. The long delay resulted from the dominance of the northern plains by the far-ranging Sioux Nation. Unlike the frontier forts that played key roles in breaking this dominance, the Black Hills post did not become a reality until the United States had conquered the Sioux, confining them to reservations.

First Lieutenant Gouverneur Kemble Warren, U.S. Corps of Topographical Engineers, was the first to recognize the strategic importance of the Black Hills to the military. He did so in 1857 while exploring the immense Indian country between Fort Laramie in present Wyoming and the Missouri River. On 30 September, Warren climbed to the top of Bear Butte, an isolated peak rising fourteen hundred feet above the plains, on the northeastern edge of the Hills. Below him was the spacious heartland of the nomadic Sioux Nation, with the Black Hills as its center. This would be the proper place, Warren determined, for the army to strike when war with the Sioux broke out. And he considered such a war inevitable. "Here they can assemble their largest force," Warren explained, "and here I believe they would make a stand." He also predicted that the Sioux would not permit occupation of the region "without offering determined resistance."[1]

Warren considered the greatest value of his explorations to be knowledge of the proper routes by which to invade Sioux country and conquer the tribe. He warned that this would require a large military force and recommended that a military post be established in the vicinity. His suggested site was north of the mouth of the Cheyenne River, which embraced the Black Hills between its south and north forks.

Although Warren's visit to the Black Hills was brief, he was there long enough to find gold "in valuable quantities."[2] His findings were supported by Captain William F. Raynolds, who led a military expedition from Fort Pierre on the Missouri River into the Yellowstone country two years later. En route, Raynolds's party found some particles of gold in a small stream northwest of Bear Butte. But the expedition, guided by the noted frontiersman Jim Bridger, continued westward without determining the extent of the gold resources.

Dakota Territory, encompassing all the land north of Nebraska between Minnesota and the Rocky Mountains, was created in 1861. Its assembly adopted two memorials to Congress relating to the Black Hills during the winter of 1865–66. One asked for funds for a geological survey to determine the extent of the region's resources. The second memorialized the secretary of war to locate a military post at the base of the Hills to control the Sioux believed to have taken refuge there. The territorial governor insisted that military protection was necessary if whites were to settle the country in and around the Black Hills. He surmised, correctly, that the Sioux would "dispute our right to occupy any portion" of that country.[3]

The army obtained additional information on the Black Hills country when two of the three columns involved in the Powder River Campaign against the western Sioux in 1865 flanked the region. One column marched from Nebraska along the east base of the Hills to Bear Butte, where a large force of hostile Sioux were believed to be camped. Finding no Indians there, the column linked up with troops that had traveled from Fort Laramie up the west side of the Hills. The combined columns then continued on into the Powder River country. Neither column penetrated into the interior of the Black Hills, but the expeditions confirmed Warren's observations about the best routes for getting to the Hills.

The army had planned to establish a Black Hills post as early as 1865. But the troops scheduled to garrison it were diverted to Minnesota by Indian troubles there. So the Dakota territorial assembly repeated its petition for the Black Hills post in 1866. Lieutenant General William Tecumseh Sherman, the army's top commander, replied that the requested post would have to wait until Congress set the size of the postwar army.[4]

Any hopes the people of Dakota had for an early opening of the Black Hills to white settlement were dashed by the Fort Laramie Treaty of 1868. It created the Great Sioux Reservation, which set aside nearly forty-three thousand square miles, including all of present-day western South Dakota, for the exclusive occupation of that tribe. The treaty contained an important exception, however, that allowed officers, agents, and employees of the government to enter the reservation in the discharge of lawful duties. But no whites were to settle there.[5] The exception provided the rationale for later government excursions onto the reservation. But it did not excuse the hordes of unauthorized whites who invaded the reservation between 1874 and 1876 and brought on the Sioux war that Warren had predicted.

In 1873, when the nation was suffering an economic depression, the Dakota territorial legislature again memorialized Congress for a scientific survey of the Black Hills. This was the only way, it contended, to determine the validity of the reports of gold. The legislature also asked that the region be removed from the Sioux reservation—claiming the reservation was being used as a haven for hostile Indians—and be opened to white settlement.[6]

Widespread drought and an invasion of grasshoppers on the Great Plains the following year gave a sense of urgency to the matter of determining the wealth of the Black Hills. Conditions in Dakota were so bad that the government authorized the army to distribute rations and surplus clothing to the distressed settlers. Many of them, lured by unconfirmed rumors of gold in the Black Hills, joined expeditions then forming along the frontier for an assault on the forbidden region. Proclamations pointing out the illegality of such enterprises were issued by both military and civic authorities but were largely ignored.[7]

The government initially honored its treaty commitment to keep the whites out of the Hills by dispatching troops to intercept the trespassers. Those discovered were arrested and their wagons destroyed. Among those captured were eighteen enlisted men from Fort Randall who had deserted to join the rush to the goldfields. They were returned to their Missouri River post for courts-martial.[8]

Although the army steadfastly carried out its unpopular mission of keeping the Black Hills closed, it quickly recognized that the task was

3

almost impossible. There were just too many gold seekers and two few soldiers available to adequately patrol the immense reservation. It also recognized that the Sioux would resist the white invasion and that war would result—as Warren had prophesied.

Lieutenant General Philip H. Sheridan, commanding the Division of the Missouri, headquartered in Chicago, in 1873 acknowledged that a military post in the Black Hills was needed. "In this way," Sheridan stated, "we could secure a strong foothold in the heart of the Sioux and thereby exercise a controlling influence over these war-like people."[9]

Sheridan's division included five geographic departments, but only two—the Departments of Dakota and the Platte—were directly concerned with affairs on the Great Sioux Reservation and its environs. The Department of Dakota, headed by Brigadier General Alfred H. Terry, was based at Fort Snelling with headquarters in St. Paul. It included the state of Minnesota and the territories of Dakota and Montana. Brigadier General George Crook commanded the Department of the Platte, which was headquartered in Omaha and which included the states of Iowa and Nebraska, the territories of Wyoming and Utah, and a portion of Idaho Territory. On these departments fell the responsibility of keeping whites out of the Sioux country and of preventing the Indians from warring on the frontier settlements.

In the summer of 1874, Sheridan ordered a military reconnaissance of the Black Hills "for the ultimate object of establishing a military post" there. Since previous government explorations had not included the Hills interior, Sheridan believed "knowledge of it might be of great value in case of Indian troubles."[10] Lieutenant Colonel George Armstrong Custer, the flamboyant "Boy General" of Civil War fame, was chosen to lead the expedition. Custer's Seventh Cavalry left Fort Abraham Lincoln, in the northern sector of Dakota Territory, on 2 July and returned sixty days later, covering 1,205 miles on the round trip.

While camped in the southern Black Hills, the expedition found gold "in paying quantities" on French Creek. En route home, the expedition camped near Bear Butte on 14–15 August, and Custer sent out a dispatch that described the agricultural and mineral resources of the Hills. What captured the greatest public attention, of course, was the news about the gold discoveries. Completely missing from Custer's voluminous and detailed reports, however, was any recommendation for a military post in the region. The main purpose of the expedition was lost in the excitement over the gold finds.[11]

General Sheridan, renewing his recommendation for a Black Hills post, later expressed regret that a fort was not established at that time. "Unfortunately for the subsequent history of Indian affairs," Sheridan wrote, "the construction of the post was not authorized until several years later, when disasters had occurred which might have been averted."[12]

The Sioux considered the Custer expedition a blatant violation of the Laramie treaty. But Generals Sherman and Terry, both of whom had served on the commission that had negotiated the treaty, asserted its legality. They pointed to the exception provided for government officers, agents, and employees on assigned missions. Sherman insisted that "the treaty permits of such explorations." Terry wrote that he was "unable to see that any just offense" was given to the Indians by these expeditions. The Sioux disagreed. They called Custer's route to the Black Hills "the Thief's Road" because many of the whites who took the region from them came over it.[13]

In any event, the immediate result of Custer's expedition was a stampede of gold seekers into the Black Hills in undisputed violation of the treaty. In the vanguard was a party of twenty-eight men, one woman and her nine-year-old son from Sioux City, Iowa, who reached the Hills in late December 1874. They erected a stockade on French Creek, near the site where Custer had found gold, and wintered there while prospecting in the vicinity. In April, the party was discovered by a cavalry patrol and escorted out of the Hills.[14] Many other prospectors, however, managed to reach the goldfields undetected. Without winter quarters in the Hills, General Crook reported, it was almost impossible to patrol the region adequately during periods of snow and cold. He proposed that an eight-company fort be established to reduce the hardship on the soldiers patrolling the region.[15]

Moreover, General Sheridan complained of the "double duty" imposed on the army—that of protecting the settlements from Indian raids as well as honoring the treaty commitment to keep whites out of the Black Hills. He recommended action to permanently settle the Black Hills question "and relieve us from an extremely embarrassing duty."[16] President Grant responded by appointing a commission to negotiate with the Sioux for their cession of the Hills.

Controversy over Custer's report of gold in the Hills, a report whose accuracy was questioned in some quarters, led the government to send out yet another expedition in the summer of 1875. Its purpose was to make a more thorough examination of the region's resources than Custer had been able to conduct during his quick trek through the Hills. The expedition was headed by two geologists, Henry Newton and Walter P. Jenney, and was accompanied by an eight-company military escort from Fort Laramie. The expedition spent five months examining the Hills and produced a wealth of technical information, including confirmation of the existence of gold.[17]

Besides gold, the Newton-Jenney expedition also found many illegal miners in the Black Hills. Some of them were evicted in August by troops under General Crook. Others were rounded up by troops under Captain Edwin Pollock, of the Ninth Infantry, who established Camp Collins on French Creek in the fall of 1875. This camp was located at Custer City, founded and named by the miners in honor of the leader whose gold reports had brought them to the Hills. Camp Collins was garrisoned by two companies of cavalry and one of infantry. It had the distinction of being the first military camp of any duration in the Hills. Although its existence was brief, it remained in use longer than the temporary camps of the Custer and Newton-Jenney expeditions. It was abandoned in November when the government suddenly shifted its policy toward the Sioux and the Black Hills.[18]

Grant's commission had failed to gain Sioux approval for cession of the Hills, so the president devised a scheme for forcing the issue. He decided that the treaty prohibition against white intrusions onto the Sioux reservation would remain in force but that no further troops would be sent out to enforce it.[19] The effect of this policy, of course, was a dramatic increase in the number of whites who headed for the Black Hills goldfields in violation of the 1868 treaty. The policy also gave the Sioux the opportunity to conduct raids on the unprotected white invaders without the fear of army retaliation.

If the Sioux went to war over the Hills issue, Grant threatened, he might find it necessary to withhold government supplies to the tribe. He reminded the Sioux that they had been provided with food and other provisions beyond the requirements of the 1868 treaty. Thus, he believed that the government would be justified in cutting off supplies if they continued to resist white expansion into the Hills. Then, in a move that made Sioux resistance a virtual certainty, the president authorized the withdrawal of the troops evicting trespassers from the Hills.[20] In addition, the Sioux hunting bands wintering on the unceded lands of Wyoming and Montana were advised to return to the reservation by 1 January 1876 or be considered hostile. Few of them complied, mainly because of the short notice given them and the difficulty of winter travel. Consequently, the army was charged with forcing their return, and the Sioux Campaign of 1876–77 was born.

That the Black Hills controversy was a significant factor in bringing on the campaign seems incontrovertible, although Sheridan contended otherwise. "It is nonsense to suppose that the Indians now hostile are so from the Black Hills invasion," he wrote. "They wanted to fight and have been preparing for it for years back. It is their profession, their glory and the only thing that stirs them up from complete idleness."[21] At any rate, the Indians opposed the illegal invasion of their Hills by stepping up their attacks on parties en route to the Black Hills or already there.

In June 1876, a small military camp was established at the mouth of Red Canyon in the southern Black Hills to offer protection to travelers coming into the region from the south. Its founding came just as Custer and the Seventh Cavalry were marching to the Little Bighorn River of Montana as part of a three-pronged force aimed at rounding up the "hostiles." The camp at Red Canyon was commanded by Captain William Collier, of the Fourth Infantry, and was garrisoned by a small force of soldiers from Fort Laramie. It was surrounded by a stockade 125 feet square, with bastions on the northeast and southwest corners. The camp was situated along the Cheyenne and Black Hills Stage Line, which had opened a station on the Cheyenne River a few miles to the southwest. Officially carried on the rolls as "Camp at the Mouth of Red Canyon," the post was known locally as "Camp Collier" for its commander. It was abandoned the following June when the stage route was relocated farther west. With its one year of existence, however, Camp Collier was the longest-lived military post in the Black Hills before the legal opening of the area.[22]

Under article 11 of the 1868 treaty the Sioux on unceded lands away

7

from the reservation were entitled to hunt there as long as enough buffalo remained to "justify the chase." Those who failed to return to their reservation as ordered were pursued by the three army columns sent by Sheridan. One, under Colonel Joseph J. Reynolds of General Crook's command, on 17 March destroyed a village occupied by Sioux and their Cheyenne allies on the Powder River. The soldiers also captured the large pony herd there. But Reynolds retreated when the Indians counterattacked and recovered most of their ponies. Three months later, Crook's force from Fort Fetterman was attacked by a large body of Sioux and Cheyennes on the Rosebud River of Montana. Although his soldiers fought off the attackers and held the battlefield, they had taken so many losses after six hours of hard fighting that Crook also retreated. Meanwhile, the two other columns, under Brigadier Generals John Gibbon and Alfred Terry, were closing in on the Indians from the north and the east, respectively.[23]

Ironically, it was Custer and his Seventh Cavalry from Terry's command who caught up with the Indians on the banks of the Little Bighorn River on 25 June. The Sioux and Cheyennes, whose encampment had been greatly enlarged by summer arrivals from the agencies, scored a great victory over Custer and his troopers on that day. He and a large portion of his regiment paid with their lives for their part in precipitating the white invasion of the Black Hills. But it was to be a Pyrrhic victory for the Indians, marking the beginning of the end of their long domination of the northern plains. The army retaliated swiftly by sending exceptionally large numbers of troops into the field against them, forcing their gradual surrender and return to the reservation.

Moreover, an enraged Congress passed an Indian appropriations act that denied government support to bands that engaged in hostilities against the whites. The act also provided that no further funds would be appropriated for the Sioux unless they relinquished their claims to the Black Hills and all the unceded lands outside their reservation.[24] Although Custer had initiated the fight at the Little Bighorn, the government justified these drastic measures on the grounds that it was the Sioux who had failed to keep the peace. Crook claimed there had not been a year since the 1868 treaty that the Sioux had not violated every feature of it. Further, he charged that the Sioux considered the treaty "binding upon us, but not on them."[25] As early as 1873, General Sherman had also complained of Sioux violations of the treaty. He asserted that they had broken it so often that Congress would be justified in abrogating the entire treaty or any part of it.[26]

By the time of the nation's centennial in 1876, the gold frenzy in the Black Hills had shifted from Custer City to Deadwood in the northern Hills. Deadwood, situated at the hub of a cluster of mining camps that lined the adjacent gulches, quickly became the metropolis of the Black Hills. Its population fluctuated from seven thousand to fifteen thousand as successive gold strikes were reported. At its Fourth of July celebration the citizens signed a memorial asking Congress to legalize their presence in the region by extinguishing the Sioux title. They also urged that troops be sent to the Hills to protect the trespassers from the Sioux. The memorial was followed by a petition signed by the mayor, the city council, and 650 citizens asking for a permanent military post in the Black Hills.[27]

Although he had twice recommended a Black Hills post, Sheridan responded by pointing out that action on the request would have to await new negotiations with the Sioux for cession of the region. Sheridan had earlier made it clear that he did not welcome citizens' petitions for posts. "If the wishes of the settlers on the frontier were to be gratified," he had stated, "we would have a military post in every county, and the army two or three hundred thousand strong." (Army strength at the time was less than 26,500.) Moreover, he contended, the army's limited appropriations required that "for every new post we establish an old one must be given up."[28]

Sheridan favored the establishment of two posts on unceded lands in the Yellowstone Valley—one at the mouth of the Bighorn River and the other at the mouth of the Yellowstone—where the Sioux hunting bands often congregated. He believed forts there would better enable the military "to meet the troubles which will originate from the Black Hills question."[29] But his requests for their authorization and funding were repeatedly ignored by the cost-conscious Congress until the humiliating defeat of Custer at the Little Bighorn.

An eight-member peace commission met with the Sioux at their reservation agencies in September and October. It explained what the Indians must do: end all fighting with the whites and give up the Black Hills in order to receive more food.[30] These were the terms mandated by Congress, the Indians were told, and the commission was powerless to change them. Not surprisingly, considering their destitute condition and their inability to support themselves, the Sioux signed away the Black Hills. But only 241 signatures were obtained on the agreement, far from the number required for additional land cessions. Under the terms of the 1868 treaty, no cession of any portion of the reservation would be valid without the consent of three-fourths of the adult males. The Black Hills Agreement (Congress had discontinued making treaties with Indians in 1871, and later pacts were termed *agreements*) fell far short of that requirement.[31]

Shortly before Congress ratified the Black Hills Agreement, the Dakota territorial legislature divided the region into three counties—Lawrence, Custer, and Pennington—and provided for their organization.[32] Ratification was completed on 22 February 1877, and the measure was signed by the president the next day. The Black Hills Agreement provided that the government would continue to supply the Sioux until they were able to support themselves. In return, the Indians agreed to the exclusion of the Black Hills from their reservation. Further, they consented to the construction of three wagon roads across the reservation to the Hills.[33] Although the validity of the agreement would later be challenged because of the shortage of signatures, its ratification sparked jubilation in the Black Hills settlements. "Those going to or returning from the Black Hills are now entitled to protection from the government," one of the frontier newspapers editorialized, "and hereafter they will receive it."[34]

The cession of the Black Hills did not end Sioux opposition, as the whites had expected. In fact, 1877 was the bloodiest year in the Hills since the whites had arrived, principally because there were more of them for the Indians to attack. Many Sioux, either not parties to the Black Hills Agreement or opponents of it, continued to raid on the settlers. These attacks occurred mostly along the foothills and continued after the ratification of the agreement. Second Lieutenant J. F. Cummings was sent to Deadwood from Camp Robinson, Nebraska, in February with Company C, Third Cavalry, to protect the settlers there. His command captured an Indian village on Crow Creek northwest of Deadwood, but the Indians escaped. Cummings recovered some stock stolen by the Indians but gave up pursuit when it appeared he was being drawn into an ambush. "Before coming here I had an idea that this Indian difficulty did not amount to much," Cummings informed his superiors, "but I have changed my mind very quickly."[35]

It was generally believed that the raiders were Sioux holdouts traveling between their diminished reservation and the Yellowstone country. Colonel Nelson A. Miles, charged with clearing the Yellowstone region of "hostiles" after the 1876 campaign, forced the surrender of the last of these bands in the spring of 1877. Only Sitting Bull, who had fled into Canada with his followers, remained unvanquished. But Miles considered the capitulation of these bands as merely "the beginning of the end" of the fighting. Unless the government exercised "wise and judicious management" of the Indians, Miles predicted, hostilities were "liable to recur at any time."[36]

The army's top brass came to the Yellowstone country in the summer of 1877 to review the Indian situation and to inspect the two new military posts under construction at the Bighorn and Tongue rivers. These forts, authorized at Sheridan's urging, had been funded by Congress the previous August when national indignation over the defeat of Custer and his men was at its peak. The post at the mouth of the Little Bighorn was named for Custer. The Tongue River fort was named for Captain Myles Keogh, also of the Seventh Cavalry, who had fallen with his commander at the Little Bighorn. Generals Sherman, Sheridan, and Terry conferred there and encountered no hostile Indians while traveling to the rendezvous from different directions. Sherman credited the absence to the strong garrisons at the two posts. He noted, "The Sioux Indians can never again regain this country."[37]

There was yet the matter of the long-delayed Black Hills fort to be resolved. The settlers there renewed their demands for a fort following sporadic Indian attacks in the valleys of Bear Butte and False Bottom creeks in June 1877. "Settlers for safety must have military protection immediately," the citizens of Deadwood wired the secretary of war, "or the agricultural interests of the Hills will be abandoned."[38]

A similar appeal was made by Territorial Governor John Pennington, who also wired Washington for troops. The governor authorized Seth Bullock, an experienced frontiersman whom he had appointed sheriff of Lawrence County, to organize militia companies until regular army

11

troops could reach the Hills. However, Pennington informed Bullock, the territorial government could not supply the companies with arms or ammunition. Nevertheless, Bullock organized six thirty-man companies of cavalry into the First District of Dakota Volunteers.[39]

The *Black Hills Daily Times,* at Deadwood, urged its readers to "Organize, Organize" on 25 July, claiming "dozens of our citizens are being slaughtered on every side by the savages." It predicted that a delay in organizing would result in the destruction of the Hills settlements. Deadwood was divided into military districts, and all abled-bodied residents were instructed to report to their assigned stations "at the first sign of trouble."[40]

None of the settlements came under direct attack, however, as the Indians confined their raids to the foothills ranches and to small parties traveling to and from the Hills communities. The fertile valleys around Spearfish, a foothills hamlet fourteen miles northwest of Deadwood, were dotted with small farms and ranches that supplied the northern Hills mining camps with food. These settlements were especially vulnerable to Indian attack, and the possibility of raids was ever present. The frightened citizens at Spearfish and Rapid City, another foothills community, built log stockades for the protection of the settlers in the event of Indian attacks. But the expected raids never materialized.

The Indian scare neared the panic stage when a particularly brutal triple killing occurred north of Bear Butte on 16 July. The victims were Frank Wagnes, his twenty-year-old pregnant wife, and her brother. They were Norwegian emigrants from Moorhead, Minnesota, who had come to the Hills over the Bismarck road that spring. The men had been putting up hay in the valleys around Deadwood but had decided to return home so that Mrs. Wagnes could have her baby there. They set out alone on the Bismarck Trail despite being advised to wait and travel with a wagon train. When their wagon neared Bear Butte the party was killed by a band of Indians. The men were not scalped, but the woman's body was mutilated.[41]

Shortly afterward, a public meeting was held in Deadwood, and again telegraphs and letters were sent to Washington demanding military protection. "The feeling here is very bitter against the government," it was reported, "which is blamed for not providing a fort to protect the industrious denizens of the Hills."[42] The enraged citizenry also petitioned the Lawrence County Commission to spend whatever it deemed necessary to provide needed protection from Indian depredations. The commission responded by offering a reward of $250 for the body of "each and every Indian, dead or alive, killed or captured" within the county.[43]

Militia activity waned after detachments of the Third Cavalry from Camp Robinson (renamed Fort Robinson in January 1878) and Fort Laramie reached the Hills in July. There were a few skirmishes between the troops and the Indians, but generally the raiders had vanished by the time the soldiers arrived on the scene. It was not the army's fault the Indians were so elusive, the *Black Hills Daily Times* pointed out, comparing the raiders to the joker in three-card monte. "Now you see it and now you don't," the newspaper explained, "and you more often don't than do."[44] Every outbreak of Indian depredations in the Hills throughout the summer and fall of 1877 brought renewed demands from the settlers for military protection. General Sheridan instructed the commanders of the Departments of Dakota and the Platte to send enough troops there to give the settlers the requested relief and to "punish the Indians."[45]

General Terry responded by dispatching detachments of the Eleventh Infantry from the Standing Rock and Cheyenne River agencies and the rebuilt Seventh Cavalry from Forts Abraham Lincoln and Totten to the Hills. Crook usually sent detachments of the Third Cavalry from Camp Robinson and Fort Laramie. Company C, Seventh Cavalry, from Fort Totten, was in the field from 14 August until 28 December guarding the stage route from Bismarck to the Black Hills. The company marched over twelve hundred miles before returning to its northern Dakota station.[46] There were also soldiers in the Hills throughout most of the rest of 1877. The Indian raids generally ceased while the soldiers were in the vicinity but resumed when the troops returned to their home stations.

"The proper thing for the government to do," editorialized the *Yankton Press and Dakotian* in the territorial capital, "is to leave these troops in the Hills where they can be made available next time they are needed."[47] The *Black Hills Daily Times,* at Deadwood, termed the government policy "a farce," predicting the settlements could expect more Indian raids as soon as the troopers were "comfortably back at their winter quarters." The newspaper also asserted that it cost more to send troops from distant posts to the rescue of the settlers than it would to build a fort in the Black Hills.[48]

General Terry, in his annual report for 1877, again recommended the establishment of a Black Hills fort. He described the neighborhood of Bear Butte as the best place for it and noted that the settlement of the Hills had created a "new frontier" that required military protection. General Sheridan agreed but claimed that he did not have enough troops to meet all the demands he was receiving from the exposed settlements and their representatives in Congress. His division had a ratio of only one man for every square mile to be protected in the Departments of Dakota and the Platte. He felt that "the little army" then defending the rapidly expanding settlements was doing the best it could under the circumstances. Besides, Sheridan believed that the Indian troubles in his division were essentially over, although he conceded that "complications" were still "liable to arise."[49]

Sheridan ordered Crook to send additional troops to the Black Hills in December in response to settlers' reports of renewed Indian depredations. Crook dispatched three companies of the Third Cavalry under Major A. W. Evans from Fort Laramie, but they found no Indians. Crook, complaining of the expense and noting that previous reports of Indian troubles there had not been corroborated, was permitted to withdraw his troops. Major Evans pointed out that any trouble with the Indians would more likely occur in the spring rather than winter. Therefore, he wrote, instead of sending troops to the Hills from distant posts, "it would be better to establish a permanent post here at once." He believed that Spearfish would be the best place for it but observed that there were also other suitable sites in the region.[50]

Surprisingly, after pushing for the Hills post so strenuously for so long, the settlers almost ruined their chances for getting it. In January 1878 a band of white renegades stole a large number of government horses at Fort Custer. The commanding officer there sent his chief of scouts, James Campbell, with a detachment of Crow scouts in pursuit of the thieves. The detachment caught up with them on Spearfish Creek and recovered fifty of the stolen horses, but the rustlers escaped into Deadwood. When Campbell went after them, he found that feelings against the Indians were so strong among the Deadwood townspeople that the lives of his Crow scouts were endangered. It took a military escort from the Third Cavalry to get them safely out of the Hills.

Crook, reporting the incident to higher headquarters, noted that previous attempts to recover stolen government and Indian stock in the Black Hills had also been unsuccessful. He blamed it on the fact that "the thieves of such property, it is believed, are sustained and supported by many people in the Black Hills."[51]

General Sherman, with requests on his desk for a Black Hills fort, was incensed. If the people of Deadwood protected horse thieves, he asserted, they could not expect troops to protect them and their property against hostile Indians.[52] Sheridan, sharing Sherman's and Crook's irritation over the matter, changed his mind about placing a post in the Black Hills despite his earlier support of the plan. Instead, he suggested a summer campaign that would place temporary infantry camps in the Black Hills as support bases for cavalry reconnaissance patrols seeking Indians. Sheridan believed this would provide sufficient protection for the settlers in the event of trouble. The controversy over settlers' harboring horse thieves was eased somewhat after Crook reported in late February that Third Cavalry troops had succeeded in recovering stolen government ponies in Deadwood. Sherman then approved Sheridan's plan for the summer campaign, and orders implementing it were issued in May.[53]

Meanwhile, appeals for a Black Hills post continued to pour into Washington. J. A. Hand, at Crook City, a foothills town northeast of Deadwood, wrote that the Sioux had remained quiet "during the few short periods when troops have been stationed among us." But no sooner had the troops departed, he added, "than our enemies are again in our midst destroying property and taking life." S. N. Wood, a Deadwood banker, proposed that a post be established on Spearfish Creek or on the Redwater or Belle Fourche rivers. This was where "depredations on the inhabitants of the Hills are first commenced," Wood wrote. Edwin Van Cise, a Rapid City lawyer, visited Washington in January and learned that Secretary of War George McCrary was in favor of a Black Hills post. He returned home and gathered three hundred signatures on petitions asking that the post be placed at Rapid City. Van Cise forwarded the petitions to Washington along with a long letter outlining why Rapid City would be the best place for the post.[54]

General Terry, noting that Rapid City was located in the foothills about thirty miles south of Deadwood, complained that the site was too far from the main roads leading into the Hills to provide the needed protection. He reiterated that Bear Butte would be a much better place for the post. Most of the population of the Black Hills was then centered at Deadwood and its environs, whereas Rapid City was sparsely settled. Nonetheless, competition between the rival communities continued unabated for the coveted post. Sheridan had six applications on his desk for new posts, as well as other demands for military protection. "It is utterly impossible to comply with these requests and demands," he wrote. "We have not the men."[55]

Actually, Sheridan's division contained eight of the army's ten regiments of cavalry and eighteen of its twenty-five infantry regiments. But his territorial command extended from the Canadian border south to the Rio Grande River, a distance of fifteen hundred miles, and from the Rocky Mountains eastward for twelve hundred miles to the Mississippi River. There were seventy-three permanent posts and camps of observation scattered throughout this vast region. Sheridan complained that the number of troops assigned to him was not commensurate with the responsibilities of his division.

However, Sherman noted that the number of troops under Sheridan at the time composed "quite two-thirds of the effective force of the whole army." He insisted that it would be "impossible to further re-enforce him [Sheridan] without absolutely stripping our seaboard, or abandoning other territories of equal value and subject to the same dangers." But Sherman sympathized with Sheridan, pointing out that the country covered by Sheridan's division had undergone more radical change in the past ten years than in the fifty years before that. "The game is nearly all gone," Sherman declared, "the Indian has been forced on to small reservations; farms and herds of neat cattle are fast taking the place of the buffalo, and every ox and steer has an owner who will fight for his property."[56]

The issue was brought to a head with a bill introduced by Senator George E. Spencer of Alabama, the chairman of the Committee on Military Affairs, on 16 April 1878. The bill authorized the Black Hills post and appropriated $150,000 for its construction. Sherman, despite Sheridan's change of position in the matter, endorsed the measure with the comment that "troops cannot exist in that region without shelter, and therefore a post seems necessary."[57]

Senator Spencer's bill did not pass Congress in its original form. But its provisions were incorporated into the Army Appropriations Act, which Congress approved on 18 June 1878. The act authorized the construction of two forts—one in the Black Hills and the other (Fort Assinniboine) on the Milk River in Montana—and provided $100,000 for each of them. In addition, Congress also appropriated $50,000 for the construction of a military telegraph line linking the Department of Dakota posts. One branch of the line would run from Bismarck to Fort Ellis, via the Missouri and Yellowstone rivers, connecting Forts Buford, Keogh, and Custer. A second branch would run from Fort Sully to Fort Keogh via Deadwood.[58]

In accordance with Sheridan's views, since two new posts had been authorized, permission was granted for the abandonment of other posts. Closed were Fort Bridger, Camp Stambaugh, and the North Platte Cantonment, all in Crook's department.

Petitions, telegrams, and letters from Deadwood, Crook City, and Rapid City, all seeking the post, had been shuffled between Congress, the War Department, and army, division, and department headquarters for months. Sheridan recognized that the post's location was a hot issue among the rival communities. He also recognized that discretion was important in reaching a decision. So he entrusted the recommendation of a site for the post to his secretary, who also was his brother, Brevet Lieutenant Colonel Michael V. Sheridan. The younger Sheridan's written orders did not specifically outline the purpose of his mission. They merely directed him to proceed to Bear Butte in connection with "the public business" and in conformance with the "special instructions" verbally given him by his brother.[59] But subsequent events left no doubt of his assignment.

The long-awaited Black Hills post—recommended by Warren twenty-one years earlier and subsequently by many others—was at last nearing reality. The search for the proper site started where Warren and others had suggested—at Bear Butte.

THE CAMP AT BEAR BUTTE

Lieutenant Colonel Sheridan arrived in Deadwood on the Bismarck stage in late May, and the purpose of his mission quickly became public. The *Black Hills Weekly Times* there broke the news that Sheridan had come to find a suitable location for the long-awaited permanent Hills fort, and the paper confidently predicted that Bear Butte would become the chosen site. The newspaper had also learned from Sheridan that troops were on their way to the Hills to establish the summer camps promised by the division commander.[1]

After viewing the country around Bear Butte and making a tour of the mines near Deadwood and Central City, Colonel Sheridan went to Rapid City. There he was taken in hand by the officers of the Rapid City Town Company, who squired him around the growing settlement and the nearby booming mining camp of Rockerville. Sheridan was quoted as being very impressed with the "very great progress" Rapid City had made during its short existence. It boasted a population of about 250, and Rapid Creek, which Sheridan described as "a very beautiful mountain stream," coursed through the community.[2]

The *Black Hills Journal* at Rapid City described Sheridan as "a very pleasant gentleman" and expressed the hope that he would "give a report to the Department in our favor."[3] He did. Writing his report on 10 June, the colonel outlined the relative merits of the Bear Butte and Rapid City sites. In his examination of the country around Bear Butte, he wrote, he had found "all that is necessary to make a comfortable, permanent post, should it be thought necessary to establish one there." The site had a constant stream, ample timber for fuel, and grass for haying and was situated near the convergence of the Bismarck, Pierre, and Sidney roads. But Sheridan added, "While a post there would cover the entrance of these roads to the Hills, I fear it may be too near the foothills to accomplish all the purposes intended by it." Further, he wrote that he regarded a post at Bear Butte "as too far to the northwest" to give protection to the fast-developing country around Rapid City.[4]

Sheridan noted that the government was then relocating the Red Cloud Agency to a point on the White River southeast of the Black Hills. "The route north for the Indians will then be directly through the Rapid Creek country," he wrote, adding that the ranches there would be enticing targets for cattle and horse raids. "A post on Rapid Creek would keep them [the Indians] east of the south fork [of the Cheyenne River] and be in a position to render assistance to all the settlers" in that region. Moreover, Sheridan disclosed, "Materials can be furnished for constructing a post on the most reasonable terms at Rapid City." Above all these considerations, he emphasized, was "the necessity for protecting the people and rendering a confidence" that would "encourage the speedy settlement of a most beautiful and fertile country." If a permanent post could not be established there, the colonel concluded, the army should either make frequent scouts along the White River or locate a summer camp there. This would allow the army to keep a close watch on Red Cloud's Oglalas and "perhaps give some assurance of peace to the pioneers" in that section.[5]

Missing from Sheridan's report was any mention of his personal involvement in Rapid City's fortunes. He omitted the fact that he had acquired twelve lots in the townsite during his short visit to the community. He paid the Rapid City Town Company five hundred dollars for nine lots in block 93 and three lots in block 98 of the original townsite.[6] Both blocks became valuable commercial property as the town's business district grew and prospered. It was suspected, but never proven, that the choice lots had been given to Sheridan in exchange for a token payment. Private investment by army officers in the real estate of budding frontier townsites was then a common practice. There were no laws or conflict-of-interest rules against such investment, and many officers took advantage of opportunities to supplement their pay with speculative ventures. It was ten years later before the Rapid City newspaper wrote about this facet of Sheridan's visit. It then disclosed that the colonel had been "treated to the best the pioneers here at the time, poor in purse and few in numbers, could afford." According to the newspaper report, Sheridan was

highly pleased with the bench north of town, and before he left he stated that he would report favorably upon that location. . . . Colonel

Mike liked the place, the good water and people he met here. Everything possible was done for his entertainment while here. . . . about the selection of the site for the post, *according to agreement* [emphasis added], Rapid City was reported upon favorably. Somehow Mike became owner of half a block of property here. He probably bought it or it was given to him because he was a good fellow. Of course, it had nothing to do with his favorable report.[7]

General Sheridan forwarded his brother's report to Sherman without comment. His endorsement of it made mention only of the troops ordered out from the Departments of Dakota and the Platte to establish summer camps in the vicinity of the Hills. He reported that Lieutenant Colonel Luther P. Bradley, Ninth Infantry, had arrived at his destination—the Big Bend of the Little Missouri River about eighty miles northwest of Deadwood—to set up one of the camps. Bradley's command consisted of four companies of his own regiment (B, C, H, and I) and five companies of the Third Cavalry (A, B, D, F, and K) from the Department of the Platte. The camp served as a depot of supply for the cavalry troops as they scouted the region for Indians and was designated Camp Devin for Colonel Thomas C. Devin, the former Third Cavalry commander who had died the previous April.[8]

On Sheridan's orders, Terry sent an advance force of five companies of infantry from the Department of Dakota to establish a second summer camp at Bear Butte. He also ordered Colonel Samuel D. Sturgis, the commanding officer of the rebuilt Seventh Cavalry at Fort Lincoln, to move his regiment to the butte. Sturgis, colonel of the regiment since 1869, had been on detached service when the Seventh marched out on the disastrous 1876 campaign and had thus escaped the fate of Custer. However, the colonel's son, Second Lieutenant James G. (Jack) Sturgis, just one year out of West Point, had been among the officers who fell with the regiment's lieutenant colonel.

Sturgis, commanding the infantry troops at Bear Butte as well as his own regiment, was instructed to divide his cavalry into scouting parties and conduct reconnaissances in all directions from the camp. The object was to provide "thorough protection during the summer and autumn of the Black Hills, and of the roads to them from Bismarck and Fort Pierre,

Colonel Samuel D. Sturgis was the commander of the famed Seventh Cavalry when it was ordered to the Black Hills in the summer of 1878 to help establish Fort Meade. He was also a central figure in the controversial court-martial of Major Marcus A. Reno. (Courtesy of Caroline Brooks Winston. Author's collection.)

from attacks by hostile Indians." His patrols to the northwest were to extend only far enough to connect with Bradley's cavalry from Camp Devin. To the north, Sturgis was to pay special attention to the region around Slim Buttes, for that was "believed to be a favorite rendezvous for hostile Sioux." At the first sign of any large gathering of "hostile Indians," Sturgis's orders directed him to concentrate his own forces "and move speedily to attack them."[9]

Captain Leslie Smith, First Infantry, reached Bear Butte with Company F of his regiment and a supply train from Fort Abraham Lincoln on 25 June. Five days later, five additional companies of infantry arrived at the encampment from Forts Sully and Randall and the Cheyenne River Agency. The 167-mile march was made over prairie that had been turned into "a sea of mud" by summer rains. The new arrivals included Companies C, I, and K, First Infantry, and D and G, Eleventh Infantry, under Captain Kinzie Bates. Smith, who had established "a pretty camp with good grazing, plenty of timber and spring water," assumed command of the entire encampment pending the arrival of Colonel Sturgis. The site was identified on orders as "Camp at Bear Butte."[10]

A party of newspapermen from Deadwood visited the camp on 2 July and reported that it was "beautifully situated on Spring Creek about two miles northeasterly of Bear Butte." The newsmen, "cordially received by the officers of the command," climbed Bear Butte and were guests for supper at the camp. "The health of the command is excellent and no desertions have yet occurred," the paper reported. "A bull train of forty wagons had just arrived and were unloading. This will be the supply camp of the Seventh Cavalry, which is expected to arrive in a few days."[11]

The gold boom then under way in the Hills did not impress Sergeant Gustav Reider of Company I, First Infantry. Writing to his wife at Fort Randall, he noted that every citizen he had met had told him "that there has been more money brought to this country than has been taken out." Moreover, Reider did not appreciate the highly touted beauty of the Black Hills. Any man who came to the Hills and returned to bring his family "to this wild country," Reider wrote, "thinks nothing of them."[12] At any rate, the Bear Butte camp soon became "a fashionable Sunday resort for Deadwooders," since the sutlers there were selling Milwaukee lager beer for fifty cents a bottle.[13]

Meanwhile, press reports that Mike Sheridan favored Rapid City for the post site shocked the citizens of the northern Hills. They deluged Jefferson P. Kidder, the Dakota delegate in Congress, and the War Department with telegrams and letters that repeated their earlier arguments for a northern Hills location. Their central arguments were that the northern Hills had the largest population, was where most of the Indian raids had occurred, and was where the Bismarck, Fort Pierre, and Sidney stage and freight routes converged.

The unexpected reaction to Mike Sheridan's report convinced Sherman that it would be wise to order another reconnaissance of the Hills to select a post site. General Sheridan, embarrassed that Sherman had not accepted his brother's recommendation, decided to make the site selection himself. He telegraphed the decision to Sherman, explaining, "It's an important post and should be in the right place."[14]

On 18 July, after a tedious twelve-day march, headquarters and Companies A, C, D, E, G, I, K, and M of the Seventh Cavalry, under Colonel Sturgis, reached Bear Butte from Fort Abraham Lincoln. They set up camp on Spring Creek on the opposite (northwest) side of the butte from the infantry camp. In honor of the colonel's son, killed at the Little Bighorn, the cavalry camp was named "Camp J. G. Sturgis."[15] Left behind to guard Cheyenne prisoners, who had been captured during the 1877 Yellowstone campaign and who were being held under surveillance at Fort Abraham Lincoln, were Companies H and L, under Captain Frederick Benteen. Lieutenant Colonel Elmer Otis, who had taken Custer's place in the regiment, also remained at the fort as post commander during Colonel Sturgis's absence. The two remaining companies of the regiment—B and F—were stationed at Forts Yates and Totten, respectively, and remained there.[16]

Two days after the Seventh Cavalry reached Bear Butte, General Sheridan and his party, which included his brother, arrived by special coach from Bismarck. It was a homecoming of sorts for Mike Sheridan, since he had been a captain of the Seventh since July 1866. He was still being carried on the regimental rolls as the detached commanding officer of Company L, although he had not served with the regiment since joining his brother's staff in 1870 with the brevet rank of lieutenant colonel.[17] The general's party also included the paymaster from Fort Lincoln, who paid the soldiers during Sheridan's visit.

While the division commander, escorted by Company E, scouted the

Second Lieutenant James G. (Jack) Sturgis, the son of the Seventh Cavalry's commander, was killed along with the regiment's lieutenant colonel, George Armstrong Custer, at the Battle of the Little Bighorn in Montana on 25 June 1876. Camp J. G. Sturgis, established at Bear Butte in the summer of 1878, was named for him. (Courtesy of Caroline Brooks Winston. Author's collection.)

region for a post site, the Bear Butte camp became a lively place after payday. The "girls and gang" from Deadwood descended on the camp, "reaping a rich harvest," which included "about all the money distributed by the paymaster." One Hills newspaper reported that drunken soldiers were "laying around over the prairies and in the woods between Crook and their camp thick as hair on a dog's back." It was said that they were having "lots of fun and . . . paying for it dearly." Finally, the camp commander placed a double guard over "the boys in blue" and expelled the visiting fun-merchants.[18]

Relations between the soldiers at the butte and the citizens of Crook City and Deadwood, the closest settlements, were generally good. There was much visiting back and forth, especially on weekends. Deadwood fielded a baseball team that played against the soldiers at both Bear Butte and Camp Devin. For some reason, the Third Cavalry team at Camp Devin was called "The Government Stockings."[19]

General Sheridan spent several days inspecting the valleys of Whitewood and Spearfish creeks and of the Redwater and Belle Fourche rivers. It was believed that he would locate the post on Spearfish Creek because it was the only stream in the vicinity with enough pure water to supply a garrison on a year-round basis. First Lieutenant Hugh L. Scott of Company I, Seventh Cavalry, described it as "the best stream in the Black Hills" and revealed that everyone thought Sheridan would locate the post there. However, Scott later reported, "Speculators put such a high price on the Spearfish land that Sheridan took his fort elsewhere."[20]

While in the vicinity, Sheridan made an official visit to Bradley's camp on the Little Missouri. He considered the region "a devil of a country" and found the soldiers there complaining that the water was "worse than the sutler's whiskey."[21] So he had Bradley move his command to a new campsite on Hay Creek, northwest of Spearfish. It was also during Sheridan's visit that the infantry companies at Bear Butte were moved to the cavalry camp on the other side of the butte.

Returning to Camp J. G. Sturgis, Sheridan learned that Scott and First Lieutenant Luther Hale of Company K, Seventh Cavalry, had made separate maps of the foothills region a few miles southwest of Bear Butte. He put the two maps together, "and upon this he located the post" about five miles from Camp Sturgis.[22] The site selected was on a plain fronting a gap in the foothills through which travelers entered the northern Hills from the prairies to the east. Sheridan considered it "the best strategic point for a military post in the entire Northwest."[23] The general rode his horse to the top of a hill northwest of the post and pointed with his sword to where he wanted the fort's buildings erected. The new post's reservoir was subsequently built on the hill.

With the post site question finally settled, Sheridan and his party went by special coach to Deadwood, where the general registered at the Welch Hotel. The *Times* there hailed his selection of the post site, predicting it would satisfy more settlers than if located anywhere else. Sheridan received old army friends residing in Deadwood, including some Civil War veterans, and also toured the mines in the vicinity with a small party of local citizens. Before leaving the Hills on 27 July, Sheridan and his officers were feted at a reception in his honor by the citizens of Deadwood. It was, the *Times* stated, an exceedingly pleasant gathering, "long to be remembered by all participants."[24]

Sheridan did not visit Rapid City while he was in the Black Hills. That may have been due to his brother's recently acquired property in that town and a consequent desire to avoid any appearance of a conflict of interest. The general was reportedly scrupulous about such matters. "Scandal never tainted Sheridan's name," it has been said, "nor did he become wealthy, though the opportunities to a man in his position were legion."[25]

Van Cise, disappointed that his appeals for a Rapid City post had been rejected, complained about Sheridan's neglect of his community. He charged that the general "was being banqueted in Deadwood when he should have been contemplating the advantages of Rapid City." The lawyer also claimed that the water was bad at the site Sheridan had selected.[26] The *Times* at Deadwood, commenting on "Rapid City's Grievance," asserted that "a large majority of the people of the Hills" were "entirely satisfied with the location of the post at its present place—more so than they would have been at any other point." It was true that the springwater at Bear Butte was alkaline and distasteful. But the site Sheridan had picked for the post was some distance from the butte and was "beautifully situated near the head of Bear Butte Creek in the vicinity of a large and ever-flowing spring of pure, cold water."[27] Despite Van Cise's protests, Sheridan's site selection was approved by Sherman and the War Department.

On 8 August, Companies H and L, Seventh Cavalry, under Lieutenant Colonel Otis, arrived at Camp J. G. Sturgis with the Cheyenne prisoners from Fort Abraham Lincoln. The Indians, led by Little Chief, numbered several hundred and were mostly old men, women, and children, "equipped with travois and accompanied by a congeries of dogs and ponies."[28] They had been on the march since 25 July and were en route to Indian Territory under military escort. There they expected to be reunited with Cheyennes under Dull Knife and Little Wolf, who had been relocated to Indian Territory the previous fall. Bear Butte was a sacred place to the Cheyennes; traditionally, tribal members went there to pray for visions of the future. Many of the prisoners climbed the butte and fasted there for three days and nights, leaving presents "to the medicine that inhabited the mountain."[29]

There was an eclipse of the sun while the Cheyennes were at Bear Butte. The Indians became excited and fired their guns to scare away the evil spirits that they believed were destroying the sun. "Their treatment was highly successful," reported Lieutenant Scott of Company I. "The sun recovered." Scott was a particular friend of the Cheyennes; at Fort Lincoln he had paid one of their chiefs sugar, coffee, and other rations in exchange for lessons on the Indian sign language. He became the army's leading expert in the hand gestures so widely understood by the plains tribes.[30]

Company K, Seventh Cavalry, relieving Companies H and L as the military escort for the Cheyenne prisoners, left Bear Butte on 11 August for Sidney Barracks, Nebraska. From there the prisoners were escorted to Indian Territory by a company of the Fourth Cavalry. Companies H and L joined the other units of the regiment at Camp J. G. Sturgis in performing patrol duty in the region.[31] The newspapers at Deadwood published many articles about the lively happenings at Camp Sturgis and Bradley's camp on Hay Creek during the summer and fall of 1878. Billy Nuttall, a Deadwood showman, erected a theater, forty by seventy-five feet, at Camp Devin and reportedly had it crowded every night. Nuttall subsequently moved the theater to the Bear Butte camp.[32]

Shortly after the establishment of Camp Devin, a Third Cavalry soldier there clubbed a fellow trooper to death in a drunken dispute over the ownership of some mess utensils. The victim was buried at the camp and his killer taken to Cheyenne for trial. One Gus Johnson, caught stealing horses at Bradley's camp, was arrested, manacled, and placed in a tent guardhouse watched by an armed sentry. Somehow he managed to escape during the night despite the shackles on his wrists and ankles, taking three horses from the picket line with him.[33]

Rustling of army horses was widespread at the time, according to the *Black Hills Daily Times*. "Every man in this country who needs a horse," the paper stated, "repairs to the nearest military camp in the foothills and takes one or two." It also reported that an officer of the Third Cavalry had picked up three stolen Company D horses and a span of army packtrain mules in the Deadwood area in one day.[34] Civilians were generally not allowed in the military camps except for short visits or on business approved by the commanders. Consequently, the "girls and gang" from Deadwood set up shop just outside the camp boundaries and did a brisk business during the soldiers' off-duty hours.

A cluster of crude, makeshift structures dotted the homestead claim of "Grasshopper Jim" Fredrick (he had acquired his nickname by living off grasshoppers in the dugout he had built near the butte before the gold rush of 1876). Just northwest of Bear Butte, not far from Camp Sturgis, the area quickly became known as "Scooptown" for the ability of its inhabitants to "scoop" the pockets of the soldiers who patronized the "fun parlors" there. Fredrick claimed to have come to the Black Hills in 1873. But Ben Ash, who blazed the trail from Bismarck to the Hills before their official opening, remembered him as a "spittoon cleaner" in Bismarck in 1874. In any event, it is known that Fredrick squatted on land near the butte before any other whites had settled there. Fredrick's homestead was near the Bismarck road, and he was one of the men who had recovered the bodies of the massacred Wagnes family in 1877. He bought liquor in Deadwood for resale to the soldiers at the Bear Butte camp and also provided the facilities for their gambling and womanizing. Fredrick was one of the best known, but least admired, of the early-day Black Hills pioneers.[35]

It was mid-August before orders were issued for the establishment of the permanent Hills post. Terry picked Major Henry M. Lazelle, First Infantry, who was then serving as the post commander at Fort Sully, for the task of laying out the military reservation. Lazelle was directed to garrison the new post with two companies of his regiment already at Bear Butte, along with two Seventh Cavalry companies selected by Colonel

Major Henry M. Lazelle, First Infantry, was the first commanding officer of the Black Hills post that became Fort Meade in December 1878. He left in May 1879 to become Commandant of Cadets at West Point. (Special Collections Division, United States Military Academy Library.)

Sturgis. However, the army intended to eventually add six more companies; hence, the quarters to be built in 1878 for the initial four companies had to be constructed "on some general plan . . . susceptible of that extension." Lazelle was told to move promptly to prevent encroachment upon the reservation by civilians. He was also instructed to quickly forward a plat of the reservation so that the president could have it set aside "without delay." Lazelle's orders further directed him to lay out the reservation in the shape of a parallelogram and to run it far enough back into the hills to assure a good supply of wood.[36]

The major initially laid out the boundaries of the new post to encompass a reserve six miles square. The boundaries were subsequently changed, however, to form an oblong roughly six miles north to south and two miles east to west. The change was necessitated by the large number of settlers who had taken up homesteads within the military reserve and by the military's desire to keep homesteaders as far from the post as possible. Settlers were establishing ranches in such close proximity to the post that the army was finding it difficult to maintain good discipline among the soldiers. With the boundary change, the *Times* explained, the ranchmen would "be kept at a sufficient distance so as not to interfere upon the military, nor be interfered with or molested by them."[37]

Ranchers around Bear Butte experienced considerable trouble with claim jumpers, who were "gobbling up every square foot of ground in the vicinity of the new post." Several owners of valuable land were driven from their claims by armed men. "Hemp will have to become fashionable in this country before long," said the *Times*.[38]

Whereas Major Lazelle was designated the commanding officer of the Black Hills post, the task of overseeing its construction was assigned to First Lieutenant George Ruhlen of the Seventeenth Infantry. Ruhlen had been the regimental quartermaster at Camp Hancock near Bismarck until its abandonment late in 1877 and was stationed at Fort Lincoln. He had directed the building of Fort Custer in Montana the previous year and had also aided in the erection of other western posts.[39]

It had taken the army a long time to place a permanent post in the Black Hills. But the Black Hillers did not mind; the post was, at long last, a reality. And it was to benefit them far beyond providing protection from Indian depredations. Ironically, with the Sioux at peace on their reservations, the construction of the Black Hills fort got under way when there no longer seemed to be a need for one.

★ 3 ★

CAMP RUHLEN

Four companies from Camp J. G. Sturgis, which were to compose the initial garrison of the new post, established a construction camp along Bear Butte Creek on 27 August, within the boundaries of the military reservation and about one-half mile north of the site selected for the post. Major Lazelle's command consisted of Companies F and K, First Infantry, and Companies E and M, Seventh Cavalry, numbering eight officers, sixty-five enlisted cavalrymen, and forty-seven enlisted infantry-men.

Officers assigned in addition to Ruhlen were Captain Thomas French and First Lieutenant Andrew W. Nave, Company M, Seventh Cavalry; First Lieutenant Charles DeRudio and Second Lieutenant James D. Mann, Company E, Seventh Cavalry; Captain Leslie Smith, Company F, First Infantry; and First Lieutenant Matthew Markland and Second Lieutenant Frank H. Edmunds, Company K, First Infantry.

General Order No. One, issued by Lazelle from the construction camp on 28 August, proclaimed that the camp would be known as "Camp Ruhlen" for its builder and also designated Lieutenant Edmunds as camp adjutant.[1] Lieutenant Ruhlen went to Deadwood for workers and sup-plies for the camp and hired Charlie Poor as the superintendent of the civilian laborers. The workers were instructed to report to the camp on 9 September with their tools and bedding, since their first task would be to build temporary quarters and mess facilities for themselves. Initially, the construction camp housed the four companies of the post garrison as well as the civilian workers.

The Northwestern Stage Company, which ran passenger stages and freight wagons between Bismarck and Deadwood, began service to Camp Ruhlen shortly after the camp's founding, charging three dollars for a one-way ticket from Deadwood to the camp and five dollars for a round-trip

31

First Lieutenant George Ruhlen, Seventeenth Infantry, was in charge of constructing the Black Hills post that became Fort Meade. The construction camp was
named for him. He also supervised the construction of several other frontier posts
and eventually became a major general. (Courtesy of Old Fort Meade Museum
Association.)

ticket. The Sidney stage soon followed suit, changing its route from Rapid City to Deadwood "to accommodate residents of the new military post on Bear Butte Creek."[2] Traffic was brisk on both lines as craftsmen seeking work and businessmen hopeful of winning contracts for supplies swarmed to the construction site.

The *Times* described Camp Ruhlen as "the liveliest camp in the Hills" in early September and reported that its economic effect on the Hills communities was already "beginning to count." In addition to providing building material for the new post, the camp offered a ready market for area farmers and ranchers who had flour, potatoes, eggs, fresh milk, pork, and beef to sell. The army also sought bids in September for eighteen hundred cords of softwood and twelve hundred tons of hay to carry the camp through the forthcoming winter. Superintendent Poor estimated that it would require a year to build the permanent post.[3]

The construction of the fort from the Camp Ruhlen site inspired speculators to promote rival townsites in the camp's vicinity. Aside from Grasshopper Jim's "Scooptown," Crook City and Deadwood were the closest settlements to Camps Ruhlen and Sturgis. But not for long. Soon a "New Town in the Foothills," at the mouth of Boulder Canyon about seven miles west of the construction camp, was being boosted in the Deadwood press. A cutoff road through the canyon was six miles shorter than the Crook City route between the fort and Deadwood. The promoters of the new town—named "Ruhlen City" for the officer in charge of building the fort—were described as energetic men. They would spare no expense, it was reported, to make their settlement "the leading town of the foothills." Charlie Collins, an Irish firebrand publisher whose newspaper, the *Black Hills Champion,* had gone under at both Central City and Deadwood, was reportedly a "prominent businessman" of Ruhlen City.[4] Collins had a penchant for championing ill-fated causes, and Ruhlen City would become one of them.

No sooner had the birth of Ruhlen City been announced than a rival townsite was reported about a mile and a half below Ruhlen City, placing it even closer to the site of the new fort than its competitor. The new contender was called "Dudley Town" for Judge E. G. Dudley, an early entrepreneur in Deadwood who owned a sawmill at the upper end of Boulder Canyon. "Both towns," the *Times* noted, "have great expectations."[5]

Newspaper reports of the founding of Ruhlen City and Dudley Town preceded the news that a third town had been surreptitiously platted even earlier, just one mile east of the post site. "Sturgis City" was laid out by Jeremiah C. Wilcox, a cousin of Colonel Sturgis's wife. Wilcox was among the fortune seekers who had flocked to Deadwood during the gold boom. Like many others, he had failed to strike it rich and was down to his last dollar and a half when he paid a visit to Colonel Sturgis at his Bear Butte camp. After walking to Camp Sturgis, Wilcox proposed "the laying out of a townsite near the new post about to be established." Sturgis agreed to be a member of the townsite company and initially invested a twenty-dollar gold piece in the enterprise. Wishing to establish the townsite with as little notice as possible, Wilcox staked out Sturgis City before daylight on the morning on 26 August. He hired a young boy to help him and used "a hundred-foot rope as a surveyor's chain and the north star for a compass" in carrying out the work.[6]

Unlike Camp Sturgis, named for the commanding officer's son, the new town was named for the colonel. Wilcox gave Arthur Buckbee of Deadwood an interest in the company for helping to guard the claim until he could complete the organization of the town company. Major Lazelle and B. G. (Barney) Caulfield, a Deadwood attorney who had previously served in Congress from Chicago, were among the investors. Each member received townsite lots in proportion to his investment. Lazelle put $232.70 into the venture. Colonel Sturgis subsequently increased his investment to the extent of acquiring several blocks of lots. Wilcox received thirty-five lots for laying out the townsite and forming the company.[7]

There had been a few squatters in the vicinity of the Sturgis City townsite before 1878. But none of them bothered to claim a legal homestead until the site of the new military post was announced. Part of the townsite covered area later claimed by Dudley for the town he planned to develop. But, recognizing the influence the army officers and Caulfield brought to Wilcox's enterprise, Dudley became a stockholder in Sturgis City rather than further promote his own town. Collins also claimed to have located on the townsite but was unable to prove it. Undaunted, he resurrected his *Black Hills Champion* to give the town its first newspaper. He also became the town's first postmaster. Like so many of his ventures, however, his newspaper and his postal appointment were short-lived, and he was soon chasing rainbows elsewhere.[8] The abortive settlements of Ruhlen City and Dudley Town quickly and quietly faded away.

Caulfield filed for a patent on the Sturgis City tract in the land office at Deadwood on 25 October. By then John Harmon, the former post trader at Fort Abraham Lincoln, had erected the first building in the new town—a general store. The first street laid out was a path linking the new post with the new town. It ran parallel to Bear Butte Creek and was named Lazelle Street, for the Camp Ruhlen commander. Wilcox, a major of the Fifth Iowa Cavalry during the Civil War, had a good rapport with the officers of Camps Sturgis and Ruhlen. He succeeded in selling lots in Sturgis City to some of them, including the ill-fated Lieutenant George Wallace of Company G, Seventh Cavalry.

When it became apparent that Sturgis City was "the coming city of the Hills," the occupants of Grasshopper Jim's "Scooptown" moved en masse to the fast-expanding community.[9] The varied services they provided were welcomed by the townsite promoters. The relocated settlers attracted prospects for town lots and also assured the neophyte city of a growing population. Less welcome was the sobriquet of "Scooptown," which followed the residents to Sturgis City and tarnished the community's reputation to the chagrin of its "better class" of citizens. Nevertheless, the town remained stuck with the unwanted nickname. The *Times* at Deadwood saw no justification for the rival town's existence, except for "the drippings" that would "fall into its lap from the military post."[10]

While Sturgis City was experiencing its initial growth, the Seventh Cavalry carried out its mission of patrolling the region from its camp at Bear Butte. Company I, First Infantry, under Captain Fergus Walker, performed escort duty for the workers building the telegraph line between Deadwood and Camp Devin. The other infantry troops at Camp Sturgis carried out routine camp duties. The construction of the new fort proceeded at a rapid pace—as many as one hundred civilians were employed on the project before the end of the year. A sawmill on the west end of the military reservation was the first facility erected. The soldiers of the garrison, believing that permanent quarters could not be built before the coming of winter, reinforced their tents with slabs from the sawmill. Some of them made temporary quarters by digging into the side of a hill and using the slabs to shore up their dugouts. Ruhlen did all he could to prepare for the coming winter, "but his principal efforts had to be devoted to sawing lumber and arranging for work on the new post."[11]

Assistant Surgeon Louis Brechemin, assigned to Camp Ruhlen in September, opened a twelve-bed provisional tent hospital for eight patients transferred from the field hospital at Camp Sturgis. Matilda McCarthy, the wife of a civilian laborer at the camp, was hired as the hospital matron. Private Albert Neihoven, Company C, Seventh Cavalry, had died at Camp Sturgis of internal bleeding on 16 August and was buried on a hill adjacent to the camp. He was later reburied in the post cemetery when it was established on a heavily wooded hill southwest of Camp Ruhlen.[12] The first to die at the Camp Ruhlen hospital was Sergeant Charles A. Hess of Ruhlen's quartermaster force on 24 September. Death was again attributed to internal bleeding. Musician Private Henry Weiss of Company B, Ninth Infantry, from Camp Devin, died at the Camp Ruhlen hospital on 29 September. While working with a crew laying the poles for the military telegraph line from Deadwood to Fort Keogh on 1 September, Weiss had been returning to camp when his wagon went over an embankment.[13] Neihoven, Hess, and Weiss were the first to be buried in the newly created post cemetery.

On 26 September, Camp J. G. Sturgis was moved about five miles to a new site in Bear Butte Valley, about two miles below Camp Ruhlen. Private A. B. Brant of Troop D, Seventh Cavalry, accidentally shot himself in the stomach while at this camp and died on 1 October. The camp was broken up on 6 October when the troops were ordered to the Pine Ridge Agency, which had been established for Red Cloud's Oglala Sioux the previous summer on White Clay Creek southeast of the Black Hills. The troops from Camp Sturgis were to assist in the pursuit of a party of Cheyennes. Unhappy with the lands allotted them in Indian Territory, the Cheyennes were attempting to return—without government consent—to their northern home. Under the leadership of Dull Knife and Little Wolf, the Cheyenne party had left the reservation while Little Chief's band, after its pilgrimage to Bear Butte, was still on its way there. Dull Knife and Little Wolf were pursued from Oklahoma, through Kansas, and into Nebraska by a large force of soldiers whose numbers increased as the Cheyennes neared the Sioux agencies.[14] From Camp Devin, Major Caleb H. Carlton took a battalion of the Third Cavalry to Fort

Robinson to join the pursuit. The rest of Bradley's command at Camp Devin returned to Fort Laramie for the winter after completing the telegraph line from Deadwood to Fort Keogh in October.

In the absence of Colonel Sturgis and Lieutenant Colonel Otis, both of whom were on detached service at the time, Major Joseph G. Tilford led the force from Camp Sturgis to Pine Ridge. His command, numbering 430, included Companies A, C, D, G, H, I, and L of the Seventh Cavalry, Companies C and I of the First Infantry, and Companies D and H of the Eleventh Infantry, all from Camp Sturgis, as well as Companies E and M of the Seventh from Camp Ruhlen. That left only the camp staff and Companies F and K, First Infantry, at Camp Ruhlen.[15]

However, the garrison was enlarged on 22 October when Second Lieutenant James S. Pettit arrived from Fort Sully with sixteen men from Company H, First Infantry, and thirty-three recruits. Eighteen of the recruits were assigned to Company F and the remainder to K. The garrison was further augmented on 29 October when thirty recruits for the absent Companies E and M of the Seventh Cavalry arrived. Pettit's detachment worked until 15 November on the military telegraph line from Camp Ruhlen to Deadwood, where the line connected to Fort Keogh. The detachment then returned to Fort Sully.[16]

Major Tilford's command was patrolling the Dakota-Nebraska border when Dull Knife and his band of Cheyennes were found on 23 October in the Sandhills country. The Indians, exhausted after their long trek and poorly clad for winter conditions, surrendered to a Third Cavalry force. With the assistance of Companies C and G of the Seventh Cavalry, the prisoners were taken to Fort Robinson to await deportation to the Indian Territory. Little Wolf's band, meanwhile, avoided the cordon of troops along the border by traveling west of the Black Hills. The following spring, troops from Fort Keogh captured them near the Little Missouri River in southeastern Montana Territory.[17]

Following Dull Knife's surrender, Tilford returned to Camp Ruhlen with his Seventh Cavalry troops. The First and Eleventh Infantry companies attached to his force returned to their home stations. On 13 November, all companies of the Seventh Cavalry except E and M, which were part of the permanent garrison, left Camp Ruhlen for winter quarters at Fort Lincoln. Major Lazelle's winter garrison, in addition to the eight officers assigned to the camp, included fifty-four men in Company E and fifty-nine in Company M, Seventh Cavalry, and forty-three men in Company F and thirty-seven in Company K, First Infantry.[18]

Cold weather and snow slowed work on the post, and some civilian laborers at Camp Ruhlen were laid off when winter conditions prevented them from working. Soldiers with building skills worked in construction from time to time and received extra pay. The first building to be completed was the guardhouse, which was first used on 8 November. It was a 63.6-by-32-foot sandstone structure with space for thirty prisoners.[19]

On 12 November the adjutant's office on the north side of the post was completed and immediately occupied. Built of Black Hills pine over a locally quarried sandstone foundation, which was the pattern followed for all the buildings, the office was 39 by 27.6 feet in size. It contained five rooms, with the two largest serving as offices for the post commander and the adjutant. The smaller rooms were used by the regimental clerk, for court-martial proceedings and for record storage.[20]

Twenty-four general orders were issued at Camp Ruhlen from the time of its establishment in August until the end of 1878, and fourteen of them pertained to garrison court-martials. Absence without leave, desertion, neglect of duty, and drunkenness were the most common offenses.[21] Other orders issued at Camp Ruhlen during its first few months involved administrative matters or camp procedures. For instance, General Order No. 4, issued on 16 September, set up the daily calls: reveille (or first call) at fifteen minutes before sunrise and taps (last call) at 8:45 P.M. Special Order No. 136, issued on 14 November, appointed a general court-martial board to begin trying cases on 21 November.

Captain Smith, First Infantry, and First Lieutenants DeRudio and Nave, Seventh Cavalry, were appointed to the Council of Administration, which was charged with dispensing nonappropriated post funds.[22] These funds, accumulated from a variety of nongovernmental sources, could be expended only on projects benefiting the entire command. Among the council's expenditures was $125 for garden seeds, which were distributed to each of the companies, enabling them to grow their own vegetables for the company messes. The Council of Administration was also charged with regulating the prices of the post trader. In December, William S. Fanshawe was appointed the post trader over twelve other applicants.

Fanshawe had succeeded Harmon as the post trader at Fort Abraham Lincoln when Harmon had gone to the Black Hills as the sutler for Camp Sturgis. When Harmon had opened his general store in Sturgis City, Fanshawe had taken over the sutlership at Camp Sturgis.[23] M. P. Clarke, of St. Paul, Minnesota, was the successful bidder to supply the new post with "Fresh Beef on the Block" for the period from 1 December 1878 to 30 June 1879. He was required to furnish beef that had been "stall-fed during one month previous to being slaughtered." In addition, he had to furnish "such number of good, fat beef cattle as may be required to accompany expeditions from the post at a price per pound not to exceed one-half the price paid for the beef on the block per pound net."[24]

Despite winter conditions, three more buildings were completed by the end of November. Two of them, each 200 by 30 feet in size, were designated as the quartermaster's storehouse and the commissary storehouse; the latter was connected to a 100-by-26-foot root cellar that was 9 feet deep. The third building was a 200-by-25-foot granary capable of storing up to eighty thousand pounds of grain.[25]

On 16 December, the first of the garrison moved into new quarters when the infantry companies occupied their completed barracks buildings. Six days later, the cavalry companies moved into their barracks, and their horses went into the completed stables. Each of the barracks was 236.6 by 25 feet, housing two companies, and was fronted by an 8-foot-wide porch that ran the entire width of the structure. Each barracks contained two squad rooms, 100 by 24 feet, as well as a first sergeant's room, a company office, and a storeroom; the barracks were heated by two large drum stoves. Natural lighting came from twelve windows and artificial lighting from candles. None of the barracks had latrines; these were two hundred yards away. Connected to each barracks was a 119.6-by-25-foot structure containing a messroom, a kitchen, a pantry, and a sleeping room for the cooks.[26]

The stables, 200 by 30 feet in size and also made of pine on sandstone foundations, were located about five hundred yards north of the barracks. Each of them had a tack room and stalls for eighty horses. Wells were dug in front of the stables, and water was reached at an average of twelve feet.[27]

By the end of December, the first set of officers' quarters was completed and occupied by Lieutenants Ruhlen and Edmunds. Officers' quarters, 33.5 by 40 feet, were two-story frame structures with a parlor, a sitting room, a dining room, and a kitchen on the first floor and four bedrooms with closets on the second floor. An outside entrance led to a 9-foot-deep cellar walled with bricks, and a shed covered the outside door to the kitchen and was used for storing firewood and for washing clothes.[28]

At year's end, the garrison comprised thirteen officers and two hundred enlisted men. In addition, there were fifty-nine women and children on the post: seven wives and fifteen children of officers, seven servants, and nine laundresses and their twenty-one children. The laundresses were the wives of enlisted men and supplemented their husbands' pay by doing officers' laundry for three dollars per month and enlisted men's for two dollars. They lived with their families in nine one- or two-room log structures built by their husbands at their own expense along Bear Butte Creek about five hundred yards north of the post.

Lieutenant Ruhlen's force of civilian quartermaster employees who were engaged in post construction numbered seventy-five at the end of 1878: fifty carpenters, ten masons, and fifteen common laborers. In addition, Ralph Bell, a contract surgeon, joined the garrison in December.[29] General Terry was on detached service at the end of 1878, so Colonel John Gibbon, commanding in Terry's absence, wrote the Department of Dakota report for that year. He characterized conditions in the department as "remarkably quiet and peaceful" with one exception. Raiding parties of Indians were still continuing "their predatory operations" in the region between the Missouri River and the Black Hills and in western Montana. But Gibbon expected that the Black Hills post and another fort scheduled to be built in the Bear Paw Mountains of Montana in 1879 would bring that under control. "These two posts," he wrote, "will aid very materially in giving protection to the large and thriving interests of the surrounding regions, by furnishing starting points for military bodies acting against hostile bands, as well as depots of supplies, both in winter and summer, for troops in the field."[30]

At the time, the Department of Dakota mustered five thousand soldiers, about one-fifth of the total U.S. Army strength authorized by Congress, serving in ninety-eight companies located at twenty-two posts scattered over more than 375,000 square miles—one soldier to each seventy-five square miles. Gibbon urged an end to the policy of scattering a large number of small posts over such a vast region. Rather, he favored "large garrisons of regimental size" as more efficient in protecting the rapidly expanding frontier.[31]

General Sheridan described the Indian situation in the Department of Dakota as "unsatisfactory" in his report for 1878. He had opposed relocating the Red Cloud and Spotted Tail agencies away from the Missouri River because the moves had placed the agencies closer to the Black Hills settlements. The Red Cloud Agency on White Clay Creek was particularly close to settled areas. "I doubt if, in the present frame of mind of the Red Cloud Indians," Sheridan stated, "that the two races can live so closely together without fighting."[32]

Camp Ruhlen remained in existence while construction continued on the post facilities, but its population dwindled quickly as permanent quarters for the officers became available. On the last day of 1878, the post was given a name of its own. General Order No. 27, issued at Department of Dakota headquarters, announced that Secretary of War McCrary had designated the post "Fort Meade" in honor of Major General George G. Meade, of Civil War fame, who had died in 1872. The same order renamed the posts at the Standing Rock and Cheyenne River agencies as Forts Yates and Bennett, respectively.[33] Fort Meade's namesake had commanded the Army of the Potomac at the time of the Battle of Gettysburg, considered the turning point of the war, and had been a close associate of Ulysses S. Grant's.

Fort Meade was established late in the army's long struggle to maintain peace between the dispossessed Indians and the land-hungry whites—two peoples who now lived side by side, two cultures that seemed destined for confrontation rather than compatibility. Yet Fort Meade had a significant contribution to make to the peace-keeping effort.

★ **4** ★

COMPLETING THE FORT

Heavy snowfalls and temperatures thirty below zero brought activity at Fort Meade to a virtual standstill in the first month of 1879. It was so cold in January that a detachment of troops scheduled to make a training march to Fort Keogh was kept at the fort on the post surgeon's recommendation. Nevertheless, despite numerous cases of frostbite, work continued on completing the remaining buildings. Construction of the post hospital began on 11 January while the last of the officers' quarters were nearing completion. Soldiers from the post tried to dam Bear Butte Creek to secure ice for summer use, but the dam failed to hold. Ice was obtained from the frozen Belle Fourche River instead.[1]

Major Lazelle and the other officers still at the construction camp moved into their new quarters on the post in February. Second Lieutenant Mann of Company E shared a set of two-story bachelor officers' quarters with Second Lieutenants Baldwin D. Spilman of Company M, Seventh Cavalry, and Charles G. Starr of Company F, First Infantry. Mann's quarters were on the first floor, while Spilman and Starr occupied the second floor. In smaller rooms on the second floor were quartered a "striker," an enlisted man who supplemented his pay by working as a servant for officers, and a cook. "Bachelors in the army always run their own mess and houses," Mann wrote his mother.[2]

The first death of the year also occurred in February. Three enlisted soldiers, charged with desertion, escaped from a sentinel at the post on the evening of 7 February. A detail led by Lieutenant Starr found the escapees in the Big Bonanza Saloon in Sturgis City. The deserters fled, and Starr fired on them. A private from Company M, Seventh Cavalry, fell wounded; the other two were captured. The wounded man died at the post several hours later. "No blame can be attached to Lieutenant Starr for his conduct," Major Lazelle wrote of the incident.[3]

The post commander was authorized in February to employ one guide-interpreter and two guides to accompany the cavalry troops on their patrols of the region. Private First Class Amos A. Stoneburner, a telegraph operator with the Signal Service, was also assigned to Fort Meade; he was needed because the military telegraph line was approaching the post from two directions—eastward from Fort Keogh via Deadwood and westward from Fort Bennett via Rapid City. Stoneburner, the lone Signal Service soldier on the post, remained at Fort Meade until transferred fifteen months later.

On 23 February, Companies E and M, Seventh Cavalry, under Lieutenants Nave and Mann, were ordered out on the trail of a band of Indians that had attacked a wagon train east of Rapid City. The force, accompanied by Contract Surgeon Bell, included ninety-one enlisted men with rations for six days. A freighter named Schramm, carrying supplies from Fort Pierre to Camp Crook, had narrowly escaped during the attack near Washte Springs. The Indians withdrew before the cavalry reached the scene, and Schramm volunteered to accompany the soldiers in pursuit. The soldiers failed to locate the Indians after following their trail along the Belle Fourche River for five days in what Mann described as the worst weather of the winter. Company E had marched 206 miles and Company M 190 miles in extreme cold, high winds, and snow by the time the force returned to the fort on 26 February. "Such is the life of the cavalry," bemoaned Mann.[4]

While the troops at Fort Meade were engaged in periodic patrols and routine garrison duties, the civilian quartermaster employees labored to complete the post buildings as weather conditions permitted. The original appropriation for the construction of the fort was exhausted, however, before all the buildings were completed. Citizens of Rapid City, still smarting over their earlier failure to win the post, petitioned the War Department to abandon the fort. Their memorial urged the establishment of garrisons in lower Rapid Valley and in the Redwater country, "where they would do some good." It was only Deadwood's "champagne and laudatory froth," the *Black Hills Weekly Journal* asserted, that had induced Sheridan to pick the Fort Meade site, "where there are no roads and no settlements to protect." Despite this opposition, a supplemental appropriation was secured, and construction continued on the buildings at Fort

Meade. The post hospital was completed and patients were admitted in April.[5]

Also in April, Major Lazelle was reassigned as Commandant of Cadets at West Point. Since there were no other field-grade officers at the post at the time, Lazelle remained until the arrival of Major Marcus A. Reno the following month. Reno, one of the most controversial officers to ever serve in the Seventh Cavalry, not excluding Custer himself, assumed command on 22 May. He was returning to his regiment after two years of suspension from rank and pay. His crime: making improper advances to Emiline Bell, the wife of Captain James M. Bell of the Seventh Cavalry, during the captain's absence from Fort Abercrombie in December 1876. The court-martial board that convicted Reno in March 1877 meted out a sentence of dismissal from the service. But President Rutherford Hayes commuted the penalty to suspension in recognition of Reno's twenty years of service during the Civil War and subsequent Indian campaigns.[6]

Reno returned to duty to find that Captain French, whose Company M had been part of the major's battalion at the Little Bighorn engagement, had just begun serving a court-martial sentence of his own. French's trial for drunkenness had ended with a guilty verdict and the captain was suspended from rank at half pay for one year, effective 15 April. French retired in February 1880, and First Lieutenant Frank M. Gibson of Company H was promoted to the captaincy of the company.[7]

Reno's service as post commander was short. In a change of stations, the field staff, the band, and Companies A, C, G, and H of the Seventh Cavalry were transferred to Fort Meade from Fort Abraham Lincoln in June and July. This gave the post an eight-company garrison, since Companies E and M of the Seventh, with Companies F and K of the First Infantry, were already there. Companies B and D of the Seventh remained at Fort Yates, F and K at Fort Totten, and I and L at Fort Lincoln. Colonel Sturgis arrived at Fort Meade with his family on 16 July and took command the next day.

At Fort Lincoln, a four-page monthly tabloid newspaper, the *Sentinel,* proclaiming itself "devoted to the interests of the U.S. Seventh Cavalry," was published by M. A. Breese. When the regimental headquarters was moved to Fort Meade, Breese solicited support for the paper both there and at Sturgis City. Among his Fort Meade advertisers were Fanshawe, the post trader; Charles F. Roth, who operated a barbershop at the east end of the band quarters; and Best and Smythe Photographers. Advertisers from Sturgis City included Harmon's General Store, Perkins' Saloon and Restaurant, Ingalls Jewelry, the Sheridan House, and Dr. H. P. Lynch, "Practicing Physician and Surgeon." The *Sentinel* featured regimental gossip from both Fort Lincoln and Fort Meade.[8]

Also coming with the troops from Fort Lincoln was the regiment's famous horse, "Comanche." Captain Myles W. Keogh of Company I had acquired the buckskin gelding in 1868 and had ridden him into the Battle of the Little Bighorn. Keogh was one of the sixteen Seventh Cavalry officers killed in that fight. Comanche, severely wounded, was the only living creature found on the Custer battlefield after the fight. He had spent almost a year at Fort Lincoln in a special bellyband sling as he was tenderly nursed back to health. Before moving the headquarters of the regiment from Fort Lincoln to Fort Meade, Colonel Sturgis issued General Order No. 7 retiring the horse from active service. The order also prohibited riding Comanche and directed that the horse be saddled, bridled, and led by a mounted trooper in all ceremonial regimental formations. "His kind treatment and comfort should be a matter of special pride and solicitude on the part of the Seventh Cavalry," the order stated, "to the end that his life may be prolonged to the utmost limit."[9]

Fort Meade, situated on a broad plain, was an open-style fort, like so many others on the western frontier. Construction was virtually complete at the time the troops from Fort Lincoln changed stations; the post included fifteen officers' buildings south of the parade grounds and five sets of barracks on the north side for enlisted men. Other buildings included noncommissioned officers' and band quarters, the adjutant's office, the hospital, a sawmill, a bakehouse, a guardhouse, a granary, the trader's store, commissary and quartermaster storehouses, stables, and shops. There were also corrals and a wagonyard near the stables.

The last of Ruhlen's construction force, down to six carpenters and one common laborer, were discharged in July. Ruhlen was then relieved as post quartermaster, and he returned to Fort Lincoln. He was succeeded by the Seventh Cavalry's regimental quartermaster, First Lieutenant Charles A. Varnum, who had a complement of twenty-six civilian quartermaster employees after Ruhlen's departure. The highest paid among

Fort Meade, with Bear Butte looming in the background, as it appeared after the initial construction was completed in 1879. The fort was established on a broad plain fronting the northern entrance to the Black Hills. The parade grounds separated the enlisted men's barracks, the adjutant's office, the guardhouse, and the stables from the officers' quarters (lower line of buildings). The road at the lower left led to the post cemetery. (Photo by Mary Murphy Haas, courtesy of Old Fort Meade Museum Association.)

them was an engineer-sawyer, who earned $135 a month. The others and their salaries were two clerks, $100; seventeen teamsters, $30; two scouts, $30 plus one daily ration; one trainmaster, one wheelwright, and one blacksmith, $60 each; and a guide, $50 plus one daily ration.[10]

At two o'clock in the morning on 3 August, the first serious fire at the new post destroyed the trader's store and the commissary. A bucket brigade was formed to combat the flames, since a fire department had not yet been organized, but it was unable to save the building. The fire loss was placed at $50,000, and Fanshawe's insurance covered only $27,000. Arson was suspected, and Fanshawe offered a one-thousand-dollar reward for information leading to the arrest and conviction of the arsonist; several suspects were questioned but were released when no case could be proven. Fanshawe quickly rebuilt his store and by November had enlarged his inventory sufficiently to advertise for off-post business. By then, the post had its own fire department.[11] Another post "first" occurred on 17 August when the wife of the hospital steward, August von Glossman, gave birth to a daughter, Sophie, at the fort.[12]

Fort Meade reached its authorized ten-company strength in September when the infantry contingent was enlarged to four companies. Companies D and H of the First Infantry arrived from Fort Sully on 9 September. Companies F and K of the regiment had been a part of the garrison from the fort's beginning.

Colonel Sturgis hosted a grand review of his troops, followed by a reception and dance at his quarters, in early September. The guest of honor was Granville G. Bennett, the territorial delegate, who had just secured an appointment to West Point for the colonel's eighteen-year-old son, Samuel D. Sturgis. It was the first major social event in the fort's brief existence and attracted many of the leading citizens of the Black Hills. The host was described in the Deadwood press as "well preserved, active and apparently a middle-aged man, round and plump as one could wish to be, with but a very light sprinkling of the silver threads among the gold." Sturgis was fifty-seven and more than a little portly at the time. Mrs. Sturgis, described in the Deadwood press as "a stout, matronly lady," suffered "a slight attack of vertigo" after the affair, "owing to over-exertion." Major Reno, on the other hand, was seen as "a prepossessing man" of prominent, intelligent, and pleasant features and as "genial in his disposition, interesting in his conversation and a man of stability."[13] The major was to prove himself otherwise during his brief tenure at Fort Meade.

Lieutenant Ruhlen returned to Fort Meade on 12 September to supervise the construction of quarters for the newly arrived infantry troops. He soon had a force of thirty-nine civilian carpenters, masons, and painters at work on the project, funded by an eleven-thousand-dollar supplemental appropriation. The quarters were completed in December, the craftsmen were discharged, and Ruhlen again returned to his home station. The only civilian workers remaining on the post were twenty-seven regular quartermaster department employees.

In mid-September, a party of officers and ladies from Fort Meade went on a four-day hunt on the Belle Fourche River, about fifty miles north of the post, returning with seventeen antelope. Ella Sturgis, the beautiful twenty-one-year-old daughter of the post commander, reportedly dispatched "a goodly share" of them. She was, according to the *Times* at Deadwood, "the best rifle shot in the West."[14] The description seems out of character compared with other accounts of her as a shy, delicate, and refined young lady. But there was no question about her attractiveness. She was "a very handsome girl, tall, slender, with large expressive gray eyes, dark skin and hair and marked eye brows, with color enough to make her brunet beauty effective."[15] And she was reported to be a talented amateur actress, performing lead roles on the stage in St. Louis as well as at Fort Lincoln.

An early morning fire on 26 September wiped out four years of uncontrolled growth at Deadwood, destroying many businesses and driving residents from their homes. In response to an appeal for help, Colonel Sturgis sent Company C of his regiment to the scene. This unit of three officers and forty-four enlisted men helped bring the fire under control and prevented looting of the evacuated homes. Sturgis also offered rations and temporary housing at the post for anyone left homeless by the fire. The offer was not accepted, however, since the victims preferred to remain close to the ruins of their homes to salvage what they could.[16] Deadwood's location at the apex of converging tree-lined gulches filled with overcrowded cabins made it especially vulnerable to fire.

Ever alert to opportunities for making good investments, Sturgis became deeply involved in the mining activities of the region. He joined a group of leading Black Hills entrepreneurs in forming the "Fort Meade Hydraulic Gold Mining Company" and became its president. Others involved in the venture included the colonel's influential friend, Territorial Delegate Bennett, and Captain Henry Jackson, the commanding officer of

Company C, Seventh Cavalry. The enterprise proposed to develop the gold-mining potential on Rapid Creek and built "a mammoth tunnel" not far from Rapid City, enabling it to "obtain access and drainage to 19,500 linear feet of the bed rock of that extremely rich auriferous stream." The company, capitalized for a half million dollars with stock selling for five dollars a share, reportedly had "an excellent mill" and also a lumberyard in Rapid City, which sold timber not needed for the mine.[17]

Colonel Sturgis's real estate and mining interests in the Hills frequently kept him away from Fort Meade for long periods. Returning from one absence, the colonel was upset to find Major Reno visiting his wife and his daughter, Ella, in the family quarters. The major had come uninvited and had spent several hours in conversation with the lovely Ella. The colonel disapproved of any alliance between his daughter and Reno. In fact, Sturgis was later to claim, Reno would not have been admitted if he had presented his card, as was customary for officers making unofficial calls at their commanding officer's quarters. Reno, who many believed could have saved Custer—and therefore young Lieutenant Sturgis as well—at the Battle of the Little Bighorn, was not on the best of terms with the Sturgis family.[18] Furthermore, the widowed major at forty-four was not considered an eligible suitor for Ella, who was less than half his age. The Sturgis family was especially protective of their daughter because her earlier romance with a young lieutenant in the Seventh Cavalry had ended tragically with the young man's suicide.[19]

Major Reno's interest in Ella was even more inappropriate than that of the unfortunate lieutenant, who had at least been a bachelor and Ella's own age. But Reno had more against him than his age and being a widower with a motherless son. His conviction for taking liberties with another officer's wife counted heavily against him with the other officers of the Seventh and their families. Then too, Custer admirers among the regiment's officers blamed him for the defeat at the Little Bighorn and for the death of the entire command. They did not welcome Reno's return to the regiment, and they had as little to do with him as possible. The Sturgis family in particular had no affection for him, since the beloved son Jack had also fallen with the troops Reno had "failed" to rescue at the Little Bighorn.

Colonel Sturgis was given the opportunity to remove the major when

Reno got himself into trouble again. The major and Second Lieutenant William J. Nicholson of Company G, Seventh Cavalry, got into a fight while playing pool on the post on the night of 25 October. Sturgis determined that Reno had been the aggressor in the affair and charged him with conduct unbecoming an officer and gentleman under the Sixty-first Article of War. Reno was placed under arrest in quarters on 28 October to await his general court-martial. To strengthen the case against the major, Sturgis added two specifications alleging misdeeds that had occurred two months earlier. One claimed that Reno had been "disgustingly drunk" at a supper at the home of the post trader on the night of 3 August, the same day that Fanshawe's store had burned down. The other specification charged that Reno had been drunk and disorderly at "a public billiard saloon" on the post on the night of 8 August.[20] These offenses had gone unreported (and unpunished) until the fight with Nicholson. To make matters worse, an additional charge would be placed against the beleaguered Reno even before his court-martial could be convened. It would, unfortunately for the major, involve Colonel Sturgis's daughter.

To some, Reno's troubles seemed to be the result of "petty jealousy" among the officers of the Seventh who would be in line for promotion if a vacancy was created by his dismissal. "Another effort will be made to weed out of the army a good and brave officer," one newspaper asserted, "whose only sin is the common one (in the army) of conviviality."[21]

While Reno was awaiting the start of his court-martial, a killing occurred to further disrupt the Fort Meade military reservation. Two lawmen, W. H. Llewllyn and Boone May, had arrested Lee (Curley) Grimes as a suspect in the robbery of a post office on the Sidney stage route and were taking their handcuffed prisoner to jail in Deadwood when a storm broke as the mounted men rode along the edge of the military reserve. According to the lawmen, Grimes asked to be released from his handcuffs to warm his hands. When the request was granted, Grimes attempted to escape by bolting his horse northward. The officers fired at the fleeing prisoner and he fell dead, just over the Fort Meade line. Llewllyn and May rode into the fort and reported the incident to Sturgis. The colonel sent a detail to bury Grimes where he had fallen and placed the two officers under arrest before turning them over to the civil authorities. Although charged with murdering their prisoner, the lawmen were the only witnesses to the

Fort Meade was built as a ten-company post. The two-story officers' quarters, constructed on the south side of the parade grounds, were first occupied during the winter of 1878–79. (Courtesy of Old Fort Meade Museum Association.)

killing, so there was nobody who could contradict their account. The pair were acquitted when brought to trial in 1880.[22]

The government telegraph line between Forts Bennett and Meade was completed in November as troops from each post worked toward each other in setting the poles. In response to a petition from the citizens of Rapid City, who believed their interests were suffering from a lack of telegraph communication, the line was run through that community. Colonel Sturgis had promised this would be done "without delay" and kept the promise by assigning troops from Fort Meade to speed the work at the western end of the line before winter arrived.[23] Rapid City was interested in the project because the government permitted private and commercial use of the line for a fee, although such dispatches were put second in priority to military messages.

By his cooperation, Colonel Sturgis managed to help overcome Rapid City's resentment at not being chosen for the post site. The fact that he was the president of the Fort Meade Hydraulic Gold Mining Company, a leading mining enterprise in the Rapid City area, as well as the commander at Fort Meade, was not lost on the town's business community. On the evening of 22 November, one hundred Rapid City businessmen signed the first dispatch over the new telegraph line. Sent to Colonel Sturgis, the message extended "greetings to Fort Meade" from "the Central Metropolis of the Black Hills." The townsmen claimed a "commercial affinity" with Fort Meade and proclaimed, "United We Stand." In reply, Sturgis wired his congratulations to "the good people of Rapid City" and predicted they would soon be getting a railroad also.[24]

The completion of Fort Meade, along with the two Yellowstone posts constructed earlier, gave General Sheridan confidence that the Indian troubles in his Division of the Missouri were over. "There has been no general combination of hostile Indians in this military division during the past year," Sheridan stated in his annual report for 1879, "and I doubt that such combinations can ever exist again."[25] Nonetheless, the Sioux were still proving troublesome. On 15 December, Colonel Sturgis received word that Indians from the Pine Ridge Agency had run off with a herd of cattle north of Whitewood Creek. The colonel dispatched Company C of the Seventh, but the unit was unable to recover the stolen cattle and returned to the post on 17 December, after covering fifty miles on the mission.[26] It was the last Indian duty of Fort Meade's first year. But there was other excitement at the fort to break the monotony of routine garrison life, excitement provided by Major Reno's court-martial, which was followed with as much interest off the post as on.

★ 5 ★

RENO'S FALL

Major Reno's court-martial brought more public attention to Fort Meade than anything else that had occurred there during the brief history of the post. The trial had elements of high drama—conflict and comedy, passion and pathos, romance and rancor—that lifted it above the ordinary case of military jurisprudence. Interest in the case extended far beyond the limits of the fort, since Reno had gained national notoriety from his involvement in the much-publicized Custer fight. To set the record straight, he had asked for and had been granted a court of inquiry to investigate the facts surrounding that engagement.

The inquiry had been held in Chicago from 13 January to 1 February 1879. Testimony was taken from twenty-three soldiers, including several officers and enlisted men from Fort Meade, and from civilians who had been at the Little Bighorn in 1876. After hearing testimony that ran the case record to thirteen hundred pages, the court determined that the conduct of the officers throughout the battle had been excellent. Although it concluded that Reno's subordinates in some instances had done more for the safety of the command than Reno, it found nothing in his conduct requiring criticism. It did not recommend that he be court-martialed. Both Secretary of War McCrary and General of the Army Sherman approved the court's findings.[1]

Despite this exoneration, Reno still found himself a frequent target of criticism when he rejoined his regiment at Fort Meade. And, in many respects, the major was his own worst enemy. No stranger to adversity, Reno had a knack for bringing it upon himself.

Born 15 November 1834 in Carrollton, Illinois, Marcus Albert Reno was the fifth of the six children of James and Charlotte Hinton Reno. His father, who was in the hotel and drugstore business in Carrollton, died when Marcus was eleven years old. His mother died three years later. The children were then divided among relatives. When Marcus was seventeen, he received an appointment to West Point through U.S. Senator Stephen Douglas of Illinois.

The young plebe, only average in his classwork, earned more than the average number of demerits for infractions of the academy's rules. He was twice suspended for such offenses as tardiness at formations, unbuttoned blouses, sitting down on guard duty, and carving his initials in a tree on the academy grounds. Following each suspension, Reno was permitted to return to the academy and join the next class. On 23 January 1856, in an incident that would have later significance, Reno was arrested by First Lieutenant William H. Wood for singing while on guard duty. He was again suspended. Permitted to join the class of 1857, he finally graduated, ranking twentieth among its thirty-eight members.[2]

Reno's first assignment as a newly commissioned second lieutenant was in the First Dragoons at Fort Walla Walla, Washington. He was promoted to first lieutenant on 26 April 1861 and to captain on 12 November of that year, when the First Dragoons reorganized as the First Cavalry. Reno participated in the defense of the nation's capital at the outbreak of the Civil War. He served in the Army of the Potomac and was brevetted major for gallant and meritorious service during the fighting in Virginia in 1863. He was General Sheridan's chief of cavalry during the Shenandoah campaign in 1864. Promoted to brevet colonel on 1 January 1865, Reno was brevetted brigadier general of volunteers on 13 March of that year. He ended the war as commander of the 12th Pennsylvania Cavalry.[3]

In 1863, Reno married Mary Hannah Ross, who was from an extremely wealthy Harrisburg, Pennsylvania, family. They had one son, Ross, born in 1864. Mrs. Reno, small of stature and in frail health, did not care much for the rigors of military life. She made frequent trips back to Harrisburg to visit her family and to escape the spartan conditions of life at the frontier posts where Reno was stationed after the war. Harrisburg became a second home to Reno too, and he joined his wife and son there whenever his military duties permitted.

Reno reverted to his regular army rank of captain after the war and served in a variety of assignments. He was an assistant instructor at West Point before he was promoted to major on 26 December 1868 and assigned to the Seventh Cavalry. He joined the regiment during its campaign against the Indians in Kansas. Reno did not participate in the Black Hills Expedition of 1874 because he was then in command of two detached companies of the regiment at Fort Totten, in Dakota Territory. From that post, Reno's command served as escort for the Northern Boundary Commission surveying the Canadian and U.S. border from Minnesota to the Rocky Mountains.

Reno was commanding the escort troops in the field in July 1874 when he received word that his wife had died in Harrisburg. He was unable to obtain leave in time to attend her funeral, and it was not until late September that his command returned from the field. He then hurried to Harrisburg, where he received a cold reception from his wife's relatives. Not being army people, they could not understand why he had been unable to obtain leave until two months after his wife's burial. Particularly cool to him were his wife's sister and her husband, who had taken over the care of his ten-year-old son. Fearing that his son was being alienated from him, Reno obtained an eleven-month leave of absence and spent part of it on a European vacation with Ross. At the end of his furlough, Reno decided to leave Ross with his wife's family in Harrisburg. The frontier was no place for a motherless boy, he reasoned, especially since Reno's military duties required him to be gone from his station for long periods of field service.[4]

Then followed Reno's participation in the Sioux Campaign of 1876 and his subsequent tribulations—the court-martial conviction resulting from his relations with Mrs. Bell and the court of inquiry into his conduct at the Little Bighorn. His European travels with Ross had been expensive, and the cost of the Harrisburg attorney who had represented him at the court of inquiry had further depleted his financial resources. By the time he returned to active duty at Fort Meade, Reno needed a regular paycheck. The major had a sizable monthly income from his wife's estate and the interest from a trust fund his father-in-law had established for Ross; nevertheless, he was frequently strapped for funds.[5]

As a widower, Reno was out of place with officers of his age and rank, who had the company of their families at the fort. So he associated during his off-duty hours with younger, single officers of lower rank, who were given to more frivolity than their older, more sedate superiors. Hard drinking and gambling were their favorite nighttime activities, and Reno was a willing, if not always a welcomed, participant. Less than six months after coming off suspension, Reno found himself in trouble again. Complicating his woes was the fact that he had become enamored of Ella Sturgis.

Reno had been handsome in his younger days and had cut an imposing figure with his fine physique, dark brown eyes, dark wavy hair, and thin, neatly trimmed moustache. But his once slim, five-foot-eleven-inch frame had become bloated from food, drink, and idleness while he was under suspension and away from the daily physical activity of military life.

On his return to duty, Reno's very presence in the regiment was an irritant to the Seventh's commander. The major's interest in the carefully protected Ella only exacerbated the situation. Colonel Sturgis had difficulty maintaining official relations with his subordinate and avoided social contact with Reno whenever possible. Although he was the junior of the Seventh's three majors, Reno was the second-highest-ranking officer on the post. Major Tilford was on detached service with Lieutenant Colonel Otis at Fort Lincoln, and Major Lewis Merrill was commanding Fort Yates. Yet despite the findings of the court of inquiry in Chicago, Sturgis could not—or would not—absolve Reno of responsibility for what had happened at the Little Bighorn. The loss of his son in that affair was undoubtedly a factor in his attitude.

Characteristically, Reno made it easy for the colonel to dispose of him. Reno's fight with Lieutenant Nicholson gave Sturgis all the excuse he needed to start the proceedings that would rid the Seventh of his unwanted executive officer. The 61st Article of War, under which Reno had been charged, provided for dismissal on conviction. The fight with Nicholson was the first specification cited in support of the charge. Surprisingly, Sturgis had added two incidents from the previous month to the charge, despite having earlier disapproved the filing of late charges against Reno under similar circumstances. The colonel's change of position probably reflected his personal interest in the case.

When Reno's sentence in the Bell case had been commuted from dismissal to suspension, some of Reno's enemies within the regiment had presented a new set of charges against him. It was alleged that he had been drunk on duty at Fort Lincoln when the regiment had returned from

Major Marcus A. Reno's long and troubled army career came to an end at Fort Meade, where his ill-fated affection for his commander's daughter resulted in his dishonorable discharge. A review of his case, long after his death, cleared his record, if not his reputation. (Special Collections Division, United States Military Academy Library.)

the field in September 1876. Further, he had been accused of insulting another officer, engaging in a fistfight with him at the officers' club and challenging him to a duel with pistols. All of this had reportedly occurred six months before Reno's court-martial on the charges involving Mrs. Bell. Colonel Sturgis, feeling that the charges should have been made at the time the alleged offenses had occurred, had refused to approve them. "They appear now with bad grace," he had explained in forwarding the charges to department headquarters. General Terry and the secretary of war had agreed, and the late charges had been dropped.[6]

Reno was now ordered to be confined to his quarters while awaiting the assembling of the officers who would sit on his court-martial board. There were not enough officers of Reno's rank or higher at the fort to form the board, so officers from other posts were assigned to the duty. Reno was given the freedom of the post for exercise purposes while awaiting the arrival of these officers. The troubled major compounded his problems by attempting to contact Ella without her father's knowledge.

On the evening of 10 November, Reno took one of his nightly walks along the path in front of the officers' quarters. Passing Lieutenant Ernest A. Garlington, who had just emerged from the Sturgises' quarters, Reno could see Ella as she sat by the window of the family's sitting room. She was the only member of the Sturgis family that had exhibited any friendliness toward him. Since her father had brought charges against him, however, Reno did not deem it wise to go to the door and seek admittance. Instead, unaware that Mrs. Sturgis was also in the room, he went to a side window of the parlor and tapped on it to attract Ella's attention. The tapping alarmed Ella, who recognized Reno through the window, and she called to her mother that Reno was outside. Noticing that he had alarmed the women, Reno hurried back to his quarters. The next morning Colonel Sturgis preferred an additional charge against his executive officer—that of window peeping.

Adding to Reno's misfortune was the assignment of Colonel William H. Wood, then commanding the Eleventh Infantry at Fort Sully, as the president of the court-martial board. This was the same officer who, as a lieutenant, had earlier preferred charges against Cadet Reno for singing on guard duty at West Point. Two officers of Reno's own regiment, Lieutenant Colonel Otis and Major Merrill, were also assigned to the court.

Major Reno lost his heart—and his commission—to the beautiful Ella Sturgis, the daughter of his regiment's commanding officer and the belle of the Seventh Cavalry. Another officer of the regiment, after a thwarted romance with Ella, committed suicide. (Courtesy of Caroline Brooks Winston. Author's collection.)

Otis, then commanding Fort Lincoln, had been promoted to fill the vacancy caused by Custer's death, despite a petition from the enlisted men of the regiment recommending Reno for the post. Merrill, who had been in Reno's class at West Point and had served in the First Dragoons with him, got himself excused from sitting in judgment on his former classmate. Major O. T. Moore, Sixth Infantry, was appointed to the court in his place.

Completing the seven-member court-martial board were Colonel W. R. Shafter, First Infantry; Lieutenant Colonel A. J. Alexander, Second Cavalry; and Majors J. D. Irwin of the Medical Department, and Joseph S. Conrad, Seventeenth Infantry.[7] Conrad, like Merrill, was a former classmate of Reno's. But he did not ask to be excused from the court, and Reno did not object to his presence on it. Assigned as Reno's prosecutor was Captain W. W. Sanders, Sixth Infantry, a Judge Advocate Corps officer from department headquarters in St. Paul. A private from Company H, Seventh Cavalry, was detailed to record the proceedings. This was a poor choice, since the private turned out to be incompetent, in several instances garbling the testimony he transcribed by longhand.

Reno, who had served on court-martial duty for three months in New Mexico in 1869, considered himself well enough versed in military law to represent himself. He had, of course, been court-martialed once before and had gained some knowledge of trial procedures during this experience. Moreover, he had observed courtroom techniques during the lengthy court of inquiry proceedings in Chicago, where he had been the principal figure. Very likely the cost of hiring civilian lawyers to represent him at the court-martial in St. Paul and the court of inquiry in Chicago, coupled with his gambling debts, left him unable to engage more attorneys. Thus his decision to represent himself may have been dictated by his financial position at the time, although the army would have appointed an officer to defend him had he requested one. In any event, Reno's lack of counsel was probably a factor in the outcome of his case. He was not as competent in this field as he believed. Few of his many objections concerning what was and what was not acceptable testimony were sustained by the court.

Although the court-martial officially opened on 24 November, it was not until the twenty-eighth that a quorum of board members was present. There were three specifications to the first charge, each alleging a separate offense that Reno had committed "to the scandal and disgrace of the military service." The first specification involved his scuffle with Lieutenant Nicholson on 25 October, when he had struck the lieutenant with a billiard cue. The second and third specifications spelled out the earlier charges against the major: being "disgustingly drunk" at Fanshawe's quarters on 3 August and being drunk and disorderly at the post saloon on 8 August. There was only one specification cited in support of the second, or additional, charge of "conduct unbecoming an officer and gentleman"— the window-peeping incident of 10 November, in which Reno was accused of seriously frightening the members of the Sturgis family. Reno pleaded not guilty to all the charges. Testimony was taken from eighteen witnesses during the ten days that a quorum of the board was present for the proceedings.

Lieutenant Nicholson was the first witness. He testified that he and Reno had quarreled over what the major still owed him after deducting what the lieutenant had lost to him in a pool game in the post clubrooms. Nicholson admitted to offering to settle the matter with his fists and to telling Reno that he could "lick him in two minutes." He said Reno had then swung at him with a pool cue, which he had warded off with his arm. The witness then described how he had grabbed Reno by the throat and wrestled him to the floor. The fracas, which Nicholson termed "a private affair altogether," had been broken up when the combatants were threatened with arrest.

According to testimony on the supper at Fanshawe's, there had been four guests there that evening: Reno, Nicholson, Dr. Bell, and Fanshawe's partner, E. W. Johnson. They had been visiting and drinking at Reno's quarters when Fanshawe, who had been in Rapid City, had returned to the post around midnight. He had invited the men over to his quarters, located next to Reno's, for a late supper. In his testimony, Nicholson said he thought Reno had drunk too much from the bottle of whiskey on the dinner table at Fanshawe's. But he added that Reno had neither done nor said anything improper that evening. His view of the evening was supported by other witnesses who testified that Mrs. Fanshawe had considered Reno to be "disgustingly drunk" because he had hiccoughed at the dinner table. Fanshawe himself testified that all five men at the supper had drunk from the single bottle of whiskey at the table. He reported that Reno, aside from being "a little under the influence of liquor," had done nothing insulting during the evening.

As for the incident on the night of 8 August, the bartender, Joseph

Smythe, testified that Reno had been drinking and had broken an interior window in the billiard room with his chair. He also testified that Reno had twice knocked coins from his hands when he had attempted to give Reno change after the major had paid for the broken window. A witness to the incident testified that he had seen worse things occur at the club and reported that the spree had passed off quietly with no disturbance to the garrison.

Much testimony was taken on the question of whether the saloon was a public or private place, since it was alleged that Reno had created the disturbance in public. Colonel Sturgis contended it was a public place open to civilians and enlisted men as well as the officers of the post. Reno pointed out that he had been commanding the post at the time the saloon had been built. Although he had issued no official orders in the matter, Reno said he considered it a private place set apart for the officers and their friends. To avoid future conflicts over the matter, Colonel Sturgis issued, while the trial was still under way, an order that set forth his rules for the management of the saloon. They prohibited gambling, set the closing hour at 11 P.M., and made the post trader responsible for maintaining order on the premises. In addition, the order directed the officer of the day to include the establishment on his rounds and to report any violations of the rules.[8]

The most serious of the charges was the alleged window peeping. Lieutenant Garlington, the regimental adjutant, had been calling on Ella on the evening of 10 November. He testified that he had seen Reno on the walk in front of the Sturgises' home. Shortly thereafter, he disclosed, Colonel Sturgis had come to his quarters and reported that Reno had been seen peering through a side window of his residence and had alarmed his wife and daughter. On the witness stand, Colonel Sturgis gave the following account of the incident:

He had retired for the night to his upstairs bedroom when he heard his wife excitedly calling for him to come downstairs. She was shouting "Major Reno!" as the colonel, clad only in his nightshirt, met her on the staircase. He rushed downstairs and found Ella cowering in a far corner of the sitting room. Ella told him she had seen Reno looking through the window at her. She was so frightened that her father feared she would be stricken with something akin to "Saint Vitus Dance." Picking up a cane in the foyer, the colonel ran out the front door in his nightclothes in search of the major. But Reno had fled. Sturgis then returned to the house, dressed, went to Garlington's quarters, and instructed him to draw up the additional charge against Reno.

In reply to questioning by the judge advocate, Sturgis disclosed that Reno was not on cordial visiting relations with his family. He also testified about Reno's earlier visit to his quarters without invitation while he was gone, declaring that Reno would not have been admitted had Sturgis been there at the time. However, the colonel added, Reno was included when all officers of the post were invited to general entertainments at his quarters. Under cross-examination, Sturgis confirmed that Reno had sent Mrs. Sturgis a note of apology that attempted to explain his reason for looking through the window. But, the colonel told the court, he did not believe the note reflected Reno's true motive for the event.

Despite Reno's protestations, Ella was then called to the stand. The defendant had offered to plead guilty to the additional charge if it would spare Ella the embarrassment of testifying. But the judge advocate declined the offer. Ella testified that she had been receiving callers in the parlor of her father's quarters all evening and had gone into the sitting room to speak with her mother when the incident occurred. She reported hearing a noise twice outside the window as she was sitting in a nearby chair.

I heard someone tap on the window. When I sat forward and looked out into the darkness and saw a face gradually appear, I sat paralyzed. My eyes met Major Reno's. He evidently saw no one in the room but myself. As from the time he appeared where he was able to see in the room his eyes were fixed on mine. I was so frightened I could not move, and was only able to cry out, just above a whisper, "Mamma, it is Major Reno." Several times I repeated his name. "It is Major Reno, it is Major Reno." When I first said it Mamma replied, "no, it is not so," as if it could not be possible. But when she saw the state I was in and when I repeated his name, she said, "Ella run." But I could not move, and it was only when I heard mother run—leave the room—and call for father, who was upstairs, I had enough strength to get out of the chair and run into the corner.

Ella further testified that her first impression on seeing Reno's face at the window was that she would be shot. "I knew that he must have feelings against father," she stated, adding that Reno looked as if he was about to do something desperate. Reno declined to cross-examine the witness, perhaps as a gesture of gallantry.

The proceedings took on a comic aspect when Reno took the stand in his own defense and questioned himself. He did not deny tapping on the window. But he denied that he had done so stealthily or surreptitiously, as claimed in the additional charge. Over the objections of Captain Sanders, he finally succeeded in entering into the record the note of apology he had sent to Mrs. Sturgis after the incident. In it he stated that he had seen Ella standing fully dressed in front of the window when he was taking his nightly walk for exercise. He wrote, "In my loneliness and thoughts of the past, I felt myself impotent to resist the temptation" of taking a closer look at her. When he found that he had alarmed the household, he quickly retreated. The fault was in the judgment, and not the heart, Reno insisted, for he had "the greatest respect and admiration" for Ella. In fact, he added, "If my face expressed any other sentiment than admiration it greatly belied my feelings." He had no intention of harming her. He explained, "[I] would rather suffer my right hand severed from my arm, than harm one hair of her head."

Over the vigorous protests of Colonel Sturgis, Captain Benteen was permitted to take the stand in Reno's defense. He testified that Reno had shown him the note of apology before sending it to Mrs. Sturgis. In his opinion, the plain-speaking witness stated, the note did not express Reno's true feelings toward Ella. "That he was dead in love with the young lady was my belief," Benteen revealed, adding that he believed Reno's motives were honorable even if his conduct had not been. Benteen's testimony was short, but it probably hit closer to the truth than anything else placed into the record. Reno had indeed acted more like a love-struck swain than someone out to harm Ella. Further evidence of his strange behavior was the fact that he had twice tapped on the window—as Ella had corroborated in her testimony. It was apparent he had wanted to be seen by her.

Benteen's testimony so enraged Colonel Sturgis that he asked the court to appoint him assistant prosecutor. He expressed dissatisfaction with Sanders's prosecution of the case, charging him with having his mind "otherwise occupied" and failing to raise objections to the admission of certain testimony. As the accuser in the case, Sturgis vehemently claimed the right to act as assistant prosecutor. In that capacity, he explained, he could call the court's attention to points of law that would prevent Benteen and similar witnesses from appearing. After a closed-session discussion of the propriety of such a proposal, the court rejected the colonel's request. The development, not surprisingly, strained relations between Sanders and the colonel. The judge advocate seemed not to have much heart for the case after that point. It may have been apparent to him by then that Ella's involvement in the additional specification was warping her father's judgment. In any event, the case continued, with Sturgis and Sanders less respectful of each other than when the proceedings had started.

Reno dismissed the first charge and its specifications as inconsequential. He had been provoked into the fight with Nicholson by the lieutenant's threat to whip him, he claimed, and had stopped fighting when both of them had been threatened with arrest. He had broken the window at the officers' club, he told the court, out of pique over missing a billiard shot and had paid for the damage. He admitted to knocking the change out of the bartender's hands but claimed it was done in the spirit of frivolity, since it had elicited laughter from other officers present. Reno also claimed that he had drunk no more than the other guests at the Fanshawe supper but had become lightheaded from coming out of the cold night air into the warm dining room. Thus he may have given the appearance of being drunk when he was not. Moreover, Reno contended, the peace of the garrison had not been disturbed by any of these incidents, and no harm had been done. The 61st Article of War, Reno insisted, was not intended to apply to "youthful frolics or trivial deviations from rectitude" but to more serious offenses.

In a moving summation, Reno claimed that it had been his misfortune to have attained "a widespread notoriety throughout the country by means of the press" as a result of the Little Bighorn fight. He stated, "A greater degree of attention will be called to what I do than other officers not so widely advertised." Nothing he had done, he asserted, reflected any real criminality on his part. A conviction based on the charges, he

65

pleaded, would be an unjust reward for his over twenty-two years of "hard and faithful service" to his country.

Reno's closing statement was so convincing that the newspapers at Deadwood and Rapid City predicted his acquittal. But they also suggested that he be transferred to some other regiment. "He will always be an element of discord in the Seventh Cavalry," the *Black Hills Weekly Journal* at Rapid City editorialized. The *Times* at Deadwood, terming the trial "a farce," wrote that Reno had been as much sinned against as sinning himself. W. H. (Hank) Wright, who had covered the proceedings for the *Times,* claimed that Reno was being persecuted "with a view to driving him from the Seventh Cavalry."[9]

Wright's daily dispatches on the proceedings had been picked up and reprinted by other newspapers. So the court's verdict was eagerly awaited, not only by the area press but by newspapers throughout the entire country. It is unlikely that any other officer facing the same charges would have received the attention given to Reno.

The court-martial board announced its findings on 12 December. It found Reno not guilty of the first charge, ruling that his actions had failed to meet the criteria of being a "scandal and disgrace to the military service" as defined by the 61st Article of War. But on this first charge it did find him guilty of "conduct to the prejudice of good order and military discipline," a lesser offense not requiring dismissal on conviction. On the additional charge—his actions at the Sturgis home—the court found Reno guilty and sentenced him to be dismissed from the service.

However, five of the seven members of the court signed a statement urging clemency for Reno. They claimed that strict compliance with the Articles of War deprived the court of all discretionary power in the matter. They were wrong about that: the board had reduced the first charge and could have done so on the additional charge also. Instead, the majority of the court recommended the defendant "to the merciful consideration of the confirming authority."

When Reno first heard the verdict, he promptly wired the secretary of war and asked to be allowed to resign his commission rather than be dismissed. On later learning that a majority of the court had recommended clemency, he withdrew the request. The *Times* prophetically predicted the plea for clemency would carry little weight with President

Hayes.[10] He had saved the major from dismissal by commuting his sentence to suspension after Reno's conviction in the Bell case. But now, only a few months after his return to duty, Reno was in trouble again, in another case involving a woman.

It took almost three months for the court's findings to work their way up the military hierarchy for review. Meanwhile, Reno remained in close arrest at Fort Meade. He spent a depressing Christmas there awaiting the decisions of the reviewing authorities.

Major Thomas F. Barr, the judge advocate of the Department of Dakota, reviewed the case for General Terry. He had been the prosecutor in the Bell case and was well aware of the major's eye for women. Nevertheless, Barr disagreed with the Fort Meade court's sentence of dismissal on the window-peeping charge. "In my opinion," Barr wrote, "the court would have been justified in acquitting him of the additional charge and specification." It was probably true, he added, that Reno had been motivated only by admiration for Ella when he had looked through the window at her. General Terry, a lawyer himself, agreed. "The finding upon this charge should not have been guilty with a recommendation to mercy," he declared. "It should have been not guilty." Terry pointed out that he did not have the authority to modify the sentence and that his disapproval of it would leave Reno without any punishment whatsoever. Therefore, he approved the findings and joined with the majority of the court in recommending that the sentence be modified.

Brigadier General William M. Drum, the judge advocate general at army headquarters, was the next reviewing officer. He believed that both Terry and Barr had been too lenient with Reno. He termed Reno's conduct in looking through the window of his commanding officer's quarters "one of the gravest violations of the obligations of a gentleman he could have committed." Nor, he added, could "such an outrageous offence as his be claimed to have been condoned and wiped out by a letter of apology, no matter how profuse." But even Drum believed dismissal was too severe a penalty "for the succession of excesses of which Maj. Reno has been found guilty." If commutation of the sentence was deemed expedient and just, Drum added, Reno's offenses past and present did not warrant "any great extent of lenity."

General of the Army Sherman joined with the majority of the court and

General Terry in recommending a modification of Reno's sentence. He proposed to the president that it be reduced to suspension for one year with loss of pay. Further, he suggested that Reno be reduced five files in the list of majors of cavalry. That would place five majors then below him in seniority ahead of him for future promotion. Moreover, Sherman recommended that Reno be confined to post headquarters at Fort Meade for the period of his suspension. Accompanying Sherman's recommendations was a less generous view of the case by Judge Advocate Henry Goodfellow of the War Department. If Sherman's proposals were accepted, he wrote, it would be best to confine Reno at a post other than Fort Meade in view of his "gross indecorum" toward Colonel Sturgis and his family. Goodfellow added the following damaging comments:

> The case, however, may be regarded as presenting the serious question of whether Major Reno's recent history in the light of this and a former trial does not demonstrate him as unfit to retain his commission.
>
> Whether he is not shown to be deficient in that respect to the female sex which is so essential a motive to every man's self respect, and whether he is not a pernicious example to younger men who should look up to an officer of his years as an example of decency and respectability rather than as a leader in vice and immorality?
>
> While the government is dismissing lieutenants and young captains, and sending wayward cadets home to their distressed mothers, should it show undue mercy to an officer of mature years who has once already disregarded [a] most impressive admonition?

President Hayes did not think so. This time, despite the pleas for clemency, the president confirmed the sentence of dismissal on 16 March. Reno's long military career, distinguished for the most part but sorely troubled in its late stages, was over. Orders were issued for his dismissal, effective 1 April 1880.

Colonel Sturgis, no doubt, was pleased to be rid of him. Yet the Reno case held ironic parallels for Sturgis. Sturgis's own military record was not without blemish. He had been the object of a board of investigation held 28 June 1864 at Memphis, Tennessee, an investigation that centered on his conduct during the Civil War.[11]

Sturgis, then a brevet brigadier general, had suffered one of the most severe Union defeats of the war at the Battle of Brices Cross Roads in Mississippi on 10 June 1864. He had been sent out with a Union command of cavalry and infantry to engage General Nathan Bedford Forrest's Confederate force, which was threatening General Sherman's lines of communications. Although Sturgis commanded a force twice the size of Forrest's, his troops were routed. During the investigation that followed, one officer testified to seeing Sturgis "very much intoxicated" in a Memphis hotel just before the departure of the troops to the front. The witness also testified that he had seen Sturgis stop a girl passing by and put his arm around her. "I became disgusted with the sight," the witness stated, "and did not wait to see more." An enlisted man who testified at the inquiry said he had seen Sturgis drinking whiskey with another officer on the day of the battle with Forrest. He declared that the troops "had little confidence" in their commander.[12] But other witnesses said Sturgis was not drunk at the time. They attributed the Confederate victory to Forrest's superior tactical skills. The investigation ended without any formal charges being placed against Sturgis. The court decided that Forrest had been so busy routing Sturgis that he had been unable to interfere with Sherman's march on Georgia. So, in a way, Sturgis had actually aided Sherman. The investigation, however, resulted in unfavorable newspaper publicity, and Sturgis requested a formal court of inquiry to clear his name. Sherman, in denying the request, informed Sturgis that his complaints were "mere topics of camp rumor reproduced by the newspapers" and that "no charges or imputations from any authorized source" existed against him. Nevertheless, Sherman permitted Sturgis to publish and circulate a letter he had written to army headquarters on 24 February 1864, defending his actions during the campaign.[13]

General Grant, in reviewing the case, noted that Sturgis had been so badly beaten that Forrest had driven him back "in utter route and confusion" for about one hundred miles. By pursuing Sturgis, Grant wrote, Forrest had been "defeated in his designs upon Sherman's lines of communication. The persistency with which he followed up his success exhausted him, and made a season for rest and repairs necessary."[14] General Sheridan, in recalling the battle, reported that Sturgis had invited him to watch as he whipped Forrest's cavalry. Having other things to do,

Sheridan had declined. But he later wrote that it had been necessary for him to send an infantry brigade to rescue Sturgis from "a serious predicament."[15] So, although he was not court-martialed, Sturgis's reputation as a field commander was severely damaged by the investigation. It explains why his superiors usually found some detached service for him whenever the Seventh Cavalry was sent into the field after he became its commander.

Fifteen years after his own similar troubles, Sturgis might have been more tolerant of Reno's conduct if his daughter had not been involved. The fact that his son had been killed at the Little Bighorn—where Reno had been the senior surviving officer—probably also motivated him to press the case against the major so vigorously.

There is no disputing the fact that Reno did drink too much and was overly fond of women—not uncommon traits among soldiers on the frontier. A once handsome officer, Reno was a hot-blooded romantic who regarded himself as attractive to women. But he exercised poor judgment in picking the objects of his affection. Emiline Bell, although having a reputation within the regiment as an unfaithful wife when Reno got into trouble over her, was a married woman.[16] And Ella was much his junior, as well as being the daughter of a superior officer who intensely disliked him. Reno's principal fault, as he himself described it, "was in the judgment and not the heart." That his dismissal may have come on the wrong charge was of little consequence to his enemies, who felt that justice had finally been done.

Reno left Fort Meade on 1 April, and his place in the regiment was filled by the promotion and assignment of Captain Edward Ball, Second Cavalry. Reno went back East and spent the remainder of his life vainly attempting to regain his commission. He even persuaded former President Grant to recommend a review of his case. However, Secretary of War Robert Lincoln, the son of the assassinated president, ruled that the law gave the president no authority for reinstating the dismissed officer. "As the number of majors of cavalry is limited by law, and the list is full," Lincoln wrote, "Major Reno could not be appointed to that grade without removing a major from service." Lincoln also noted, "A decision made under one president is not liable to be reviewed and annulled under the administration of another."

Several private bills for Reno's reinstatement were introduced in Congress but died in committee for lack of support. Reno married Isabell Ray, a government clerk, in 1884, but they quickly separated. They both filed for divorce, and Reno protested a court order requiring him to make fifty-dollar-per-month support payments to his wife. He claimed that his annual income was scarcely three thousand dollars at the time. Reno was working as a special examiner in the Bureau of Pensions in Washington when it was discovered that he had cancer of the tongue. He died on 30 March 1889, before his divorce became final, and was buried in an unmarked grave in the Glenwood Cemetery. Only his son, Ross, and hired pallbearers attended the graveside funeral.[17]

Reno's death came almost thirteen years after the historic Battle of the Little Bighorn, where so many men of his regiment had fallen. But in a sense his life had ended there too.

★ **6** ★

CHANGING THE GUARD

Shortly after Reno left Fort Meade, the permanent garrison of the post was reduced by 11 officers and 297 enlisted men, due to the transfer of the four companies (D, F, H, and K) of the First Infantry in May 1880 to posts in Texas. Companies F and K had been part of the garrison from the beginning, D and H since September 1879. It would be August before the troops were replaced. Left at the post were the headquarters staff, the band, and six line companies of the Seventh Cavalry—A, C, E, G, H, and M. The other four companies of the Seventh (B, D, F, and L) were posted to Forts Yates, Totten, or Abraham Lincoln.[1]

The first federal census in the Black Hills was taken in June 1880. It established Lawrence County, which contained Fort Meade, as the largest of the three Black Hills counties. It had a population of 13,200, of which 3,677 were in the county seat. That gave Deadwood the distinction of being the largest community in southern Dakota, outstripping even the territorial capital at Yankton.[2]

At Fort Meade, the census taker counted 525 persons, including 141 civilians. The civilian employees of the Quartermaster Department numbered only 29, so the majority of the civilians counted were either the wives, children, or servants of the officers or the family members of the enlisted men. The garrison still included a number of veterans who had fought at the Little Bighorn, but most of the soldiers enumerated had joined the regiment during the intervening four years. One hundred and fifty-two people on the post were of foreign birth. Only Colonel Sturgis and his wife, Jutie, along with three servants, were found residing at the post commander's quarters when the post census was taken. The servants were Katie Costello, a twenty-one-year-old married white woman, John C. Collins, a fifty-eight-year-old single white man, and Lizzie Warren, a twenty-eight-year-old single black woman. The two unmarried Sturgis

Fort Meade gave birth to the town of Sturgis City, one mile west of the post. A number of officers stationed at the fort, including the post commander, became major property owners in the town. Three wagon roads to the northern Black Hills converged here, and the townspeople did a lively business with freighters and soldiers. (Photo by O.A. Vik, courtesy of Old Fort Meade Museum Association.)

daughters, Ella and fifteen-year-old Mary, were away at the time, as was eighteen-year-old Samuel, who became a plebe at West Point on 1 July.

The population of Fort Meade was far greater than that of the nearby community it had brought into being—only sixty persons resided in Sturgis City, including Jeremiah C. Wilcox of the townsite company, his wife, Perlia, and their five children. Wilcox was identified as a real estate agent. An additional forty persons were counted in the Sturgis precinct, which included the environs of the town and the fort. Some of these residents had homesteaded in the area before the establishment of the fort, but most of them had settled there when the post was founded.[3]

Detachments of the Seventh Cavalry were frequently dispatched into the field during the summer of 1880 in response to reports of Indian depredations. Scouting missions were particularly numerous in the vicinity of the Belle Fourche and Little Missouri rivers north and west of the Black Hills. Colonel Sturgis proposed the establishment of a two-company summer camp in the area "for the purpose of patrolling the country between the Bismarck road and the Little Missouri River." The colonel, however, was doubtful that it was Indians who were causing the trouble. "The outskirts of civilization," he noted, "are infested by horse thieves and fugitives from the law who disguise themselves as Indians and carry away many horses and cattle."[4]

Permission for the camp came in June, and Sturgis sent Companies E and G of his regiment to the Little Missouri River in Montana. The camp was named Camp Hodgson for Second Lieutenant Benjamin H. Hodgson of Company B, Seventh Cavalry, who had been killed at the Little Bighorn. An eighty-six-mile march for the troops from Fort Meade, the camp was the base of operations for scouting missions in that region until August, when it was abandoned. There were no engagements between these troops and the Indians that summer.

Fort Meade became a ten-company post again in August when four companies of the Twenty-fifth Infantry Regiment arrived to replace the transferred First Infantry companies. The Twenty-fifth was one of two infantry regiments whose enlisted ranks were composed solely of blacks. It had been stationed in Texas since 1870 and came to the Department of Dakota in April 1880 in exchange for the First Infantry. Colonel George L. Andrews, with headquarters and Companies F, G, and I, took station at Fort Randall. Companies C and E were assigned to Fort Hale, a post established in 1870 on the Missouri River at the Lower Brule Agency and abandoned fourteen years later. Assigned to Fort Meade were Companies A, D, H, and K, and they reached the post on 17 August, which increased the permanent garrison by 8 officers and 187 enlisted men.[5] Captain David Wilson, the first chaplain to be assigned to Fort Meade, reported to the post on 5 September. His daughter, Jeannie, a graduate of Western Maryland College, was hired to teach school for the officers' children at the post.

In the spring of 1881, Colonel Sturgis was appointed the superintendent of the Soldiers' Home in Washington, D.C., a post he would hold for four years. The regiment's lieutenant colonel, Otis, then on detached service as the commanding officer at Fort Lincoln, became the acting commander of the Seventh. Consequently, the headquarters of the regiment was temporarily transferred from Fort Meade to Fort Lincoln when Sturgis left the post, and Captain David D. Van Valzah, Company D, Twenty-fifth Infantry, became the post commander at Fort Meade. He was succeeded in August by Major Ball, Reno's replacement, of the Seventh.[6]

Companies A and H of the Seventh Cavalry, along with Company A of the Twenty-fifth Infantry, performed patrol duty in the Little Missouri River country throughout most of 1881. Companies C and M of the Seventh served as escorts for the hauling of government supplies from Fort Pierre to the post, while Companies E and G provided protection for the Northern Pacific Railroad crews operating in Montana. Company G was later detailed to the School of Cavalry Instruction at Fort Leavenworth, Kansas, and left, under the command of Lieutenant Wallace, on 10 November.

Fire destroyed the quarters occupied by Company A, Twenty-fifth Infantry, and Company H, Seventh Cavalry, in late November. The fire originated in one of the kitchens, and a strong wind carried embers that set the grass aflame on the parade grounds. However, the soldiers kept the flames from spreading to other buildings.[7]

Both cavalry and infantry companies engaged in routine garrison duties at Fort Meade during the remainder of 1881. The fatigue details often included cutting firewood for the fort at wood camps established in the timber tract reserved for the military reservation. Situated about five miles southeast of the fort, this timber reserve, established in 1881 and enlarged in 1889, covered 5,208 acres in what later became the Meade District of the Black Hills National Forest.

By the end of 1881, the government had supplemented the original appropriation for the construction of Fort Meade by fifty-seven thousand dollars. The additional amount was spent on such improvements as the hospital, a reservoir, and another barracks for enlisted men. Post facilities then consisted of twenty-three sets of officers' quarters, ten barracks for the enlisted personnel, a headquarters building, eight stables, one bakery, two quartermaster storehouses, one commissary, one band quarters, the

hospital, four buildings for noncommissioned officers, two shops for mechanics, the sawmill, an ammunition magazine, the guardhouse, and a
building that doubled as a school for children of post personnel and as a
church. The post cemetery had also been fenced. Five thousand cords of
wood per year were needed to heat the post buildings. The post's horses
annually consumed 1,700 tons of hay, 750,000 pounds of corn, and 1,500
pounds of oats.

Leaving Major Tilford in command at Fort Abraham Lincoln, Lieutenant Colonel Otis returned the headquarters of the Seventh to Fort Meade
in July 1882 and assumed command of the fort as well. In addition to
Company G, which was at Fort Leavenworth, four other companies of the
Seventh were absent from Fort Meade for long periods in 1882. Companies A and C marched 412 miles to Fort Sisseton in eastern Dakota
Territory, arriving there on 23 May and returning to Fort Meade on
29 August. Company H guarded work parties of the Northern Pacific in
Montana from May to September. And Company M performed escort duty
from June to October for the U.S. Geodetic Survey as it surveyed the
boundaries between Wyoming, Nebraska, and Dakota, marching more
than 1,200 miles on that duty.[8]

Fort Meade's garrison was enlarged in November when Captain Edward G. Mathey's Company K of the Seventh arrived from Fort Totten in a
change of stations. Since the cavalry barracks destroyed by fire the previous year had not yet been rebuilt, Mathey's soldiers worked at building
their own quarters until 15 December, when they resumed normal garrison duties.[9]

The transfer of Company K to Fort Meade brought Lieutenant Hugh L.
Scott, who had mapped the boundaries of the post in 1878, back to the
Black Hills. Scott, previously of Company I, had married the daughter of
Major Merrill of the Seventh's headquarters staff. He was less than en-
thusiastic about the change of stations. It was a four-hundred-mile march
from Fort Totten to Meade by way of Fort Lincoln, where Scott picked up
his wife and daughter, under winter conditions. He wrote of the trip:
"After a long march in great cold, wet, and discomfort, we arrived at Fort
Meade. We had left comfortable brick two-story barracks, the best in the
Northwest, to march four hundred miles through inclement weather to a
post where there were no quarters for us and we had to start building our

own of logs, in winter. There was apparently no emergency to cause this change of station and it seemed nothing but a wanton disregard of the comfort of troops."[10]

Scott later complained about a stage trip his wife and son would take from Fort Pierre to Fort Meade the following spring. The Bismarck stage had attracted most travelers bound eastward from the Hills in the fort's first years, but the Fort Pierre route became favored when the Chicago and Northwestern Railroad tracks reached the other bank of the Missouri River at Pierre in 1880. The Northwestern Express and Transportation Company transferred its stage operations from Bismarck to Pierre that same year when awarded the contract for carrying the mail to the Black Hills from Pierre. Scott's wife and son took the stage to Fort Pierre en route to visit her family in Philadelphia and made good time going out over the frozen ground. The return trip was made in warmer weather and was, Scott wrote, "one of the hardest trips any one ever had." They were seven days and nights on the stage because of the condition of the soil, which rolled "up on the wheels like glue when wet." The four big horses pulling the stage, Scott reported, "would pull about five hundred yards and stop, out of breath, the wheels glued up with gumbo." The journey could not be continued until the "gumbo" was laboriously removed.[11]

The Seventh Cavalry lost one of its most experienced officers in 1882 when Captain Benteen was promoted to major and assigned to the Ninth Cavalry, which was composed of black soldiers. Benteen's place in the Seventh went to Lieutenant DeRudio, who was promoted to captain on 1 February 1883.

Recreational activities for the troops at Fort Meade at the time included baseball games between the companies, horse racing, theatrical productions, and the varied attractions of the post trader's saloon and the bawdy houses in Sturgis. The post surgeon frequently treated both cavalry and infantry soldiers for knife and gunshot wounds, some of them fatal, sustained "in drunken brawls in Sturgis City."[12] "Many are the cutting and shooting affrays recorded against the town," the *Black Hills Journal* at Rapid City asserted, "and *The Police Gazette* would do well to have a regular correspondent within its confines."[13]

Many of the officers of the fort, Lieutenant Scott among them, spent their free time on hunting leaves. The army at that time encouraged officers to take hunting leaves, providing they turned in maps of the country traveled. During the hunting season, Scott and his friends often took advantage of the opportunity to hunt and explore the Black Hills region. "I turned in maps of the country for two hundred miles about Fort Meade in every direction," he wrote.[14]

Concern with sanitary conditions, including the quality of the water supply, was reflected in the post surgeon's monthly reports throughout the 1880s. The doctor went so far as to propose that the fort be abandoned if the water supply was not improved. One report noted that the water of Bear Butte Creek, which supplied the fort, was running red from mine tailings dumped into it by miners at Galena. Another complained of pine slabs and a dead cat being found in the creek; another drew attention to cattle crossing the creek above the point where water was drawn for the post. The gradual growth of Sturgis City, whose sewage emptied into Bear Butte Creek above the fort, was also a constant concern to the post authorities.[15]

The fort's waterworks, which included a system of pipes that carried creek water to a reservoir eighty feet above the pump house, were started in 1881 and finished in 1883. The system cost $8,140 and was supplemented by a twenty-one-foot well at the post sawmill. Containing between six and seven feet of pure water during the wet season, the well was insufficient for the post's needs during dry periods. Water restrictions were then imposed. Both the post surgeon and the Seventh Cavalry's regimental quartermaster made repeated requests for a dependable supplemental water supply.[16]

Finally, after three years of negotiations, three thousand dollars was appropriated to purchase a twenty-one-acre tract containing an excellent supply of pure spring water. These springs had originally been intended as part of the military reserve, but they had been left out through a survey error. Meanwhile, William McMillan, a pioneer of the region, homesteaded the tract containing the springs. He deeded them to the government on 2 April 1888, after accepting the appropriated sum.[17]

In 1883, the post surgeon found fault with the "filthy conditions" of the quarters formerly occupied by the commissary sergeant. Before the surgeon's arrival at the post, the sergeant had lost a child to diphtheria, and his quarters had then been disinfected and overhauled. But they soon reverted to their previous "primitive filthy conditions," and the surgeon recommended that the quarters be burned down. The unhappy sergeant later became the post's first suicide victim on 3 November 1883. The surgeon also reported an infant's death from malarial fever on "Laundress Row," also known as "Soapsuds Row." The surgeon asked the post commander to put a stop to the laundresses' habit of washing clothes in Bear Butte Creek above the post's water intake.[18]

In another of his monthly sanitary reports, the surgeon noted that replacing the board roofs on the "loghouses" occupied by Troop K (cavalry companies were renamed troops in 1883), Seventh Cavalry, and Company H, Twenty-fifth Infantry, had stopped the roofs from leaking. But he recommended that the floors, which had been ruined by the water leaks, be replaced before winter set in again. His report for September 1883 included a notice of the death, from cholera, of the infant daughter of a Seventh Cavalry band member.[19]

The post's waterworks were extended into the hospital bathroom and kitchen on 3 November. The next day the sawmill, which contained the pump house supplying the post with water from the creek, was destroyed by fire. The cause of the fire, which had started at four in the morning, was not determined.[20]

Detachments from Fort Meade made marches to Fort Pierre in the spring of 1883 to pick up horses for the cavalry and recruits for both the cavalry and the infantry units. Lieutenant Scott commanded a detachment sent into the Powder River country in April in pursuit of Crows under Crazy Head; they returned to the fort on 26 May after intercepting the Crow band and escorting them back to their reservation. Fatigue details from both the cavalry and the infantry companies spent much of the summer of 1883 cutting firewood at the wood camps.[21]

Otis was promoted to the colonelcy of the Eighth Cavalry in April. He was succeeded as post and regimental commander by Lieutenant Colonel Andrew W. Evans, who had just been promoted from major, Third Cavalry, and assigned to the Seventh. Evans's tour at Fort Meade was brief, since he retired in September. Tilford was then promoted to lieutenant colonel and assumed command of his regiment and Fort Meade in November, at the same time that General Sheridan was promoted to succeed the retiring Sherman as the commander in chief of the army. General John

Schofield took Sheridan's place as the commander of the Division of the Missouri, which included Terry's Department of Dakota.[22]

The seven posts in southern Dakota—Meade, Sisseton, Randall, Hale, Sully, Bennett, and Camp at Rosebud Agency—were part of Terry's middle district, headed by the commanding officer at Fort Abraham Lincoln. The army abandoned many of the military telegraph lines linking its Department of Dakota posts in 1883–84, in keeping with its policy of turning this activity over to private companies as they extended their poles to the frontier communities. The Fort Bennett to Fort Meade line was among those abandoned during this period. Communication services for Fort Meade were then provided by the Black Hills Telegraph and Telephone Co., established in 1883.[23]

Although it had been a thriving town since 1878, Sturgis City did not get its first newspaper until 1883. The founders were Charles Moody, who was the son of Judge G. C. Moody, and John Elliott, who had been a compositor for the *Black Hills Daily Times* at Deadwood and who had a ranch near Bear Butte. Volume 1, number 1 of the *Sturgis Weekly Record* came off the presses on 27 July and soon began a regular column on happenings at Fort Meade: "The Boys at Meade—A General Collection of the Cream of the News from the Post (Specially Reported)." The headline was soon shortened to "Garrison Gossip." The publishers gave Fort Meade happenings attention in keeping with the fort's importance to the community. Many articles dealt with the troubles the soldiers experienced in saloons and houses of ill repute, and others devoted considerable space to the social activities of the fort.[24]

Tilford held the dual posts of regimental and post commander at Fort Meade until June 1885. Colonel Sturgis, relieved from his assignment at the Soldiers' Home, returned to the fort on 26 June and took command the next day. During Colonel Sturgis's second tour of duty at Fort Meade, racial trouble broke out between the black troops of the Twenty-fifth Infantry and the townspeople of Sturgis City. A private from Company D, Twenty-fifth Infantry, had been killed by a black prostitute in Sturgis City in October 1884 while Tilford was the post commander. But the woman was acquitted on the grounds of justifiable homicide, and no other trouble ensued, probably because both principals were black.[25]

The situation was different when Corporal Ross Hallon of Company A was accused of murdering Dr. H. P. Lynch in Sturgis on the night of 22 August 1885. Hallon frequently beat one Minnie Lewis, and she sought treatment from Dr. Lynch. The doctor advised her to report the beatings to the authorities at Fort Meade, and Lewis informed Hallon she would do so if he continued knocking her around. Incensed at the doctor's interference, Hallon borrowed a pistol from a soldier in his company and wore the blouse of another man in order to conceal his corporal's chevrons. Then, according to circumstantial evidence brought against him, he went to Lynch's drugstore and fatally shot the doctor. A coroner's jury ruled that Lynch "came to his death at the hands of Hallon," and the soldier was arrested on 23 August.[26]

Hallon was taken to jail in Sturgis, where he was placed under the custody of Deputy Sheriff William Souter. The deputy engaged Norman McAuley and John P. McDonald to guard the prisoner until he could be brought to trial. On the night of 25 August, a group of armed men appeared at the jail and advised the guards to go home. "McAuley has a family and McDonald hopes to have one," the *Sturgis Weekly Record* later reported. "Consequently, neither one of them looked back and they are not sieves today."[27] Hallon's body was found hanging from a tree west of town the next morning. A detail of the Seventh Cavalry under Lieutenant Scott cut down the body and brought it to the fort for burial in the post cemetery. A three-man coroner's jury ruled that Hallon had come to his death "by strangulation, or some other climactic disease, at the hands of parties unknown."[28]

This was the second hanging of a prisoner taken from the Sturgis jail by a mob. The first was Alex Fiddler, a white man described as "a dissolute character" among the unsavory hard cases who frequented the Sturgis saloons and bawdy houses. Fiddler had been accused of beating and robbing a German emigrant in June 1884. He was being held in the jail when masked men forced the guard to turn him over. He was hanged at a tree on the west edge of town, a tree thereafter known locally as "Fiddler's Tree." It was on this same tree that Hallon's life also ended.[29]

When word of Hallon's fate reached Fort Meade, some soldiers of his company armed themselves and started to town. Colonel Sturgis, however, sent a detachment of the Seventh Cavalry to return them to the fort. The incident created considerable tension between the black soldiers and the people of Sturgis, so the troops were kept at the fort until tempers cooled. The explosive situation was exacerbated by the existence of two Sturgis establishments that catered to the black soldiers. One was a dance hall owned by Abe Hill, a black man, and the other an adjoining bawdy house owned by John Dolan. The feared explosion occurred there during the night of 19 September when a group of soldiers of Company H, Twenty-fifth Infantry, fired into the two buildings from the street. A visiting cowboy, Robert Bell, of York, Nebraska, was killed in the melee.[30]

Colonel Sturgis was hosting Caulfield, the lawyer for the Sturgis Townsite Company, at his quarters when word reached him of the incident. Sturgis immediately convened a board of investigation to look into the affair, and Caulfield, angered by the assault on the town in which he was promoting settlement, sent President Grover Cleveland a long letter giving details on the deaths of Lynch, Hallon, and Bell. He also advised the President that the Twenty-fifth Infantry was "composed in part by a set of reckless desperadoes," and he proposed it be transferred to some other station. "These colored soldiers infest Sturgis at night and are the support of a lot of vile Negro girls and women who congregate at a drinking den called a 'Dance House,'" Caulfield informed the president. "I understand that rows and fights are of constant occurrence in and about this house, and the people of the town are kept in constant dread, by the firing of pistols and all the yells of these Negroes at night."[31]

Caulfield conceded that Sturgis had a fair share of "scoundrels" who tended to "congregate in such towns from different locations for the purpose of fleecing and robbing the soldiers about pay day." However, he claimed the "good citizens of the town were not responsible for them."[32] Annie Tallent, the first white woman in the Black Hills, spent the last years of her life in Sturgis City and wrote about the community's "era of disorder, crime and speedy retribution." During the first decade of its history, she remembered, "it was by no means always a shining example of morality and good order." In fact, she added, Sturgis City frequently presented "scenes of mad recklessness that outrivaled in lawlessness even the worst days of the early mining camps," and "these conditions were occasioned in good part by the riotous behavior of some of the men at Fort Meade. Whiskey flowed like water and after imbibing several copious draughts of the fiery fluid, they proceeded to paint Main Street in all sorts of livid color."[33]

President Cleveland referred Caulfield's letter to the secretary of war, who sent it down through channels to General Terry for comment. At the same time, the secretary was also receiving petitions from Sturgis for the removal of the black troops from Fort Meade.[34] He also asked for General Terry's recommendation on the advisability of granting the request. Terry, meanwhile, waited for the findings of the board of investigation that Sturgis had appointed. The board, consisting of three officers of the Seventh Cavalry and two of the Twenty-fifth Infantry, went into Sturgis to examine the body of Bell and the bullet holes in the buildings owned by Hill and Dolan. They also spent two days taking testimony from sixteen witnesses. The board's findings were that Private John Taylor of Company H had been involved in an argument with Hill; that Taylor had left Hill's saloon threatening revenge; that Taylor had returned with a group of up to twenty armed soldiers from his company and, after calling for the soldiers inside the saloon to get out, had fired up to one hundred shots into Hill's place, some of the bullets also striking Dolan's building; that Taylor and Pierce Greer, also of Company H, had directed the firing; that Bell had been killed by a rifle bullet fired by Taylor, Greer, Evans Morris, or Smith Watson, all of Company H, or "others in collusion with them." The board also found that the incident had been confined entirely to the places run by Hill and Dolan and had been perpetrated solely by members of Company H.[35]

Sixteen soldiers of Company H were taken to the guardhouse following the board's investigation. Four of them—Privates Watson, Taylor, Greer, and Morris—were taken to the Lawrence County jail to await trail on charges of inciting the violence and killing Bell. The other twelve men were released. General Terry, responding to Caulfield's letter to the president, termed it "a just and temperate account of the occurrences." But he also took exception to the Deadwood attorney's claim that Hallon had assassinated Dr. Lynch. Terry, also a lawyer, wrote that the evidence against Hallon was "by no means conclusive." He pointed out that the hanging of Hallon had thwarted any attempt to determine his guilt or innocence. Moreover, the department commander did not favor the removal of the black troops from Fort Meade.[36]

Terry, reminding his superiors that he had had considerable experience with black troops, stated: "I have always found them as well behaved and as amenable to discipline as any white troops we have." He termed the situation at Fort Meade "unfortunate" and expressed the view that it was undesirable for military posts to be located as close to a town as Fort Meade and Sturgis. "But the post was established before the town was founded," Terry noted, "and I do not think that there would have been a town but for the post." He expressed confidence that the officers of the post would do their best to prevent crime if the civil authorities in Sturgis would do likewise. Houses of ill fame were, of course, illegal under the laws of Dakota Territory. But Terry added:

Not withstanding the law, there are, in the town, two brothels, which would appear to have been established for the express purpose of catering to the taste and pandering to the passions of the colored troops, for they are "stocked" with colored prostitutes— negresses and mulattoes. They are, I am assured, places of the vilest character and it was at one of them that the affray of September 19th occurred. Had no such place existed it is most improbable that any affray would have occurred, and if the people of Sturgis City suffer such places to exist they must, I submit, expect the natural result of their existence—frequent broils, and from time to time, the commission of the most serious crimes. And I submit further that, until the people of the town shall have suppressed these dens, which equally debauch the troops of the post and threaten their own safety, they will not be in a position to ask the government to change its garrison.[37]

Terry's views were endorsed by his superiors, and the black troops remained at Fort Meade—for the time being.

In the meantime, a grand jury convicted Hill of running a disorderly house. He was fined $250 and sentenced to thirty days in the county jail. The sentence did not amount to much more than a slap on the wrist, and he was soon back in business at his dance hall. The grand jury also cleared Souter of any negligence in failing to prevent Hallon's hanging. Taylor, Watson, Greer, and Morris were brought to trial in Deadwood, and all but Watson were convicted. The convicted soldiers were sentenced in 1886 to life imprisonment. Before they could be transported to the state penitentiary, however, Greer and Morris escaped with several other prisoners. They were never recaptured. Taylor, unable to join in the escape because he had been in a different cell, was taken to the penitentiary at Sioux Falls, where he later died.[38] Relations between the citizens of Sturgis City and the black troops at Fort Meade remained strained for quite some time after these "affrays." But there were no further incidents serious enough to bring renewed violence.

Colonel Sturgis was on leave from Fort Meade from 17 November 1885 until 10 April 1886, and the command of the regiment and post reverted to Tilford during the colonel's absence. On 11 June, Sturgis retired, at the age of sixty-four. A week later, at the home of his eldest daughter, in Prairie du Chien, Wisconsin, he gave Ella's hand in marriage to John D. Lawler. The bridegroom was a prominent real estate developer and banker at Mitchell, in eastern Dakota. Jerusha Sturgis, writing of her husband's departure from Fort Meade, claimed that the men of the regiment were devoted to him and that "there was scarcely a dry eye" when he left.[39] The *Black Hills Weekly Journal,* pointing out that Sturgis should not be blamed for the poor location of Fort Meade because he had not made the selection, had high praise for him. "Since he has been stationed here," it editorialized, "he has entered heart and soul into all the great enterprises of the country, and done all that in reason could have been expected of him towards protecting the interests of the settlers of the Black Hills."[40]

Taking over the command of the Seventh Cavalry and the fort after Colonel Sturgis's retirement was Colonel James W. (Tony) Forsyth. A West Pointer of the class of 1851, Forsyth had served as military secretary and aide-de-camp to General Sheridan until assigned as second in command of the First Cavalry in 1878. His promotion to a full colonelcy on the date of Sturgis's retirement brought him to the command of the Seventh. Forsyth arrived at Fort Meade on 26 July and found 17 officers and 337 enlisted men of the Seventh present for duty. In addition to the field staff and the band, the cavalry troops at the post when Forsyth arrived included Troops A, C, E, H, K, and M of the Seventh. The regular garrison also included 6 officers and 138 enlisted men in the four companies of the Twenty-fifth Infantry.[41]

The occupational skills of the men in the Seventh Cavalry at Fort Meade at the time are revealed in the listing of "mechanics" in the regiment's monthly reports. Their numbers ranged from a low of eight in

Troop K to a high of sixteen in Troop M. Under this heading came such trades as baker, blacksmith, bricklayer, butcher, carpenter, clerk, cook, engineer, horseshoer, machinist, painter, plasterer, plumber, printer, sawyer, schoolteacher (there was only one in the regiment), shoemaker, stonemason, tailor, tinsmith, and wheelwright. All but twenty-one of the regiment's enlisted personnel fell into one of these categories. Fifteen civilian employees of the quartermaster department were at the post when Forsyth took command. One was Daniel Newell, the blacksmith, who had been wounded in the Little Bighorn fight while serving with Captain Myles Moylan's Company A. He was one of many former soldiers who became civilian employees of the post following their discharge at Fort Meade. As a civilian employee, Newell was paid sixty dollars a month, and he lived in a cabin he had built himself at the fort.[42]

In August 1886, Lieutenant Scott's long association with the post came to an end. He was placed on detached service for two years of recruiting duty for the cavalry at Philadelphia. He put his horses, a cow, and other property up for sale at an auction at the fort before departing. "When my old buffalo horse was bid up higher than his cost," Scott later recalled, "he seemed to look at me with reproach and say, 'After all our times together among the buffalo, are you really going to sell me?' and I withdrew him from the sale, although I needed the money."[43]

There were several changes of station for the Seventh Cavalry troops after Colonel Forsyth's arrival on the post. Troop A was reassigned to Fort Keogh and Troops E and H to Fort Yates in October. Taking their place were Troops B and D from Fort Yates and G from Keogh. Troop L remained at Fort Buford, where it conducted extensive scouts in the Yellowstone Valley.

The beginning of the end of the Seventh Cavalry's association with Fort Meade came in July 1887. Colonel Forsyth, with his headquarters staff, the band, and Troops C, D, G, and M, was reassigned to Fort Riley, Kansas, where the regiment had been organized in 1866. Their departure on 25 July left Troops B and K of the Seventh and the four infantry companies remaining at the post. Household goods and other personal property of the transferred personnel were sold at public auction on 17 July. Tilford assumed the command of the cavalry units left behind, and he again became the post commander as well.[44]

Fort Meade's garrison was reinforced in August by three other troops of the Seventh. Troops F and L joined the garrison from Fort Buford and Troop I from Fort Totten. In September, Tilford had trouble with Abe Hill, who had opened a saloon and dance hall on the boundaries of the military reservation after losing his liquor license in Sturgis. The townspeople had failed in their efforts to have the black troops removed from Fort Meade, so they got rid of Hill instead—or so they thought—by forcing him off Main Street. He merely moved his operations closer to the fort, which was only a mile from Sturgis to begin with. The debauchery there became so notorious that Tilford placed sentinels on the roads leading to Hill's place to prevent soldiers from going there. Hill protested to the secretary of war, and Tilford was asked to justify his actions. He replied that Hill's place was "disorderly and disreputable, and housed a number of women of bad repute, who were in the habit of exposing themselves to the public gaze in prostrate positions, and otherwise conducting themselves in a scandalous manner, so that respectable people could not pass on the highway without being subjected to such insult as such state of affairs offered." Tilford added, "The place had become the resort of the disorderly elements among the enlisted men of this garrison, where they could assemble and carouse, and numerous frays must inevitably have occurred to the prejudice of the service." Tilford also informed higher headquarters:

This man, Hill, was conducting a place of the same nature in the town of Sturgis, on Main Street, at which the trouble originated which resulted in the people of that town forwarding a petition for the removal of the colored troops from Fort Meade. It had become so disreputable that his license to do business in the town was re- voked. Recently he was given a license by the authorities of Sturgis to carry on his business again, but on condition that it should be removed from the central or main part of the town, and it was established as already stated.

My object in posting sentinels on the roads at this point (one branch of road is in front and one in rear) was to prevent all soldiers of this garrison from entering this house or appearing on the roads in its vicinity. No civilians were interfered with or molested in any way. I thus expected to break up all traffic at Abram Hill's saloon, for it depended upon the soldiers of the garrison for its business and support.

Since the receipt of your letter the Board of County Commissioners has revoked Hill's license to sell liquors, and I have taken the guard off the roads, believing the end in view has been obtained.[45]

Tilford's strategy worked, with the help of the County Commission. Reports of Tilford's vigorous campaign against Hill were carried regularly in both the *Sturgis Weekly Record* and the *Sturgis Advertiser*. The latter newspaper, the community's second weekly, had begun publication on 1 July 1887, with I. R. Crow as publisher. It was printed in the same building where Charlie Collins had issued his first—and only—edition of the *Black Hills Champion*. The *Advertiser* published an open letter from Tilford to the County Commission on 12 October. In it, the post commander threatened to close the road across the military reservation if something was not done about Hill's establishment. Consequently, the liquor license for the Halfway House, as Hill's place of business was known, was revoked. Deprived of a license and the soldiers' trade, Hill had to look elsewhere for business. Hill suffered another setback in 1888, when City Ordinance No. 8 prohibited houses of ill repute in Sturgis City.[46]

Tilford's strong stand against the shady elements of the Sturgis business community made him so popular that a new town was named for him. The Fremont, Elkhorn, and Missouri Valley Railway Company pushed its rails from Rapid City to Sturgis City in October 1887. The Pioneer Townsite Company, a founder of many railroad towns in southern Dakota, established a hamlet along the tracks some six miles south of Sturgis City in January 1888. The new town was named Tilford, and James Howard, the first postmaster at Fort Meade, quit his post to become the first postmaster there.[47]

Howard was succeeded as postmaster at Fort Meade by C. M. Garlington, the post trader. Fanshawe, the original post trader, had sold out in 1882 to go into business at Rapid City. He had been succeeded by E. A. Packard, until J. W. Skiles had taken over in 1885. Garlington became the post trader in 1886 and held the post until 1889, when Jordan B. Cottle took over the store and the saloon. Cottle's tenure was short-lived; he was given ninety days to close his operations that same summer. The secretary of war had been urged earlier not to appoint another post trader but did not act on the suggestion until 1889. "There is no need for a trader's post at the post," the *Sturgis Advertiser* editorialized, "as the merchants of this city can easily supply the demand." The newspaper noted that Fort Meade's monthly payroll was twenty thousand dollars, "a large portion of which" was "instantly circulated" in Sturgis.[48]

Activities at the post in early 1888 included the formation of Jack G. Sturgis Post No. 47 of the Grand Army of the Republic (G.A.R.). The post was named for the same Seventh Cavalry officer whose name had been given to the Camp at Bear Butte ten years earlier. The G.A.R. members met on the first and third Saturday evening of each month in Library Hall at Fort Meade.[49]

The tenure of the Seventh Cavalry at Fort Meade, which had begun with the establishment of Camp Sturgis at Bear Butte in 1878, ended in the summer of 1888. And so did the tour of the black Twenty-fifth Infantry. Its transfer from the post was attributed to the needs of the service and not to the earlier petitions from Sturgis requesting its removal. Orders came in May transferring the black soldiers to posts in Montana; Companies A and D were assigned to Fort Custer, Companies H and K to Fort Missoula. The soldiers marched to the Sturgis depot and left the Hills by train on 29 May. The *Sturgis Weekly Record* was not displeased with their departure. "While the officers were a first-class set of men," the newspaper stated, "yet Sturgis is not very sorry to lose the rank and file."[50]

Troops A, E, and H of the Seventh Cavalry returned to Fort Meade from Forts Keogh and Yates in May 1888. They had just settled into their quarters when orders were received for all of the Seventh's troops at the post to join the regiment's companies previously sent to Fort Riley. On 22 May, Tilford gave his daughter's hand in marriage to Second Lieutenant George H. Cameron of the Seventh. Held at the post chapel, the wedding was the last social event at the post for the regiment's officers.

Troops B, E, I, and L left the post under Tilford on 1 June. The next day, Major John M. Bacon left for Fort Riley with Troops A, F, H, and K. There were then no troops remaining of the companies that had seen Camps

Sturgis and Ruhlen evolve into Fort Meade. Chris Meyer and J. S. Wenke of Sturgis got the contract for moving the regiment's property to the Kansas post. They were paid $14.87 per hundredweight for moving seventy-five thousand pounds of material. The teamsters were required to furnish their own rations and to forage for the expedition.[51]

Going to Kansas with Troop I was the honored regimental horse, Comanche. "He is a pensioner of the War Department," the *Sturgis Weekly Record* wrote of him shortly before his departure, "and is almost daily here in Sturgis on a visit for exercise." Noting the departures of the infantry and cavalry troops, the *Sturgis Weekly Record* wrote: "The kindliest feelings go with the officers and men. Both regiments have been with us so long that we hardly know what to do without them."[52]

New units would be brought to Fort Meade to replace these troops. Few of them would know the excitement and drama experienced by the companies that had served there during the stormy first decade of the fort's existence.

★ **7** ★

THE NEW GARRISON

R eplacing the departed troops at Fort Meade in the summer and fall of 1888 were units of the Third Infantry and the Eighth Cavalry. They came from stations in Montana and Texas, respectively, and maintained Fort Meade as a ten-company post.

Companies B, C, F, and I of the Third Infantry, under Major George E. Head, arrived at the post on 31 May before the last units of the Seventh Cavalry had departed. The contingent counted 8 officers and 158 enlisted men. Companies B, F, and I came from Fort Missoula and Company C from Fort Custer. The rest of the regiment, with the exception of Company G, which moved to Fort Sisseton, was transferred to Fort Snelling.[1]

Coming to Fort Meade with the Third Infantry troops was Lieutenant Colonel G. T. Alexander, Medical Department, who became the post surgeon. Major Head assumed the command of the post, since Alexander, although outranking him, was a medical officer. Command assignments were not generally given to medical officers except in unusual circumstances. The infantrymen performed routine garrison duties until 1 July, when a severe thunderstorm washed away two bridges across Bear Butte Creek on the military reservation. They then engaged in emergency flood duty at the post and in Sturgis City.[2]

The Eighth Cavalry came to Fort Meade after making what was described at the time as the longest continuous march of mounted troops in army history. Units of the regiment, stationed at a number of Texas posts, assembled at Fort Concho, near San Angelo, and left there on 12 May for the seventeen-hundred-mile overland march to Fort Meade. Lieutenant Colonel J. K. Mizner was in command during the march in the absence of Colonel Elmer Otis, who was on sick leave. The regiment was divided into three battalions, each containing four troops, for the march. Reveille was sounded at 4:45 A.M. after each night's camp, and the "Forward March" call resuming the trek came promptly at 6 A.M.

"Our rations were hardtack, bacon and black coffee, except when we reached a post," Private William G. Wilkinson, Troop G, wrote of the march. "Then we would get some fresh beef and real bread, and that was a real treat." Wilkinson also reported that it was "an unwritten rule" that the wagons carrying the food were required to reach each day's camp on schedule, despite any obstacles encountered along the trail. "Give a soldier plenty to eat," Wilkinson stated, "and he will put up with almost any other hardship without complaint."[3]

At Fort Riley, the regiment traded transportation with the Seventh Cavalry, which it was replacing at Fort Meade. It also picked up some fresh horses and mules at the Kansas post. En route to Dakota, weather permitting, the regimental band gave impromptu performances whenever camp was pitched near a town. While the regiment was still on the march, forty recruits arrived at Fort Meade in early August. A twenty-six-man advance detachment of the regiment reached Fort Meade in late August. The main column, which was under Mizner and included the regimental headquarters, reached Fort Meade on 3 September.[4]

Shortly after its arrival, half the regiment was detached to other Department of Dakota posts. Troops E and K were sent to Fort Buford, H and L to Fort Keogh, and F and G to Fort Yates. Wilkinson figured that his troop, commanded by Captain E. G. Fechet, had marched twenty-two hundred miles since leaving Fort Concho. It had also crossed seventeen rivers on the long journey from Texas to Fort Yates via Fort Meade. For Troop G, the trip had taken two days less than four months. Even though they had endured many hardships on the march, Wilkinson wrote that the men were sorry when it was over. The scenery was constantly changing on the march, and the daily routine was not as monotonous as garrison life at an isolated army post.[5]

Left at Fort Meade, in addition to headquarters and the band, were Troops A, B, C, D, I, and M. The cavalry garrison numbered 27 officers and 360 enlisted men.[6]

The Eighth had no sooner settled in when word was received that General Sheridan, who had selected the site of the post a decade earlier, had died. He was succeeded as army commander by General Schofield. Sheridan's death prompted a series of promotions for generals of lower rank and brought on a number of shifts in departmental commands. The command of the Department of Dakota evolved to Brigadier General Thomas H. Ruger.[7]

Nelson A. Miles, the hero of the successful roundup of Indians in Montana during the 1876–77 campaign, had been promoted to brigadier general in 1880. He was commanding the Department of the Columbia on the West Coast when Sitting Bull, whom Miles had chased into Canada in the earlier campaign, returned to surrender. The elusive Hunkpapa Sioux chieftain, leading a starving band of 185 followers, laid down his arms at Fort Buford on 19 July 1881. He was taken to Fort Randall, where he was held prisoner for two years before being allowed to settle on the Standing Rock Agency. Ironically, it was Miles who was promoted to major general (despite being junior in rank to other generals in the division) and placed in command of the Division of Missouri when Crook died in 1890. Thus, Miles would soon lead another campaign against the Sioux Indians—a campaign that would again involve his old foe and indirectly result in Sitting Bull's death.[8]

While the Eighth Cavalry's colonel, Otis, was still on sick leave, his daughter died in childbirth at Fort Meade on 20 November 1888. She was the wife of Second Lieutenant DeRosey Carrall Cabell of Troop C, Eighth Cavalry, whom she had married at Fort Davis, Texas, the previous year. Their baby daughter survived. Mrs. Cabell was buried at the post cemetery.[9]

Otis did not return to Fort Meade until 26 April 1889. Since he had formerly served with the Seventh Cavalry at the post, Otis was well known to the citizens of Sturgis City, and he took an active part in its affairs. He became an officer in the Catholic Knights of America and spoke at the cornerstone-laying ceremony at St. Martin's Academy in Sturgis in July. The academy, established atop a hill on the western edge of Sturgis, was a girls' school operated by Benedictine Sisters from Switzerland and had been founded by Peter Rosen, the pastor of the Catholic Church in Sturgis since 1888.[10]

While Otis commanded the post, the sisters felt free to solicit funds there for their struggling little school. After his retirement, however, the regimental adjutant informed the academy's mother superior that he "did not deem it proper for Sisters to be in the vicinity of the pay table" seeking donations on paydays. But he also advised her that the enlisted men

General Nelson A. Miles, who led the army's campaign against the Indians after the Battle of the Little Bighorn in 1876, was the commanding officer of the Department of the Missouri in 1890–91 when the last major engagement between the army and the Sioux took place in South Dakota. Miles, earlier a national hero, found himself the target of severe criticism by the settlers of the region, who felt he had not acted forcefully enough in directing the campaign. (Courtesy of Old Fort Meade Museum Association.)

would be informed of the sisters' desire for subscriptions.[11] Until late in 1887 the soldiers had been paid every two months. The schedule was then changed to monthly pay periods. "It is hoped that by placing small amounts more frequently in the soldiers' hands," the army's adjutant general explained, "the temptation to periodic dissipation may be lessened, discipline thereby furthered and the number of desertions diminished."[12]

Relations between the Eighth Cavalry and Third Infantry companies and the residents of Sturgis (the town dropped "City" from its name during this period) were generally good. The "higher class" of Sturgis citizens succeeded in getting the town board to enact a number of reforms aimed at cleaning up the town. Ordinances were adopted that outlawed opium dens and houses of ill fame, driving some unsavory characters from the town. But there were still many nearby saloons that catered to the soldiers and in which prostitutes, with the discreet connivance of the saloon owners, plied their trade.

The eastern sector of Lawrence County, which included Sturgis and Fort Meade, was split off and formed into a separate county in 1889. Sturgis became the seat of the new county—named Meade, like the fort, for General George Meade. Although sparsely settled beyond Sturgis, Meade County was geographically the largest in southern Dakota.[13]

Also in 1889 the Great Sioux Reservation was divided into smaller separate reservations. The reservation encompassed forty-three thousand square miles west of the Missouri River even after the 1877 cession of the Black Hills. The 1889 agreement established six reservations— Standing Rock, Cheyenne River, Lower Brulé, Crow Creek, Pine Ridge, and Rosebud. Under its terms, the Indians relinquished all lands between the White and the Cheyenne rivers, except the Lower Brulé Reservation, and all lands between the 102nd and 103rd meridians east of the Black Hills. The Indians were given individual land allotments on their reservations, and nearly eleven million acres of "surplus" lands were thrown open for homesteading. In exchange, the Indians were to receive $1.25 per acre as homestead claims on the ceded land were taken up. In addition, the educational benefits of the Fort Laramie Treaty of 1868 were to be extended another twenty years. Despite considerable opposition to the allotment system among the tribes, the required consent of three-fourths of the adult male Sioux was secured. Agreement was achieved largely by approaching the Indians on an individual basis, away from the general councils, where opposition was strongest. General George Crook, one of the commissioners negotiating the agreement, played a major role in getting the Indians to sign it.[14]

Both Red Cloud and Sitting Bull had opposed the cession of additional Indian land and claimed the Black Hills had been stolen from the Sioux. Crook dismissed the charge with the claim that the Sioux had received more benefits than promised them under the treaty of 1868. The new agreement, said Crook, gave the Sioux more than the land was worth and was the best deal they were likely to get. "Instead of complaining about the past," Crook noted, "they had better think of the future." The veteran frontier commander died shortly after the agreement was approved.[15]

Another significant event of 1889 was the division of Dakota Territory into the separate states of South and North Dakota. The separation took effect on 2 November. South Dakota's constitution ceded the military reservations of Forts Meade, Randall, and Sully, by then the only posts remaining in the state, to the federal government.

Since the establishment of the post, there had been considerable controversy over the eligibility of civilian residents of Fort Meade to vote in local elections. They had done so in Sturgis City's first election in 1878, giving rise to fraud charges and demands for throwing out the returns. But by 1889 fewer civilians were living at Fort Meade. In July 1889, the post commander reported, "The only civilians living on the reservation are authorized employees of the Quartermaster Department, the post trader and his employees, a few tailors working for the troops and one barber, who are allowed to reside on the post as long as employed as stated."[16] The Quartermaster Department carried sixteen civilians, ten of them teamsters, on its payroll that month. The issue of election eligibility was later settled by the South Dakota Supreme Court, which ruled that residents of the Fort Meade reservation were not citizens of the state for election purposes.[17]

First Lieutenant Quincy O'M. Gillmore, Eighth Cavalry, the post quartermaster, in 1889 compiled a comprehensive report on the buildings that had been constructed on the fort since its establishment. The report listed seventy-three structures and described each of them in detail. It disclosed that the commanding officer's quarters, a two-story frame building constructed of native pine, had been built in 1879 at an initial cost of $2,884. Repairs and improvements over the years had brought its total cost to $3,664.96. The post hospital was a two-story frame building with surrounding porches, constructed in 1879 as a single-story building. It initially contained one ward with twelve beds. An additional ward for twelve beds was added in 1880, and the second story was added in 1888. The building was sixty by forty feet, with two wings twenty-four by forty-eight feet in size. Each wing contained two wards. The ground floor also contained a dispensary, two offices, a dining room, one special ward, a steward's room, the kitchen, a bathroom, and a hall. The second floor contained one ward twenty-four by forty feet in size, an isolation ward, one nurses' room, a large storeroom, a washroom, a linen closet, and halls. The initial cost of the building was $5,016, but with improvements the overall cost rose to $10,235.06.

Gillmore's report disclosed the government had spent a grand total of $152,082.59 on buildings and facilities for the fort during the first eleven years. It had saved considerably by using enlisted men in the construction of many buildings and by using native lumber finished at the post sawmill. However, the fort had also employed a sizable force of civilian tradesmen during its initial construction period.

A number of structures had been moved or diverted from their original purpose since the fort had been built. One of these was Fanshawe's former residence, where Reno had supped with such unforeseen consequences. It was a one-story frame cottage of native pine with porches in front and on the sides, forty-one by thirty-five feet in size with a wing thirty-three by thirty-three feet. It contained seven rooms, each sixteen by sixteen feet in size, as well as a kitchen, a hall, a closet and servant's room, and a cellar under the kitchen. Fanshawe had spent $2,800 on its construction. The government bought it for $1,750 in 1885 and spent an additional $865.28 to convert it to quarters for field-grade officers.

The post commander's office, a thirty-nine-by-sixty-foot building containing seven rooms, had been built in 1879, enlarged in 1882, and moved in 1884. The original guardhouse, built north of the line of enlisted men's barracks in 1879, had been moved in 1884 and enlarged in 1889. The reservoir, a cylindrical brick structure with an elliptical cemented base, was enclosed by square stone walls and covered by a shingled truss roof. The building was fifty-five by thirty-five feet in size and had a capacity of 77,950 gallons of water. It had been constructed in 1880 at a cost of $2,115 and roofed in 1881 at an additional cost of $82.50.

Since the water supply for the fort was a continuing problem, Gillmore's 1889 description of the reservoir is worthy of special mention. He wrote that water from Bear Butte Creek was pumped through four-inch pipes to a filter in the pump house and then to a reservoir eighty feet above the pump station. From there the water was carried through four-inch pipes to the buildings of the post. There were also eighteen fire hydrants on the post. The waterworks, started in 1881 and completed two years later, cost $8,140, exclusive of the reservoir. Gillmore concluded his report with a description of the post's drainage system. Consisting mainly of surface drainage, the system also included three ditches that carried water off the post: one, behind the officers' quarters, that led to a deep ravine; another, west of the post, that returned water to Bear Butte Creek; and a covered ditch, on the south side of the parade grounds, that carried water to the north side.[18]

Five troops of the Eighth Cavalry and two companies of the Third Infantry participated in a "Camp of Instruction" on the Little Missouri River from 22 August to 19 September. Otis designated the summer training site, seventy-seven miles northwest of the fort, as Camp Chambers. Colonel Alex Chambers, Seventeenth Infantry, had been a West Point classmate of Otis's and had died the previous year.[19]

In November, Otis reported that he had planned and constructed "the finest building for a canteen in the U.S. Army." It included a theater with a twenty-by-forty-foot stage, two dressing rooms, seating for three hundred, a library on one side and a reading room in front, a small billiard room for the officers, a twenty-four-by-fifty-nine-foot general amusement room, a twenty-four-by-twenty-foot barroom, a refreshment room, a kitchen, a sleeping room, a storeroom, and an office near a fifteen-by-thirty-foot root house. Otis contracted a debt of fifteen hundred dollars for the construction of the building but expected to pay it off with canteen receipts. "Not one dollar of the fund for barracks and quarters has been used," Otis boasted.[20]

The post commander, while conscious of the recreational needs of the troops under his command, was also a strict proponent of the military caste system. The post chaplain, who doubled as the superintendent of schools, permitted the children of civilians working at the post to attend school with the children of officers and enlisted men. Otis chastised the chaplain for not first consulting him. He directed the chaplain to "cease the practice," adding it was all right to let these children attend school with the children of the enlisted men but not with those of the officers. Class distinctions were thus impressed on the students at an early age.[21]

There was little break in the routine of garrison life at Fort Meade during the first few months of 1890. The Fort Meade Minstrels and Variety Company, organized by the soldiers, was the featured attraction at the theater in the new canteen. The post chaplain, who had irritated Otis with his school policies, retired in April and was not replaced until the following January. His successor was Edward J. Vattman, a Catholic priest, who also became the post's superintendent of schools.[22]

Mizner was promoted to the colonelcy of the Tenth Cavalry in April and joined his new regiment at Fort Apache, Arizona. Major Edwin V. Sumner, Fifth Cavalry, was promoted to lieutenant colonel and took Mizner's place in the Eighth. Sumner was on special duty in the Department of the Missouri at the time, however, and did not report to his new regiment at Fort Meade until November. By that time the troops at Fort Meade were deeply involved in the Indian campaign that so sharply broke the monotony of their ordinary garrison duties that year. It was a campaign that would provide the first real test of the fort's usefulness in contending with the Sioux.[23]

☆ **8** ☆

BLOOD ON THE SNOW

S trangely, the events leading up to the first major campaign by the Fort Meade troops against the Indians took place in faraway Nevada. There a Paiute Indian named Wovoka, the son of a tribal prophet, had a curious dream while sick with fever during an eclipse of the sun.

Following his illness, Wovoka described his dream: "When the sun died, I went up to heaven and saw God and all the people who had died a long time ago. God told me to come back and tell my people they must be good and love one another, and not fight, or steal, or lie. He gave me a dance to give my people."[1]

If the Indians obeyed these instructions and performed this new dance, Wovoka explained, God would restore the happiness of the old days and there would be no more trouble with the whites. Wovoka's message was a blend of the teachings of his prophet father and of the Christian doctrines he had learned from the white family that had raised him after his father's death. It stressed peace and brotherly love.

Indians from widely scattered tribes came to Nevada to learn of Wovoka's dance and preaching. A seven-member Sioux delegation visited Wovoka in the spring of 1890 and learned the dance, known as the "Ghost Dance" because it spiritually united the dancers with their dead ancestors.

Possibly due in part to language difficulties, Wovoka's message was reinterpreted by the Sioux delegates. Kicking Bear, of the Miniconjou Sioux from the Cheyenne River Reservation, seemed especially innovative in his interpretation. He was reported to claim that Wovoka, whom Kicking Bear described as the "Messiah," had promised that the whites would disappear in two seasons if the Sioux would perform the dance that had been given to them. Moreover, Kicking Bear claimed that the dancers could not be injured by bullets if they wore "ghost shirts," gaily painted white cotton blouses, in confrontations with soldiers.

The Sioux receptiveness to the "Ghost Dance religion" may in part be ascribed to the depressed condition of their lives on the newly created reservations. The government reduced their rations in 1890 in the hopes of forcing the Indians to become more self-supporting. But drought ruined their crops, and hunger was soon widespread on the South Dakota reservations. Some Sioux adopted the Ghost Dance in the hope that it would bring back the old days when great herds of buffalo provided them with ample sustenance. Soon the Ghost Dance was being danced on all the South Dakota reservations. It was most prevalent among Red Cloud's Oglalas at Pine Ridge, Short Bull's Brulés at Rosebud, Big Foot's Miniconjous at Cheyenne River, and Sitting Bull's Hunkpapas at Standing Rock.[2]

With increasingly tense conditions on the Sioux reservations, the army was charged with keeping the Indians under closer surveillance. Troops C, I, and M, Eighth Cavalry, and Companies F and I, Third Infantry, left Fort Meade on 6 April to establish a "camp of observation" at the forks of the Cheyenne River. The five-company battalion was commanded by Captain A. G. Hennisee, Eighth Cavalry, with Captain W. C. Bartlett in charge of the infantry contingent. The force numbered 9 officers, an assistant surgeon, and 258 enlisted men. Its mission was to keep an eye on the Miniconjou bands of Big Foot and Hump camped on the western fringes of the Cheyenne River Reservation. Their villages were on Deep Creek and Cherry Creek, respectively, not far from the point where the Belle Fourche River merges with the Cheyenne. The soldier encampment at the forks was named Camp Cheyenne.

On 23 April, Troops A and B, Eighth Cavalry, left Fort Meade under the command of Captain A. B. Wells to establish a camp at Oelrichs, just outside the western boundary of the Pine Ridge Reservation. The mission of this force of 4 officers and 108 enlisted men was to "keep a lookout for Indians leaving the Pine Ridge Agency to join Cheyennes in Montana."[3] These soldiers remained at these points all summer and kept a close watch on Indian movements by sending out frequent scouting patrols. Indians attempting to leave their reservations without authorization from their agent were turned back.

An army reorganization in 1890 reduced General Miles's Division of the Missouri to only the Departments of Dakota and the Platte. General Ruger's Department of Dakota continued to comprise the two Dakotas,

Minnesota, and Montana. Brigadier General John R. Brooke headed the Department of the Platte, headquartered in Omaha. His jurisdiction included the states of Nebraska, Iowa, Colorado, Wyoming, part of Idaho, and the Territory of Utah. General Schofield also ordered the skeletonizing of two troops of each cavalry regiment in July. So officers and enlisted men of Troops L and M, Eighth Cavalry, were assigned to other troops of their regiment, and troop-strength ceilings were temporarily suspended to accommodate them. The surplus noncommissioned officers were carried on the rolls as attached personnel until vacancies occurred. Commissioned officers on prolonged leave or detached service were transferred to the skeletonized troops. The effect was to beef up the troops that were below strength and to consolidate the absent personnel into inactive units. The order resulted in some major inter-regimental transfers in the troops stationed at Fort Meade in August and September, including those on detached service in the field at Camp Cheyenne and Oelrichs.[4]

Also in 1890, the army authorized the enlistment of Indians as scouts for six-month periods at the same pay and allowances as cavalry troopers. Fort Meade would have need of them before 1890 ended.

Many factors were involved in the Sioux "outbreak" that occurred that fall. The commissioner of Indian affairs listed twelve, including unkept treaty promises; the inability of the Sioux to quickly adapt to an agricultural culture; poor crop conditions; reduced rations; epidemics of pneumonia, measles, and whooping cough that resulted in many deaths on the reservations; and the reduction of the Great Sioux Reservation by the agreement of 1889, which had been opposed by many influential Sioux. In addition, the commissioner stated, the "Messiah Craze" (as the Ghost Dance was often termed by whites) added "the fervor of fanaticism" to the Sioux discontent. He described the movement as fostering the beliefs that "ghost shirts were invulnerable to bullets" and that "the supremacy of the Indian race was assured." Consequently, he claimed, the Indians who accepted the new faith adopted "an attitude of sullen defiance."[5]

Unrest was especially prevalent at Pine Ridge, where a politically appointed agent with no previous Indian experience was in charge. Dr. Daniel F. Royer, a former member of the territorial legislature, owed his appointment to the patronage of U.S. Senator Richard F. Pettigrew. Royer's attempts to stop the Ghost Dance at Pine Ridge earned him the derisive name "Young-Man-Afraid-of-Indians." When the Indian Office asked the Dakota agents for a list of "troublemakers" on their agencies, Royer came up with the most names—sixty-five.[6]

Agent Royer was unable to cope with the situation. "The only remedy for this matter is the use of military," Royer wired Washington in October. General Miles visited the Pine Ridge Agency later that month to arrange for the transfer of Cheyennes back to their Montana reservation. He listened to the complaints of the tribal leaders and left convinced that the excitement would soon die down. It was a view shared by Dr. Valentine T. McGillycuddy of Rapid City, an agent at Pine Ridge from 1879 to 1886 who had dealt with Red Cloud's unruly Oglalas without the use of troops. He had taken charge just after the Indians had left the warpath and were still unaccustomed to regulated agency life.[7]

McGillycuddy favored letting the Indians dance themselves out, believing they would stop by themselves when they saw that it did not produce the miracles expected. "Were I still agent here," McGillycuddy stated, "I should let the dance continue. . . . If the Seventh-Day Adventists prepare their ascension robes for the second coming of the Saviour, the United States Army is not put in motion to stop them."[8]

Royer was a novice in dealing with Indians, though, and in mid-November the frightened agent reported the Ghost Dancers at his agency were "wild and crazy." He wired the Indian commissioner: "We need protection and we need it now. . . . nothing short of 1,000 soldiers will settle this dancing." He proposed the arrest of the leaders among the dissidents and their confinement at "some military post" until the matter was "quieted." And, he pleaded, "This should be done at once."[9]

Finally, the War Department was convinced of the seriousness of the situation. It had the responsibility of suppressing any outbreak, and by the end of November troops were dispatched to both the Pine Ridge and the adjoining Rosebud reservations. Although the trouble spots were in General Ruger's Department of Dakota, Miles found it more expedient to assign troops from the closer Department of the Platte posts. Units of the Ninth Cavalry and of the Second, Eighth, and Twenty-First infantries were dispatched to the two reservations from Forts Robinson, Niobrara, Sidney, and Omaha in Nebraska. The force, commanded by General Brooke, was later augmented by the arrival of additional troops from as far west as Fort Keogh in Montana, as far south as New Mexico, and as far east as Forts Leavenworth and Riley in Kansas. Among the latter troops was the Seventh Cavalry, which had been so soundly defeated by the Sioux fourteen years earlier, and an artillery battery.

There were already Department of Dakota troops stationed at the Standing Rock and the Cheyenne River agencies. And soldiers from Fort Meade were in the field at Camp Cheyenne and Oelrichs, keeping watch on the Indians in those regions. They had been there since April, and any hopes they had for returning to the comforts of Fort Meade were dashed when buffalo coats were hauled out to them in preparation for a winter campaign.[10]

Besides, in addition to the security the troops in the field provided, the farmers and ranchers adjacent to the reservations welcomed the opportunity to sell their products to the soldiers. It was charged that the settlers around Oelrichs and Camp Cheyenne had exaggerated the hostility of the Indians in order to keep the troops nearby. "The monthly pay of these troops let loose such a dazzling deluge of money," one newspaper asserted, that these settlers "couldn't let them go." In the case of Camp Cheyenne, the paper claimed: "Every man, woman and child between Smithville and Pierre who had anything to sell, or who could make moccasins or anything else liable to be needed, united in a petition setting forth the dangers from Indians if the troops should leave. So they will be kept there."[11]

But it was the frantic appeals for troops from Royer at Pine Ridge, rather than any petitions from settlers, that kept the soldiers in the field and brought additional troops from distant posts. Every sign of Indians outside their reservation brought calls for troops—just as in 1876–77, when the Black Hills settlements had been getting started. One such scare resulted in the first deaths of the campaign, but they could not be blamed on the Indians. A report of Indians near Minnesela, on the Redwater River northwest of Fort Meade, sent Troop D of the Eighth Cavalry scurrying to the vicinity on 25 November. The *Sturgis Weekly Record* questioned the motives behind the appeal. It accused the settlers there of inventing the Indian scare so that they would have a few soldiers as customers for beer "and other necessities of life." The newspaper claimed, "There never was any danger from an Indian outbreak and none exists now."[12]

Two members of Troop D, finding no saloons open in Minnesela on Thanksgiving Day, went to the drugstore and obtained a bottle of wood alcohol. They spiked their coffee with it, and on 28 November the troop returned to the fort with their dead bodies, which were buried in the post cemetery. Troop D members later erected an obelisk over the graves as a tribute to the two indiscriminate drinkers. Late in 1890, when the newspaper at Minnesela complained about the absence of troops in that vicinity, the *Black Hills Journal* wrote: "The military authorities evidently have in mind the fate of the two enlisted men of the Eighth, who died there recently, and probably think Minnesela is a good place to keep away from."[13]

To avoid a jurisdictional dispute between Brooke and Ruger, General Miles returned to Dakota to take personal command of the developing Indian campaign. He set up his headquarters in the Harney Hotel at Rapid City, where he could be in quick telegraphic communication with his commanders in the field. Accompanying the general was a coterie of newspapermen, who would send back sensational dispatches from "the seat of the war." Since Colonel Otis at Fort Meade was about to retire, Miles ordered Sumner to take field command of the Eighth Cavalry. Sumner, relieved from detached service, was described as "an old Indian fighter" who believed that "only dead Indians are good Indians."[14] He arrived at Fort Meade on 21 November and left there for Camp Cheyenne on the thirtieth, accompanied by Troop D of his regiment. It was an eighty-five-mile march to Camp Cheyenne, which Sumner reached on 3 December, taking over command from Captain Hennisee. His mission was to keep Big Foot's village under control and give assurances of safety to the people in the region. He was "also to put a stop to the unauthorized going back and forth of parties between the upper and lower Sioux reservations."[15]

Sumner set up a system of couriers at the ranches between the camp and Fort Meade for speedy communication with his superiors. The settlers who had taken up homesteads in the region were happy to cooperate. They feared an Indian uprising and welcomed the security that troops stationed nearby gave them.

A thirty-man platoon of Light Battery F, Fourth Artillery, under Captain George B. Rodney, arrived at Fort Meade by rail from Fort Riley on 28 November. A detachment from the unit, under First Lieutenant Adelbert Cronkhite, was assigned to the camp that Colonel Eugene A. Carr of the Sixth Cavalry had established at the mouth of Rapid Creek. Carr's regiment, traveling in eighty railcars, had come to Rapid City from the Department of Arizona to bolster the forces Miles was ringing around the reservations. The rest of the artillerymen went with Captain Rodney to join Sumner's command at Camp Cheyenne.

In addition, nineteen Crow Indian scouts, under First Lieutenant Samuel C. Robertson, First Cavalry, were attached to Fort Meade from Fort Custer. Ten of the scouts were assigned to Carr's camp. The other nine went to Sumner, who also employed as a guide Eb Jones, a veteran cowboy familiar with the Indians of the Cheyenne River Reservation.[16]

In December, Captain Wells's battalion of the Eighth Cavalry at Oelrichs was enlarged by a company of the Fifth Cavalry from Texas. On the ninth, Wells was ordered to move his three-company battalion to Buffalo Gap, near the mouth of French Creek. That placed Wells on the railroad between Chadron and Rapid City west of the Pine Ridge Reservation. Soon Miles had more than three thousand soldiers either on or surrounding the western Sioux reservations.

On the Pine Ridge Reservation were eight troops of the Seventh Cavalry, eight companies of the Second Infantry, and one company of the Eighth Infantry. At Rosebud were two troops of the Ninth Cavalry and portions of the Eighth and Twenty-first Infantries. Between the two agencies were seven companies of the First Infantry. Colonel Tilford of the Ninth Cavalry, formerly of the Seventh, was stationed north and west of the Pine Ridge Reservation, with portions of the First and Second cavalries along with units of his own regiment. Carr's Sixth Cavalry was stationed on Rapid Creek east of Rapid City. Sumner's three troops of the Eighth Cavalry and two companies of the Third Infantry from Fort Meade, along with the attached artillerymen and Indian scouts, were at the forks of the Cheyenne River. Seven companies each of the Seventh and Seventeenth infantries from Forts Bennett and Sully were stationed along the Cheyenne River between its forks and the Missouri River. It was the greatest assemblage of army might on the northern plains since the decisive Indian Campaign of 1876–77.[17]

All these troop movements, of course, had an alarming effect on both the Indians on the reservations and the settlers living on their borders. In fact, it was the troops' arrival that set off the unfortunate chain of events that brought the campaign to such a bloody conclusion. The massing of so many troops caused many Indians to withdraw into the Badlands to continue the Ghost Dance away from the soldiers and their scouts. They assembled on a Badlands plateau, known as the Stronghold, which was surrounded by terrain so rough that troops could not approach undetected. Some Indians took livestock from the ranches bordering the Cheyenne River to feed those who had taken refuge in the Stronghold. This exodus of Indians from their agencies, in turn, alarmed the settlers, who rushed to nearby communities where militia units were formed for self-protection.[18]

Although the reports of war and the rumors of war with the Indians were vastly exaggerated, "Home Guard" units were organized in almost every Black Hills community. One such scare had a settler rushing into Rapid City and shouting, "The Indians are coming, the Indians are coming!" When he had calmed down and more details could be obtained, it was learned that he had seen some Indians heading toward Rapid City in a top buggy. "If the Sioux have adopted, along with the Messiah Craze and the Ghost Dance, the habit of going on the war path in top buggies," the *Journal* commented, "of course, there is no use trying to fight them."[19]

Leaders of the Home Guard units viewed the situation more seriously. With the backing of community officials, they sent urgent appeals for arms and ammunition to Governor Arthur C. Mellette. The governor, however, was getting mixed signals about the need for arms. McGillycuddy, a militia colonel on the governor's staff, visited Pine Ridge and conferred with tribal leaders. He informed Mellette, "Settlers need apprehend no trouble." But M. H. Day of Rapid City, one of the organizers of the Home Guard, telegraphed Mellette that Indians from the Pine Ridge Reservation were raiding ranches along the Cheyenne River. He asked for arms and ammunition for the settlers in that area.[20]

Mellette appointed Day as his aide-de-camp with the rank of colonel and directed him to manage the Hills campaign. The governor instructed McGillycuddy to provide Day with 150 guns and 5,000 rounds of ammunition sent to him from the capital. Although he saw no need for it, McGillycuddy reluctantly complied. Day was ordered to distribute the ordnance, and Mellette advised him to "be discreet in killing the Indians." The governor later complained of being maliciously attacked for arming the settlers and conceded that he might have been "doing wrong." But, he added, "I would rather save one person, man, woman or child from being killed than to be Governor for life." Mellette informed Day that the federal government was going to disarm the Indians. "When that is done," the governor stated, "the excitement will subside and not before."[21]

Day distributed the guns to settlers in the exposed region between the Cheyenne River, the northern boundary of the Pine Ridge Reservation, and the Black Hills. He also sent out militiamen on patrols along the river, and some of them ventured onto the Indian reservation. Their mission, the *Journal* reported, was "to dispatch the roving bands [of Indians] to their happy hunting grounds."[22] Day claimed the arms were needed because Indian raids along the Cheyenne between Spring and Battle creeks, south and east of Rapid City, had driven many settlers from their homes. But the settlers returned home after being issued arms. Day assured the governor, "The settlers feel very grateful for the arms and the protection they afford them."[23]

With the troops at his command, General Miles did not need any support or interference from militiamen. With Governor Mellette's concurrence, Miles issued instructions ordering Day to keep his men off the reservation or face military arrest. Day's force, composed of fifty mounted ranchers and their hired hands, was instructed to confine its activities to the area west of the Cheyenne River. The militiamen were told that "when the military saw fit to make a move they would be pleased to accept their company and until such time they would be considered out of place" on the reservation.[24]

Although the presence of troops had halted participation in the Ghost Dance near the agencies, the ritual was still being performed at Big Foot's and Hump's villages on the Cheyenne River and at Sitting Bull's camp on the Standing Rock Reservation. Hump, the chief of police at the Cheyenne River Agency, had given up his post to join the Ghost Dancers at his village at the mouth of Cherry Creek, some sixty miles west of his agency. The dancing there had frightened away some of the inhabitants of Cheyenne City, located on ceded land on the opposite bank of the river from Hump's settlement. But an emissary from General Miles, for whom Hump had performed scouting services during the 1877 campaign, persuaded him to abandon the dance. He came into Fort Bennett with his band early in December and enlisted as a scout for the troops.[25]

Kicking Bear had brought the Ghost Dance to Sitting Bull's band on the Grand River in October, and the Hunkpapa leader promptly embraced it. James McLaughlin, the agent at Standing Rock since Sitting Bull's surrender in 1881, sent his Indian police to eject Kicking Bear from the reservation. Unlike the inexperienced Royer, McLaughlin had been with the Indian Office since 1871 and was confident that he knew how to deal with the Sioux. His wife was part Sioux, and he had been an Indian agent since 1876. Although Fort Yates was located at his agency, McLaughlin preferred to keep order with Indian police rather than troops. The agent tried to dissuade Sitting Bull from the Ghost Dance, but he and Sitting Bull had a mutual dislike for each other, and his efforts failed. McLaughlin had undermined Sitting Bull's influence with the Hunkpapas by appointing more tractable Indians to positions of influence on the reservation. He had also allowed Sitting Bull to go on tour with William F. (Buffalo Bill) Cody's Wild West show in 1885 as a means of removing the Indian's influence from the reservation. It was during this tour that Sitting Bull was touted as "the killer of Custer" and regained the public notoriety he had earned in the widely publicized campaign that had forced him into Canada.[26]

On his return to Standing Rock, Sitting Bull and the equally strong-willed McLaughlin became open enemies and had frequent confrontations. Sitting Bull may have seen the new religion in part as a way to recoup the prominence he had held among his people before being placed under McLaughlin's reservation rule. In any event, McLaughlin decided it would be best to again remove the stubborn old warrior from the reservation. He proposed that he send Indian police to arrest Sitting Bull at a time when winter weather would minimize the likelihood of resistance. Over his objections, however, General Miles sent Buffalo Bill to Standing Rock in November to persuade Sitting Bull to come in. Cody and Sitting Bull were friends, and McLaughlin resented the showman's presence on his reservation. So the agent conspired with Lieutenant Colonel William F. Drum, the commander at Fort Yates, to delay Cody's trip to Sitting Bull's village. Then, claiming Cody's mission was unwise at that time and citing fears that it might precipitate violence, McLaughlin and Drum succeeded in getting Cody's orders countermanded.[27] Cody was understandably angry at being thwarted. He had been looking forward to reaping a publicity bonanza by bringing in the celebrated Sioux leader without bloodshed.

On 12 December, Drum received orders to arrest Sitting Bull. McLaughlin, however, talked him into letting the Indian police handle the matter, with the troops in reserve. It was initially decided that Sitting Bull would be taken when his followers came to the agency for their rations. But word reached McLaughlin on 14 December that Sitting Bull was planning to join the Ghost Dancers on the Pine Ridge Reservation. So that evening the agent dispatched the Indian police, under Lieutenant Henry Bull Head, to Sitting Bull's camp, some forty miles southwest of the agency headquarters, to effect the arrest. Drum, whose command consisted of two companies of his own Twelfth Infantry and two troops of the Eighth Cavalry, assigned the supporting role to the cavalry units. Captain Fechet was sent out with one hundred men from Troops F and G to establish a camp on Oak Creek within a few miles of Sitting Bull's home. The detachment, equipped with Hotchkiss and Gatling guns, marched with a four-horse spring wagon and a Red Cross ambulance to Oak Creek under the cover of darkness. It was prepared to aid the police entering Sitting Bull's village the next morning if needed. According to reports, the Indians had performed the Ghost Dance in the village until late the previous evening.

At daybreak on 15 December, Lieutenant Bull Head's force of thirty-nine policemen and four volunteers descended on Sitting Bull's sleeping camp. They entered his log house and arrested him in his bed. While Sitting Bull was dressing, his seventeen-year-old son, Crow Foot, chided him for submitting to arrest so peaceably. Meanwhile, the village had been aroused by all the activity, and about 150 of Sitting Bull's followers crowded around their leader's cabin. As Sitting Bull was being led outside, one of his followers shot Lieutenant Bull Head, and another shot Sergeant Shave Head. As he fell, Bull Head fired a shot into Sitting Bull. So did Sergeant Red Tomahawk. Sitting Bull dropped to the ground dead. The firing quickly became general, and the Indian police backed into Sitting Bull's house with their wounded. They threw Crow Foot out the door and shot him dead as he hit the ground. One of the policemen then braved the heavy fire to mount Sitting Bull's horse and speed out of the village for help.[28]

Captain Fechet rushed his troops to the scene. He drove the besiegers away by firing shells from his Hotchkiss gun into the timber between the river and Sitting Bull's cabin, the area where the dead Hunkpapa's followers had sought cover. As the Sioux fled southward across the Grand River, Fechet halted the pursuit and returned to the village. There, the captain reported, he saw "evidence of a most desperate encounter." He later wrote: "In front of the house, and within a radius of fifty yards, were the bodies of eight dead Indians, including that of Sitting Bull, and two dead horses. In the house were four dead policemen and three wounded, two mortally. To add to the horror of the scene the squaws of Sitting Bull, who were in a small house nearby, kept up a great wailing."[29]

Lieutenant Bull Head and Sergeant Shave Head died from their wounds. They were buried with honors in the agency cemetery, along with the four other Indian policemen killed. McLaughlin, who had favored cutting off ration allowances to the Ghost Dancers, lamented the fact that his suggestion had not been adopted. If it had, he asserted, "the dancing would have broken up and Sitting Bull arrested without bloodshed."[30] Both McLaughlin and Captain Fechet had high praise for the conduct and courage of the policemen during the engagement that had cost fourteen lives. Except for Sitting Bull, the dead of the Grand River village were buried near where they fell. Sitting Bull's remains were brought to Fort Yates for burial. "The surviving Indian police and their friends," Fechet reported, "objected so strenuously to interment of Sitting Bull among their dead that he was buried in the cemetery of the post."[31]

The death of Sitting Bull created a sensation in the country's newspapers. He had been perhaps the best-known Indian in the country because of his long exile in Canada following the Custer fight and his stubborn refusal to sign any peace treaties. His reputation as a renegade was also exploited during his travels with Buffalo Bill's Wild West show, which brought him tremendous public exposure. Even the skeptics among the newspaper publishers closest to the Sioux reservations began taking the situation more seriously after Sitting Bull's death. At Sturgis, the *Record* reported that Otis had received orders "to have every available man at Fort Meade sent to the front." The situation, the newspaper noted, seemed "to be getting worse instead of better."[32]

After the fight on the Grand River, some of Sitting Bull's followers fled toward the Cheyenne River Reservation, seeking refuge with Big Foot's Miniconjous. "It is desirable that Big Foot be arrested," Sumner, at Camp Cheyenne, was advised by Ruger on 17 December. Ruger also instructed Sumner to send Big Foot to Fort Meade for imprisonment.[33] Big Foot, at this time, had started down the Cheyenne River with his band for Fort Bennett to draw rations. As he neared Hump's village at the mouth of Cherry Creek, Big Foot learned of Sitting Bull's death from the Hunkpapas who had eluded Fechet's troops. Most of the fugitive Hunkpapas continued on to Hump's camp, where they were persuaded to go to Fort Bennett and surrender their arms. The remainder joined Big Foot's band.

Sumner caught up with Big Foot on 20 December and found him apparently cooperative. Rather than arresting him on the spot, Sumner instructed the Miniconjou leader to gather up his people and return with them to Camp Cheyenne. Captain Hennisee counted 333 Indians with Big Foot. The count included 38 refugees from Sitting Bull's village, 14 of them warriors. On 22 December, Sumner's troops escorted the band back toward Camp Cheyenne. On reaching Deep Creek, however, Big Foot asked permission for his people to return to their homes rather than continue on to the soldiers' camp. He argued that they had done nothing wrong and predicted trouble if the soldiers tried to force them to camp away from the comforts of their homes. Sumner concluded that he had to either accede to Big Foot's wishes or fight him. In the case of a fight, Sumner also concluded, he would be the aggressor. "What possible reason could I produce," he asked, "for making an attack on peaceable, quiet Indians on their reservation and at their homes, killing perhaps many of them and offering, without any justification, the lives of many officers and enlisted men."[34] Consequently, Sumner decided not to force the issue and permitted the Indians to go to their homes. Although Big Foot had offered to go to Camp Cheyenne, Sumner allowed him to return to his village after eliciting a promise that Big Foot would come to the camp the next day with the Hunkpapa fugitives for a council.

As Sumner saw it, other than participating in the Ghost Dance, Big Foot had caused no trouble during the many months his village had been under observation by the soldiers. And the chief had frequently visited Camp Cheyenne after Sumner had taken command. The camp commander's trust in Big Foot belied his reputation as an Indian fighter who

Lieutenant Colonel Edwin Voss Sumner commanded the Fort Meade troops stationed at Camp Cheyenne in the winter of 1890–91. Sumner had the opportunity to arrest the Miniconjou Sioux chief, Big Foot, but instead permitted the chief to leave with his followers. Big Foot led his band to Wounded Knee Creek, where it suffered heavy casualties from troops that had been part of the original Fort Meade garrison. (Courtesy of the National Archives.)

believed that only dead Indians were good Indians. Miles, on the other hand, considered Big Foot and his people defiant and treacherous and issued orders advising commanders not to trust them. Sumner found Miles's opinion "quite the opposite of mine." He saw nothing in his orders to indicate that Big Foot's people were hostile. In fact, he interpreted his orders as instructing him to prevent their becoming so.[35]

The fact that the commander had brought Big Foot back to the forks of the Cheyenne led Sumner's superiors and the area press to believe that the Indian was a prisoner, when he actually was not. "The uprising is nearly a thing of the past," the *Record* at Sturgis predicted. "The Indians have not wanted to fight, nor do they now."[36] Miles also believed Sumner had Big Foot under arrest and sent him this message: "I think you had better push on rapidly with your prisoners to Meade, and be careful they do not escape, and look out for other Indians."[37] Sumner, receiving the

113

message on the night of 22 December, replied that Big Foot was coming in the next morning and that, if he did not, troops would be sent to his home to pick him up. Sumner also sent John Dunn, a rancher who knew Big Foot, to the Miniconjou village with an interpreter. Dunn's instructions were to inform Big Foot that it would be best if he led his people to Fort Bennett. If he did not, the rancher informed Big Foot, Sumner's troops would fight him if necessary.[38]

Big Foot sent word back to Sumner that he wanted to go to the agency but that his young men were against it. They wanted him to accept an invitation from the Oglalas to come to Pine Ridge instead. Learning that the Standing Rock Indians whom Big Foot had promised to bring in the next day had already left the Miniconjou camp, Sumner decided it was time to act. While he pushed his command up the Cheyenne River toward Big Foot's village on the twenty-third, four companies of the Seventh Infantry from Fort Sully, under Colonel Henry C. Merriam, were closing in on the village from downstream. Three other companies of the Seventh were stationed at Fort Bennett to guard the Standing Rock Indians who had surrendered there.

On the twenty-fourth, Sumner received a direct order from Miles to arrest Big Foot. The order authorized him to round up the whole camp if necessary and instructed him to "disarm them, and take them to Fort Meade or Bennett."[39] The order came too late, however, since Big Foot had given in to the demands of his young men and had slipped away to the south during the night.

Sumner believed the Indians had learned that Colonel Merriam's troops were moving up the Cheyenne toward them and had fled south to avoid capture. On their way, Sumner later pointed out, Big Foot's band had passed through settled country "without committing any depredation or harming anyone."[40]

"Big Foot shied his breech cloth at Col. Sumner and lit out for the bad lands," a soldier at Camp Cheyenne wrote to the *Record*. He claimed that Big Foot had no more than one hundred men with him, whereas Sumner had three troops of the Eighth Cavalry and two companies of the Third Infantry. The anonymous soldier implied that Sumner had kept his troops in camp because he knew that a Christmas meal was en route from Sturgis. The writer reported that "our venerable old friend, Ed Hammon," and a woman identified only as "Aunt Molly" had ridden into camp from Sturgis with Christmas presents "and a layout for the officers of C Troop." But the disgruntled soldier also expressed surprise that Big Foot had deceived Sumner after making so many friendly visits to Camp Cheyenne. "What a diabolic old wretch that Indian must be," he wrote, "after eating and drinking all summer with the kids here."[41]

The letter writer, although critical of Sumner, thereby inadvertently confirmed that Big Foot had been friendly and cooperative while being watched from Camp Cheyenne since April. "All thought of these Indians going south had been abandoned by me," Sumner explained, "and I thought they would either go peaceably to the agency or fight."[42] The embarrassed commander sent Troop C on Big Foot's trail and immediately notified Carr, on Rapid Creek, that the fugitives were heading in his direction. He also dutifully—and no doubt reluctantly—informed Miles that Big Foot had left the area.

An enraged Miles ordered Merriam, then camped with his infantrymen near the mouth of Cherry Creek, to take command of all the troops along the Cheyenne. The division commander, Merriam was informed, was "much embarrassed that Big Foot [was] allowed to escape" and directed Merriam to use his forces "to recapture him." Miles also reprimanded Sumner by reminding him that his orders to arrest Big Foot were positive and that he had missed an opportunity that would not likely be repeated. "Endeavor to be more successful next time," Miles instructed the chagrined Eighth Cavalry field commander.[43]

Sumner's confidence in Big Foot brought undeserved ridicule on the troops from Fort Meade. Back in Sturgis, for instance, the *Record* reported that Governor Mellette had appointed Miles Cooper, a member of South Dakota's first legislature, as a colonel on his militia staff. The paper predicted that Cooper, who owned a ranch near Bear Butte, would "place a cordon around Fort Meade" for its protection. Sixty guns and nine thousand rounds of ammunition were sent to Sturgis for distribution to settlers along Bear Butte Creek and the Belle Fourche River, "where they will do the most good." One of these guns, the newspaper stated sarcastically, was "situated within three miles of Fort Meade, so it is safe."[44]

The guns, mostly fifty-caliber Long Toms, were given, for $1.15 in express charges, to any farmer who wanted one. The *Record,* reporting on

115

the formation of a local Home Guard unit, jocularly described it as composed partly of "dismounted cavalry and part of mounted infantry."[45] Apart from the militiamen that Day had patrolling the Cheyenne in Pennington County, the Home Guard units performed no real service. Day's "rangers" were characterized in one Rapid City newspaper as "swaggering bullies" just interested in killing Indians. But the *Journal* defended them as threatened ranchers engaged in protecting their families and homes. "They are not under arms for the purpose of shedding blood unnecessarily," the *Journal* insisted. Rather, they were "some of the best men in the Black Hills" and were motivated only by an unselfish desire to make the country safe.[46]

At the time of Big Foot's flight, seven companies of the Seventeenth Infantry from Fort D. A. Russell in Wyoming were being stationed along the western border of the Pine Ridge Reservation. The regimental headquarters, under the command of Lieutenant Colonel R. H. Offley, arrived in Rapid City by rail. Seventeen wagons transported the regiment's equipment "to the front." First Lieutenant Edward Dravo of the Sixth Cavalry set up heliograms on the high hills between Miles's headquarters in Rapid City and Carr's camp on Rapid Creek to speed communications. The system was intended to eliminate long rides by couriers between the two points.[47] All except Troop C, Eighth Cavalry, of Sumner's command, spent Christmas at Camp Cheyenne. Troop C observed the holiday in Big Foot's deserted village and returned to the main camp the following day. Miles, although angered that Sumner had permitted Big Foot to flee, decided to delay any action against him until after the campaign was over. The end came closer on 28 December.

On that day a battalion of the Seventh Cavalry, under Major Samuel M. Whitside, found Big Foot's band moving west of the Badlands toward the Pine Ridge Agency. Whitside, commanding four troops of his regiment and supported by a platoon of the First Artillery, intercepted the Indians and demanded their unconditional surrender. Big Foot, weary and ill with pneumonia, complied without resistance. Whitside moved the band, consisting of 120 men and 230 women and children, to Wounded Knee Creek some twenty miles northeast of Pine Ridge. When General Brooke at Pine Ridge learned of this, he gave orders that the Indians be disarmed before they were brought into the agency. Colonel Forsyth was dispatched with four more troops of the Seventh Cavalry, plus another platoon of the First Artillery, to Wounded Knee to enforce the order. On reaching Whitside's camp, Forsyth assumed command and placed his troops in positions to prevent the Indians' escape. The combined forces of Forsyth and Whitside, including the attached Indian scouts and artillery, numbered more than five hundred men.[48]

On the morning of the twenty-ninth the soldiers began disarming the Indians. Despite the overwhelming number of troops surrounding them, it was later claimed that a medicine man named Yellow Bird exhorted the Miniconjous to use their guns rather than surrender them. He reportedly threw some dust into the air as a signal for the resistance to begin. A shot was fired, and pandemonium erupted in the camp as the soldiers and Indians engaged in close combat.

The army had the advantage both in manpower and in firepower. The Hotchkiss guns of the artillery, strategically situated atop a nearby hill, sent two-pound explosive shells crashing down on the camp, "mowing down everything alive."[49] When it was all over, 146 Indian men, women, and children lay dead on the snow-covered battlefield. Among them were Big Foot and Yellow Bird. An additional 51 Indians were wounded, and some of them later died. There were also 25 dead and 37 wounded among the soldiers. Some of these wounded also died later.[50]

News of the event engendered a long-lasting controversy among advocates and opponents of the army's policies on Indian affairs. It was widely heralded by some that the Seventh Cavalry had avenged their terrible beating by the Sioux fourteen years earlier on the Little Bighorn. Defenders of the army, particularly within Dakota, charged that the Indians had brought the disaster upon themselves. These claimed that the Indians' faith in a new religion and supposedly impenetrable ghost shirts was the cause of the calamity.[51]

The Indians who had been in the Badlands with Short Bull of the Rosebud Brulés and Kicking Bear of the Cheyenne River Miniconjou Sioux were en route to Pine Ridge to surrender when they learned of the Wounded Knee slaughter. They turned back and sent parties out to harass the troops. Until Wounded Knee, the "Messiah campaign" had been relatively tame, considering the number of combatants involved. The only casualties before 29 December were the fourteen Indians killed in the fight at Sitting Bull's camp and the two soldiers from Fort Meade who had consumed wood alcohol.

Among the Seventh Cavalry casualties from the Wounded Knee fight were several soldiers who had served at Fort Meade when it was first established. Captain George D. Wallace, who still owned property in Sturgis, was the only commissioned officer killed. Lieutenant Garlington, one of Ella Sturgis's many callers when the Seventh was at Fort Meade, was shot in the elbow. Gustav Korn, a blacksmith who had been Comanche's caretaker at Fort Meade, was among the enlisted men killed.[52]

Lieutenant James Mann, who had also served at Fort Meade, was fatally wounded on the day following the Wounded Knee engagement, when a small band of Indians ambushed eight troops of the Seventh Cavalry under Forsyth at the Drexel Mission, north of Pine Ridge. The Indians were believed to be from Short Bull and Kicking Bear's forces, who had intended to surrender until learning what had happened to Big Foot's band. They gained the heights above Forsyth's command and were threatening to wipe it out when a relief detachment of the Ninth Cavalry arrived from Pine Ridge. In addition to Mann, one private was killed and several other soldiers wounded.[53]

Miles arrived at Pine Ridge on 31 December to take charge of the turbulent situation. He conferred with Red Cloud of the Oglalas and found him willing to come into the agency with his band for a surrender of arms. Miles also learned from Red Cloud that Short Bull's Brulés were adamant against surrender and were preventing other former Ghost Dancers from giving up. Kicking Bear was allied with Short Bull and was also determined to continue to resist.

One of Short Bull's men, Kills-the-Enemy, lived up to his name on New Year's Day. He was in a party of Brulés that intercepted Henry Miller, who had been working with a group of herders on White Clay Creek and was coming into Pine Ridge for supplies. Miller was persuaded to give up his revolver, and then Kills-the-Enemy shot him dead. The victim was stripped, and Kills-the-Enemy dragged the body through the Indian village behind his pony. Miller was the only white civilian casualty of the campaign.[54]

Another Brulé, a young Carlisle Indian School graduate named Plenty Horses, struck the last blow for the Sioux when a detachment of Cheyenne scouts, under First Lieutenant Edward W. Casey, was assigned to keep close watch on the Indians camped in the valley of White Clay Creek. The Cheyennes had been brought down from Fort Keogh in November to serve with the troops that Miles had assembled on the Pine Ridge Reservation. On 7 January, Lieutenant Casey and White Moon, one of his scouts, set out for Red Cloud's camp to seek a parley with the Oglala chieftain. They were met en route by Plenty Horses and another Brulé named Broken Arm, who escorted them to the outskirts of the Indian camp. There they were joined by a mixed-blood relative of Red Cloud's, Pete Richard, who had been sent out as an emissary to advise Casey to turn back. The young braves of the camp were unruly, Casey was told, and it was dangerous for him to remain in the vicinity. The lieutenant, indicating he would return with troops, turned his horse to leave when Plenty Horses fired a bullet into the back of his head, killing him instantly.[55]

White Moon, in a precarious position himself, grabbed Casey's horse and sped away from the scene. He reported Casey's death to Lieutenant Robert N. Getty, the second-in-command. Getty took a detachment of his Cheyenne scouts back to the Indian village to recover Casey's body. He also attempted to arrest Plenty Horses, who had taken refuge in the village, but the Indians refused to surrender him. With increasing numbers of soldiers closing in on them from all sides, however, the Indians recognized the futility of continued resistance. They surrendered to Miles at Pine Ridge on 15 January. Both sides paused to count their losses and perhaps to reflect on the circumstances that had resulted in so much bloodshed.[56]

Miles, chagrined that another subordinate had apparently bungled, suspended Forsyth. He ordered a court of inquiry to investigate the Seventh Cavalry commander's conduct during the 30 December fight in White Clay Valley, as well as at Wounded Knee. He believed that Forsyth had disobeyed specific orders not to allow his troops to mingle with the volatile Indians. In November, Miles had instructed Brooke: "Do not allow your command to become mixed up with Indians, friendly or otherwise. Hold them all at a safe distance from your command. Guard against surprise or treachery."[57] The order had been relayed to the commanders under Brooke, including Forsyth. Miles had repeated the admonition on 7 December, adding that the prohibition applied "not only in a military sense but in a diplomatic." This directive had also gone to the field commanders. Forsyth's failure to follow these instructions at Wounded Knee, Miles charged, may have resulted in some of the military being shot by their own comrades. The firing, particularly from the artillery pieces, had been indiscriminate and devastating. Miles felt the large number of Indian women and children killed along with the warriors had constituted needless slaughter.[58]

Forsyth, on the other hand, pointed out that there had been no way to disarm the Indians without getting among them. Further, he added, "I did not anticipate any armed resistance because of the overwhelming display of force." He attributed the Indians' apparent recklessness to their faith in the invulnerability of their ghost shirts, which had not previously been tested under fire. Forsyth also noted that it had been difficult for the troops to distinguish between men and women in the close quarters of the unexpected melee, with dust and smoke shrouding the field.[59] Secretary of War Redfield Proctor and Commanding General of the Army Schofield accepted Forsyth's explanation. They decided, "The interests of the military do not demand any further proceedings in this case."[60]

By direction of the president, Forsyth was restored to his command. Moreover, Schofield stated that the conduct of the entire Seventh Cavalry at Wounded Knee was worthy of special commendation. Medals of Honor for heroism were awarded to twenty-one soldiers who had participated in the engagement; accompanying citations were exceedingly brief and shed little light on the actions justifying the medals. They typically stated, "Extraordinary Gallantry," "Distinguished Bravery," or "Distinguished Conduct"—and generally nothing more.[61]

McGillycuddy, when asked who was to blame for the slaughter at Wounded Knee, replied: "Whoever fired that first shot. After that, nothing short of the Almighty could have stopped the killing." He also was critical of Royer for bringing troops onto the reservation, terming the agent's appointment a mistake on the part of the Indian Office. "Royer is a failure as an Indian agent and every man in the Indian Service knows it," McGillycuddy charged. "He was inexperienced and unfit for the office." Had an experienced agent been appointed, McGillycuddy asserted, "the trouble could have been averted without calling out the troops."[62] Later, James Mooney, of the Bureau of Ethnology, conducted an investigation of the Wounded Knee affair and concluded that on the fateful morning of the fight, the Indians had desired to surrender and be at peace. Further, the soldiers in good faith had expected to escort them to the agency without trouble. However, Mooney did believe that Yellow Bird had precipitated the firing. The "first shot was fired by an Indian and . . . the Indians were responsible for the engagement." He believed that the soldiers were justified in returning the fire but added that "the wholesale slaughter of women and children was unnecessary and inexcusable."[63] Other commentators have not been so confident; some claim that an accidental discharge set off the firing, and others have charged that the army fired the first shot.

Miles was disappointed at the way Proctor and Schofield disposed of the charges against Forsyth. If Forsyth's conduct was justified, there was little chance of succeeding in a case against Sumner. Miles had planned to bring Sumner up on charges too, but he abandoned the idea after his inspector general determined there were insufficient grounds. Although he had had Big Foot in hand as late as 22 December, Sumner did not receive the direct order to arrest him until two days later. By then the Miniconjou chieftain and his band had already fled onto the Pine Ridge Reservation.[64] Sumner's lapse was in trusting Big Foot after being advised against it by the division commander. It was a mistake in judgment that could be excused on the basis of his past experience with Big Foot. Unexplained was why Sumner had failed to consider General Ruger's message of 17 December as an order to arrest Big Foot. The department commander had indicated that such an arrest would be desirable, and Sumner had had the opportunity.

Miles himself did not escape blame for the conduct of the campaign that had culminated in the Wounded Knee bloodbath. Settlers along the Cheyenne River were enraged when Miles suspended Forsyth after the tragic engagement. They criticized Miles for directing the campaign from his Rapid City hotel and for not taking personal command in the field earlier than 31 December.

At a public meeting held at Hermosa on 14 January 1891, a resolution was passed that chided Miles for damaging "the honored name of Col. Forsyth" by removing him from command pending an investigation into Wounded Knee. Another resolution accused Miles of pursuing a "weak and vacillating policy" during the Indian campaign. The assembly voted to present Miles with a leather medal "as a lasting testimonial to the indignation and chagrin" the settlers had for "him and his policy." The decoration was described as five inches in diameter, "bound with red tape, ornamented with a white feather" (a symbol of cowardice), and gilded with a star that carried an inscription accusing Miles of "inactivity" in the field. The *Record* reported that the medal was presented to Miles (in absentia) by Black Hills residents who were "disgusted" with his conduct of the campaign.[65]

It was rough treatment for an officer who had earlier been a national hero. Miles's overall handling of the campaign was generally supported in the region, however, especially by experienced frontiersmen like McGillycuddy. But many settlers near the reservation felt Miles had not moved forcefully enough against the Indians when he had had so many troops at his disposal. They approved of Forsyth's conduct despite the bloodshed that had resulted. His return to the command of the Seventh was characterized in the Black Hills as a vindication of his actions. "Public sentiment," the *Sturgis Advertiser* reported, "has always been with him and against General Miles in this case."[66]

Miles would further alienate his Black Hills critics with his sympathetic view of Sioux grievances. This feeling was exacerbated when Miles went to great lengths to assure Plenty Horses a fair trial for the death of Lieutenant Casey. The general clearly did not deserve the harsh denunciations of the disgruntled settlers at Hermosa, who may have had their own reasons for wanting the region cleared of Indians.

FRONTIER JUSTICE

Four days before the end of the fighting on the Pine Ridge Reservation, a killing that occurred off the reservation added a tragic footnote to this last campaign between the U.S. Army and the Sioux. The victim was an Indian named Few Tails, a relative of the respected Oglala headman Young-Man-Afraid-of-His-Horses. This influential chief had not taken part in the clash on the Pine Ridge Reservation and had been instrumental in persuading the Ghost Dancers to surrender to Miles. Few Tails and his wife, Clown, with One Feather and his family, had been granted passes by Agent Royer to go hunting in the vicinity of Bear Butte. One Feather's family consisted of his wife, Red Owl, and their two daughters, one a teenager and the other an infant.

Few Tails and One Feather had a successful hunt and filled their two wagons with the freshly killed game. En route to Pine Ridge with their families on 10 January, they camped for the night on the Belle Fourche River at the mouth of Alkali Creek, a small stream flowing through the Fort Meade military reservation to the Belle Fourche (and about midway between the fort and Camp Cheyenne, where troops under Sumner and Merriam were stationed). Peter Quinn's ranch, where Sumner had set up a courier station, was about seven miles away. Sergeant Frank Smith of Troop I, Eighth Cavalry, visited the Indian camp while en route from the fort to Quinn's ranch. Few Tails showed Smith his pass, and the sergeant continued on to the courier station. A group of cowboys also visited the Indian camp before nightfall but left after looking around.[1]

On the morning of 11 January, the Indians broke camp and started toward Pine Ridge with two spare ponies tied to their wagons. They had gone only a short distance when they were fired on by a group of men concealed behind a knoll close to the road. The first volley struck Few Tails, in the lead wagon with his wife, and he fell dead. The two horses pulling the wagon were also hit and dropped to the ground. Another volley sent bullets into Clown's breast and leg. She sought refuge beside the stalled wagon as One Feather fled from the ambush in the second wagon. Red Owl was wounded as the wagon sped away, with the children huddled in the wagon bed for safety.

The attackers, all white men, mounted their horses and raced after One Feather's wagon. With his pursuers closing in, One Feather turned the reins over to his wounded wife, grabbed his rifle, and jumped onto the back of one of his spare ponies. He fired on the whites as they approached, giving his wife enough time to get away; she drove the wagon to a defensive position on Elk Creek.

One Feather, turning back frequently to return the fire of the whites and slow them down, reached Elk Creek shortly after his wife and managed to hold off the attackers. After the initial ambush, one of the whites had gone to the courier camp at Quinn's ranch seeking help from the soldiers. He also picked up some cowboys along the way. The four soldiers at Quinn's were told that the Indians had been stealing horses and had fired on the whites when caught and that a large party of Indians was involved in a running fight with the settlers. Sergeant Smith, who knew that only the two Indian families had been camped in the region, was not at the station at the time to challenge the report. So two of the soldiers agreed to accompany the growing posse to Elk Creek, where One Feather was making his single-handed stand.

With the odds so great against him, the besieged Indian decided to abandon his precarious position. He mounted his oldest daughter on a horse, placed his infant daughter in her arms, swung his wounded wife up behind him on his own horse, and rode away to the south in a dash for freedom. The game-filled wagon was left behind. Remarkably, the fleeing Indians succeeded in escaping.

Meanwhile, the twice-wounded Clown, lying beside the wagon where the ambush had taken place, was forgotten. With her dead husband in the wagon, the bleeding Clown remained beside it all day and through the cold of a January night. The next morning she found that one of the injured horses of the wagon team was not dead. She managed to mount him and ride to a homestead on Elk Creek, about fifteen miles away. She knew the people living there and hoped to get treatment for her wounds. She reached the house on the evening of 12 January, but rather than giving her the expected aid, the whites ordered her away at gunpoint.

More dead than alive, Clown reached the beef corral east of the Pine Ridge Agency on the morning of 18 January— a week after being wounded and more than one hundred miles from where she had been shot. She was given emergency treatment at the field hospital of the Sixth Cavalry, stationed near the corral, and then taken to the agency hospital at Pine Ridge. Amazingly, she lived to tell about her terrible ordeal. So did One Feather, Red Owl, and their oldest daughter. They reached the Rosebud Agency on 24 January, thirteen days after the ambush, by making a laborious trek through the snow-blanketed Badlands. The infant had died of starvation and exposure. This helpless child was the final victim of the madness that gripped western South Dakota during the tragic winter of 1890–91.[2]

When word of the ambush and the fight with One Feather reached Camp Cheyenne, Colonel Merriam sent Second Lieutenant F. C. Marshall of Troop I, Eighth Cavalry, to investigate the affair. Marshall found the wagon containing Few Tails's body on the morning of 12 January, but the wounded Clown had already left on her painful journey to Pine Ridge.

Marshall also inspected One Feather's abandoned wagon on Elk Creek. Finding a branding iron in the wagon, the lieutenant was at first inclined to believe the story of the attackers—that the Indians had been part of a larger party engaged in stealing horses in the vicinity. But on further investigation, Marshall reported that all the evidence indicated the Indians had been ambushed and Few Tails had been killed "in cold blood." He further stated, "I am now convinced that this was a small party of Indians returning to Pine Ridge from a hunt, who committed no depredations until fired upon; there is nothing to indicate a large band."[3]

An observer at Camp Cheyenne, who saw the bullet-ridden, blood-soaked Indian wagons when they were brought to the soldier camp, wrote, "It seems very strange that some people could not see that Indians with wagons and women were not on the warpath." Colonel Merriam, in reporting Marshall's findings to Miles, termed the attack on the Indians "unprovoked."[4]

The men who had ambushed the Indians were identified as the brothers Andrew, Peter, and Nelson Culbertson and James Julfs, John Netland,

and Alva Marvin, all area ranchers or cowboys. Merriam wrote, "The Culbertson brothers are reported to be horse thieves and at least one of them having served out a sentence in prison for that crime."[5] Miles, fearful that the killing of Few Tails might bring on a renewal of hostilities at Pine Ridge, also had the incident investigated by his inspector general. These findings supported those of Marshall and Merriam. Miles was thus in a poor position to demand that the Sioux turn over to the government for punishment those responsible for the deaths of Lieutenant Casey and the civilian herder, Miller. Article 1 of the 1868 treaty required the Indians to surrender any of their people committing crimes against citizens of the United States, soldier or civilian, for trial under U.S. law. But the same article committed the government to prosecute any "bad men among the whites" who committed crimes against the Indians.[6]

Consequently, when Miles asked Young-Man-Afraid-of-His-Horses to surrender the killers of Casey and Miller, the chief refused. Instead, he promised to have his young men shoot the pair if Miles would have his soldiers do the same to the murderers of Few Tails. "And then," he told Miles, "we will be done with the whole business."[7] Miles, of course, could not consent to the proposal, however reasonable under the Indian code of justice. But he did promise to press vigorously for the prosecution of Few Tails's murderers. Casey and Miller had been killed on the reservation, so these cases fell within the jurisdiction of the U.S. courts. But Few Tails had been killed off the reservation, in Meade County, and the prosecution of his slayers would have to be sought there. Miles sent the findings of the army investigations to Governor Mellette with a request that Few Tails's killers be brought to trial. He also joined with the army investigators of the incident in labeling the killing unprovoked murder. Satisfied that Miles would do his best to bring Few Tails's slayers to justice, Young-Man-Afraid consented to the arrest of the killers of Casey and Miller.

Meanwhile, with the Ghost Dance troubles over, Miles sought to have the control of the Sioux agencies turned over to the army. The citizens of Chadron, Nebraska, not far south of the Pine Ridge Agency, backed Miles's proposal with a petition of support to the president and the secretary of war, a petition that also proposed the appointment of Indian agents "be removed from the field of politics." Although the proposals were not adopted, Miles was permitted to place an army officer in charge

of the Sioux agencies. President Benjamin Harrison, on the recommendation of the commissioner of Indian affairs, removed Royer as the agent at
Pine Ridge on 8 January. The officers assigned to the other agencies were
instructed to work with the civilian agents in maintaining order on the
reservations.[8]

On 21 January, Miles held a grand review of his troops at Pine Ridge to
demonstrate the magnitude of the frontier army available to him. Then he
sent his troops back to their home stations or on to new assignments.
"Thus ended what at one time threatened to be a serious Indian war,"
Miles commented in his report of the campaign. "The frontier was again
assured of peace and safety from the Indians who a few weeks prior had
been a terror to all persons living in that sparsely settled country."[9]
Mooney, in his analysis of the campaign, noted that only one white non-
combatant (Miller) had been killed and that no depredations had been
committed off the reservations. "The panic among the settlers of both
Dakotas, Nebraska and Iowa was something ludicrous," he wrote. "The
inhabitants worked themselves into such a panic that ranches and even
whole villages were temporarily abandoned and the people flocked into
the railroad cities with vivid stories of murder, scalping and desolation
that had no foundation whatever in fact."[10]

Mooney's assessment overlooked the fact that Few Tails was a noncom-
batant too. Mooney put the campaign cost at the lives of forty-nine whites,
all soldiers except for Miller, and more than three hundred Indians. Most
of the dead had been killed during the Wounded Knee fight. The campaign
had also been costly in unexpected government expenses. The army's
Quartermaster Department estimated that $1.3 million had been spent
on the campaign. The estimate included the costs of transporting the
troops to the reservation and back to their posts, supplying them in the
field, providing extra clothing for the winter campaign, and purchasing
replacements for horses worn out by the campaign. In addition, buying
supplies for the troops cost more in the field than at their posts, where
goods were furnished at contracted prices. The final cost of the campaign
to the government was estimated at about two million dollars.[11]

With the troops ordered back to their respective stations, Sumner
returned to Fort Meade from Camp Cheyenne on 22 January. He assumed
the command of the post the next day, when Colonel Otis left for St. Paul

to appear before the army retirement board. All Eighth Cavalry and Third Infantry troops in the field were back at Fort Meade by the twenty-sixth.

Second Lieutenant Joseph C. Byron, Troop A, Eighth Cavalry, was sent to Pine Ridge late in January to recruit a company of Indian scouts. That he had only limited success was not surprising, considering the Indians' ill will toward the army after the Wounded Knee affair. The post rolls carried eighteen Indian scouts in January, but only half that number when Byron returned to Fort Meade in March.[12]

The permanent garrison of the fort was reduced when Company B, Third Infantry, left on 1 February for a change of station to Fort Sully. A measure was adopted in the state legislature in February urging the South Dakota congressional delegation to use its influence to get the garrison and quarters of Fort Meade enlarged. The proposal was sponsored by State Senator John Potter of Sturgis and was unanimously approved, but it failed to halt the diminution of the garrison. The fort lost all its infantrymen when Companies C and F of the Third were transferred to Fort Snelling in March and June, respectively. The transferred companies were not immediately replaced, leaving only the field staff, the band, and six troops of the Eighth Cavalry at the post.

Colonel Otis retired in February, and the command of the regiment and the post remained with Sumner. Colonel James S. Brisbin of the First Cavalry, a Pennsylvania editor and lawyer who was thrice wounded during the Civil War, was transferred to the Eighth in April. But his tenure as regimental and post commander was brief. He was in ill health and reportedly "too fat to ride anyhow." Brisbin arrived at the fort in late April, immediately applied for a leave of absence, and left for the East on 31 May. He never returned.[13] The command of the Eighth and of the fort remained with Sumner for the rest of 1891, except for brief periods when subalterns served during his absence.

The return of the troops to the fort from the field also brought back the Indian scouts who had served under Sumner and Carr. In addition, the Cheyenne scouts from Montana, formerly commanded by the murdered Lieutenant Casey and then by Lieutenant Getty, camped at Fort Meade en route to their home station. With them was a large band of Cheyennes who were being escorted back to the Tongue River Agency after visiting Red Cloud's Oglalas at Pine Ridge. The sizable Indian encampment at the

Cheyenne Indians returned from the Sioux reservation at Pine Ridge, South Dakota, to their own reservation on the Tongue River of Montana in February 1891. Under army escort, they passed through Sturgis after breaking camp at Fort Meade. They were accompanied by a company of Cheyenne scouts who had aided the army during the "Messiah Craze," which had culminated in the bloody Wounded Knee engagement. (Courtesy Mrs. Freeman E. Steele. Author's collection.)

post attracted considerable attention among the citizens of Sturgis, and many of them visited the camp.

Each of the Indian scouts received about fifty-five dollars at the pay table in February. In company with other Cheyennes, the scouts made a "general rush for the stores" in Sturgis before striking out for Montana. "Every Waterbury watch in the place was taken and dozens more could have been sold," the local newspaper reported. "Potter sold all the shawls in the store, and there are not enough quilts around town to keep people warm. There was also a great run on cheap gloves and white hats." It would be a long time, the newspaper predicted, before Sturgis would "see so many Indians on Main Street again. There were about 400 in all."[14] No more Indian scouts were carried on the post returns at Fort Meade after June 1891.

The Sioux at Pine Ridge, assured by Miles that the killers of Few Tails would be brought to trial, surrendered Plenty Horses to the government on 18 February. Another Indian, identified both as Young Skunk and as Leaves-His-Woman, was arrested for the murder of Miller. Lieutenant Byron commanded the military escort that brought the two prisoners by train from White Clay Creek to Fort Meade, where they were placed in the guardhouse pending indictment.

Dr. McGillycuddy was the foreman of the grand jury, which met for six days in March and determined that the army had arrested the wrong man in the death of Miller. Charges against Young Skunk were dropped. McGillycuddy enlisted the aid of Fast Horse, an old friend from the doctor's days as the agent at Pine Ridge, to learn who actually had killed Miller. Fast Horse learned that the killer was a Rosebud Indian, Kills-the-Enemy, the son of Yellow Robe. He had left the Pine Ridge Reservation to return to Rosebud for a visit and was expected to return in about a week. McGillycuddy passed the information along to the attorney general, but subsequent events led the authorities to decide against prosecuting Kills-the-Enemy.[15]

There was no case of mistaken identity in the killing of Lieutenant Casey. Not only had the murder been committed in the presence of witnesses, but Plenty Horses freely admitted to the deed. The young Brulé explained that he had been an outcast among his people since returning to the reservation from the white man's school at Carlisle. "I shot the lieutenant so I could make a place for myself among my people," the Indian confessed. "Now I am one of them. I shall be hung and the Indians will bury me as a warrior. They will be proud of me. I am satisfied."[16] The confession left the grand jury with no choice but to indict the prisoner. The foreman, McGillycuddy, knew of Miles's promise to also push for the arrest of Few Tails's killers. So he persuaded the jury to support Miles's position, and in a letter to U.S. Judge A. J. Edgerton, the jury urged the government to "spare no expense" in seeking convictions of the killers of Few Tails. The letter also requested that the U.S. district attorney for South Dakota be instructed to assist in the prosecution of the case.[17]

Judge Edgerton, recognizing that prejudice against the Indians was strongest in the Black Hills counties, set Plenty Horses's trial for April in the U.S. district court in Sioux Falls. The change of venue angered some Black Hillers, and the *Daily Times* charged that Edgerton "doesn't like the Hills people, and there is no love lost."[18] Relations between the civil authorities and the military also became strained when Sumner refused to surrender Plenty Horses to Deputy U.S. Marshal F. S. Fry when he came to the fort to take charge of the prisoner. Sumner explained he was under orders from Miles to hold the Indian as a prisoner of war until Few Tails's murderers were arrested by the local authorities.

Miles, determined to honor his commitment to the Sioux, was not convinced that Few Tails's killers would be punished under state law, especially since W. B. Sterling of Huron, the U.S. district attorney for South Dakota, had turned the case over to Meade County for prosecution. Sterling's action, the *Daily Times* predicted, meant that Few Tails's killers would "never be punished, and probably never even brought to trial."[19]

The civil authorities complained to Washington of Sumner's refusal to surrender his prisoner, and the secretary of war countermanded Miles's order. Meanwhile, Sterling was directed by the U.S. attorney general to assist the Meade County state's attorney in prosecuting Few Tails's killers. Thus all sides in the dispute were placated; the marshal got his prisoner, Miles's promise to the Indians was honored, and the grand jury's recommendations were accepted.

Deputy U.S. Marshal Chris Matthiessen secured Plenty Horses from the Fort Meade guardhouse and took him by train to Sioux Falls. The prisoner arrived at the penitentiary in shackles, which had been placed on his ankles at Fort Meade and which had to be removed by the city blacksmith. According to the Sioux Falls newspaper, Plenty Horses's father was a well-to-do Indian rancher on the Rosebud Reservation and would spare no expense in defending his son. The newspaper also reported, "[Plenty Horses] takes his imprisonment stoically and looks upon his probable execution in a matter of fact way that indicates an astonishing amount of nerve."[20]

Living Bear, Plenty Horses's father, may have been wealthy in Indian terms, but he lacked the necessary capital in white man's currency to finance a costly legal battle. However, Plenty Horses received legal assistance from an unexpected source. Sumner, who had been impressed with the young Indian while he was imprisoned at Fort Meade, notified the Indian Rights Association in Washington, D.C., of Plenty Horses's plight, and that organization agreed to pay whatever costs were incurred in defending him. George P. Nock and D. E. Powers, Sioux Falls attorneys, were engaged to represent him.[21]

Plenty Horses's trial opened on 23 April with Sterling as the chief prosecutor, aided by Assistant U.S. District Attorney Charles Howard of Redfield and Captain J. G. Balance of the army's judge advocate corps. Two judges—Edgerton and O. P. Shiras of Dubuque, Iowa—were on the bench, with Shiras serving as the presiding magistrate. The trial attracted national attention, largely because of the recent publicity given to the Sioux campaign by "war correspondents" on the scene. Plenty Horses was interviewed in his cell by J. J. McDonough, a reporter for the *New York World,* and reiterated what he had earlier told the grand jury: he had killed Lieutenant Casey to make a place for himself in his tribe after being ostracized for going away to the white school. Plenty Horses was twenty-two years old at the time and had returned to the reservation from Carlisle two years earlier. He confided that the education he had received during his five years at Carlisle had not benefited him on the reservation. On the contrary, it had alienated him from the other young men of his tribe. He denied taking part in the Ghost Dance but admitted that, as a member of Two Strikes's band, he had taken part in the Drexel Mission fight. Plenty Horses told the reporter that one of his cousins had been killed at Wounded Knee and that he had been angered when the bodies of a number of Indian women and children had been found miles from Wounded Knee after the fight.[22]

McDonough also appeared as a witness at the trial, testifying that Plenty Horses had freely confessed to the killing. The courtroom was packed for the trial, with many women among the spectators. White Moon and Pete Richard also testified on the circumstances of Casey's death. Philip H. Wells, Forsyth's interpreter and chief of scouts who had been knifed in the nose during the fighting at Wounded Knee, was another witness. Wells testified about relations between the Indians and the

Plenty Horses, a young Brulé Sioux, was held prisoner at Fort Meade while awaiting trial for the killing of Lieutenant Edward W. Casey (see chapter 9). This photo
was taken on the Fort Meade parade grounds. (Courtesy of the Library of Congress.)

army at the time of Casey's murder and reported that a state of war existed between them. Wells also expressed his opinion that the Indians at
Wounded Knee would never have fought the soldiers "if they had not been
under the impression that their ghost shirts were impenetrable by the
white man's bullets."[23]

The parade of witnesses prompted the *Argus-Leader* to report: "[The trial] is worth more to Sioux Falls than the Capital is to Pierre. Every day the court is in session here Uncle Sam pays out over $500 in juror and witness fees. So far during this session over $3,000 had been paid out in witness fees alone."[24] On 29 April, after twenty-four ballots had been taken, none of which were closer than eight to four, the jury reported that it could not agree on a verdict. Six jurors had voted for conviction on the murder charge and the other six for a manslaughter conviction. Judge Shiras dismissed the jury and set a new trial for 25 May, also at Sioux Falls. The *Argus-Leader* summed up the public's reaction to the outcome of the first trial by stating, "The sympathetic approve, the prejudiced denounce, and the thinking men are divided."[25]

Between Plenty Horses's two trials, Meade County, pressured by the federal government, finally moved to try the case against Few Tails's killers. A grand jury was convened in Sturgis in May, with Mayor John Monheim as one of its members. It returned indictments against Pete, Nelson, and Andrew Culbertson, Alva Marvin, and James Julfs. John Netland, previously identified as among the men attacking the Indians, was not charged. On 20 May, five days before Plenty Horses's second trial was to begin, the indicted men were arrested and placed in the county jail. Julfs was allowed to return to his ranch under bail to participate in the roundup of horses. But the other four defendants were held in jail pending the opening of the circuit court.

With both the grand jury and the circuit court in session at Sturgis, the local bar owners decided that "discretion was the better part of valor" and agreed to temporarily "close their hospitable doors." Prohibition was in effect in the state at the time, and the Enforcement League was actively seeking out violators. Thus, the *Black Hills Daily Times* reported, "Sturgis is dry for the first time in history."[26]

Alexander McCall, the state's attorney for Meade County, was well aware that "the eyes of the whole nation" were on the Few Tails murder case. He did not object to the assistance of the U.S. district attorney in prosecuting the case. But he asked that the federal government be equally as helpful in financing it, claiming that Meade County was poor and could not afford a long and expensive trial.

Reaction to the widespread attention the case was attracting was greeted differently by the two local newspapers. The *Record* resented the interest shown in the case by "outside papers" and predicted: "The authorities of this county will do just about as they see fit. They hardly need advice from other sections of the country." The *Advertiser,* on the other hand, reported there was no doubt a crime had been committed and expressed a "desire to see the guilty punished." The good name of South Dakota, it added, demanded "that justice be done." The competing newspapers would also take opposite positions when the case ended.[27]

The *Black Hills Daily Times* at Deadwood, reflecting the anti-Indian bias of its readers, predicted that the jury trying the white men would act "in a manly way." The newspaper explained that the jury would base its verdict strictly in accordance with the law and the evidence and predicted that "no sickly sentimentality or prejudiced feeling for or against the parties" would govern the jury.[28]

Captain Frank D. Baldwin of General Miles's staff was a surprise witness when the second trial of Plenty Horses opened in Sioux Falls. He had been to Pierre to urge the governor to issue a proclamation prohibiting the sale of weapons to Indians, an activity the legislature had failed to ban. Plenty Horses's attorneys had asked Miles to testify about conditions on the reservation at the time of Casey's murder, but since Baldwin was already in the state, he took Miles's place on the stand. He reported that 281 guns had been taken from the Indians participating in the Wounded Knee fight. He also reported, "The Indians have never been more completely subdued than they are now." He asserted, "The Indian trouble is all over forever."[29]

Baldwin's testimony supported the main argument of the defense attorneys: Plenty Horses had killed Casey while the officer was spying on the Indian village at a time when a state of war existed between the army and the Sioux. Baldwin denied that Casey was a spy but admitted that the officer had been "reconnoitering" the Indian camp. He also revealed that 1,000 infantrymen, 1,200 cavalry soldiers, and 125 artillerymen were on the reservation during the campaign against the Sioux Ghost Dancers. Yes, Baldwin stated, war "with a capital 'W'" existed at the time.[30]

In further support of the point, the defense attorneys entered into evidence Miles's order directing that Plenty Horses be held at Fort Meade as a prisoner of war. Forty-four witnesses took the stand during the two-day trial, including White Moon and Richard, who had witnessed the fatal shooting of Casey. Sumner also came from Fort Meade to appear as a witness, relating what Plenty Horses, while a prisoner at the post, had said about the killing. But it was Baldwin's testimony that decided the case—to the chagrin of the prosecuting attorneys, who resented his appearance as a witness without being subpoenaed.[31]

On 28 May, Judge Shiras directed the jury to return a verdict of not guilty against the defendant. He explained it was his opinion, not shared by Edgerton, that the defense had proven that a state of war had indeed existed on the reservation when Casey was killed. He said the various conflicts that had taken place on the reservation between the Indians and the troops were really battles. "If they were not," the judge told the jury, "it would be hard to justify the killing of the Indians at Wounded Knee and other places." He also said it was unlikely that Casey would have been tried for murder if the circumstances had been reversed and he had killed Plenty Horses. "The killing of Casey was a cruel act," Shiras commented, "but it was an act of war." The jury, without leaving the courtroom, quickly acquitted the defendant as directed. The verdict "was greeted with cheers by the vast audience," and "it took several minutes before Judge Edgerton and Marshal Fry could establish order."[32]

Plenty Horses, who was described as "the coolest person in the room," signed autographs for one dollar apiece and was released. Enjoying his role as a celebrity, Plenty Horses consented to be photographed with a large group of principals in the case while still in Sioux Falls. Photographed with him, in addition to his lawyers and Indian supporters, were the prosecution attorneys, the marshals, and several witnesses who had testified against him. Wells and White Moon were among the latter. Plenty Horses had achieved his objective—he was accepted by his people and returned to Rosebud as a hero.[33]

The acquittal created a sensation in South Dakota as well as elsewhere. But it was not the only melodramatic aspect of the trial. White Moon, angered that the court had freed Casey's killer, went to his room in the Merchants Hotel and stabbed himself in the left breast. The *Argus-Leader* attributed the Cheyenne scout's act to his remorse for not killing Plenty Horses when the youth had shot Casey. It reported that White Moon's wife had accused him of cowardice and had vowed not to return to his tent until he brought her the scalp of Casey's murderer. "Rather than

Plenty Horses, front row center, posed with a large group of his trial principals following the directed verdict, which acquitted him of murdering Lieutenant E. W. Casey. The group included his prosecutors and his defenders, as well as witnesses who testified for and against him. (L.T. Butterfield photo courtesy of the South Dakota State Historical Society.)

return to his empty tent on the reservation," the newspaper stated, "he chose to die in the room where he had been quartered during the trial."[34]

With the release of Plenty Horses, the government decided it was useless to pursue the prosecution of Kills-the-Enemy for the death of Miller. The herder, like Casey, had been killed on the reservation when the Indians and the government were at war. Shiras's rationale for ordering Plenty Horses freed would equally apply to Miller's killer. The only difference was that Casey had been an army officer whereas Miller had been a civilian on the reservation at his own risk.

Immediately after Plenty Horses's acquittal, speculation began on its probable effect on the forthcoming trial in Sturgis of the killers of Few Tails. Sterling, who had failed to convict Plenty Horses, noted, "It will be impossible to convict the slayers of Few Tails." Although prophetic, it was a startling statement, considering that the case had not yet gone to trial and that Sterling was to assist in the prosecution. But it was an opinion that was widely shared. "The effect of the acquittal on the rest of the Indians will be bad," said South Dakota's U.S. Senator Pettigrew, who had met with the president shortly before the verdict was announced. "I was wholly surprised when I heard of the outcome of the trial." Pettigrew had told the president, who had expressed an interest in the case, that the verdict could not be other than guilty. "The Indian who did the killing," the senator declared, "was not entitled to be treated like an enemy against whom war had been declared."[35]

William A. McMichaels, the Meade County clerk of courts, predicted it would be "mighty hard to convict a white man for killing an Indian in any of the Black Hills counties." The *Record* at Sturgis wrote that the acquittal of Plenty Horses ended "the cases against the white men" charged with killing Few Tails. "To convict or punish in any way the men who, in Meade County, shot an Indian almost at the same time, would be an unwise and unjust thing to do. The prisoners will be discharged."[36]

The *Army and Navy Journal* chided the *Record*'s editor for not seeing the difference between the two cases. "Killing the armed leader of the party reconnoitering upon the position of an armed camp," it stated, "is very far removed from the slaughter of a peaceful party returning from a hunting expedition. Guerrillas and bushwackers are not soldiers, and murder is not war." The *Record*'s editor replied that he had "lived out West too long" to advocate the conviction of whites for killing an Indian when the court had condoned an Indian's murder of a white man. Nearly every newspaper in the state, and many outside the state, joined in the debate. They were generally in agreement that it would be difficult, if not impossible, to convict the killers of Few Tails under the circumstances.[37]

Others took issue with Judge Shiras's contention that a state of war had existed. But the *Times* at Deadwood supported the judge on this point, reminding its readers that many eastern newspapers had sent correspondents "to the seat of the war." It also pointed out that a great many soldiers, plus a large force of the Nebraska and South Dakota militia, had been needed to suppress the trouble. "If it wasn't war," the newspaper asked, "what was the U.S. Army and the state militia in the field for?"[38]

It took over three days to select "twelve good men and true" for the jury after the Few Tails trial opened in circuit court in Meade County on 22 June. Sixty-five potential jurors were interviewed before the jury was seated. All but two of the twelve jurors selected were farmers or ranchers. McCall, assisted by Sterling and South Dakota Attorney General Robert Dollard, conducted the prosecution, using all their peremptory challenges. The defendants' attorneys—the Sturgis lawyers, Charles Polk, Thomas E. Harvey, Ralph Kirk, and Wesley Stuart, assisted by W. H. Parker of Deadwood—disqualified fourteen potential jurors. Judge Charles M. Thomas presided. Wells served as interpreter for the prosecution and George Carson for the defense. In a surprise move, without stating the reason, the prosecution dropped the charges against Julfs. He was described as "a well to do stockman and influential citizen" of the county.[39]

It was late in the day when the first witness, Clown, took the stand in the packed courtroom on 26 June. She was the only witness testifying that day. She identified Andy Culbertson as being among the men who had visited the Indian camp on Alkali Creek the night before the attack. She then told how her husband had been killed and how she and Red Owl had been wounded from ambush. The most dramatic moment of the trial came when the prosecutors asked her to exhibit her wounds. It was reported that the sympathies of the crowd, which previously had been with the prisoners, swung to Clown when she bared her scarred breast. "It was noticed," a newsman wrote, "that the stern judge and sterner jury, made up of the bone and sinew of the frontier, was noticeably affected."[40]

Unfortunately for the prosecution's case, One Feather could not be found to corroborate Clown's testimony. While the trial was still under way, the *Record* reported that Clown had been seen on the streets of Sturgis having lice removed from her hair by her daughter. The pair was described as "two of the oppressed whom the philanthropists of the east would fain take to their bosoms and embrace."[41] Similarly, the prosecution attempted to discredit the defendants, although not in equally as bad taste. It disclosed that two of the Culbertson brothers had been indicted in Bon Homme County for horse stealing in 1882 but had been "acquitted through a technicality."[42] Three of the defendants testified in their own behalf, telling substantially the same story. They claimed that the Few Tails party had been part of a large band of Indians who had been stealing horses in the vicinity. When the defendants had asked for the return of the stolen horses, the prisoners testified, the Indians had fired on them. They also claimed that Few Tails had been killed and Clown and Red Owl wounded in the return fire.[43]

The *Sturgis Advertiser* editorialized that the defense attorneys were making "an excellent fight" and had public opinion on their side. "A great many people honestly believe Indians have no rights that a white man is bound to respect." The *Advertiser* further stated that the defendants would probably be "sent up" for perjury if acquitted for the killing because of their estimates of the number of Indians involved in the fight. "Entirely too much swearing has been done as to the number of Indians in the county the day Few Tails was killed," the newspaper commented. "Everyone who was familiar with the excitement that prevailed at that time all through the settlements must admit that the superabundance of courageousness did not exist anywhere as boasted by several witnesses. . . . The stories told by the witnesses for the defense is [*sic*] quite conflicting as to the number of Indians, which is not at all surprising for the reason that everything would look like an Indian about that time." Moreover, the *Advertiser* wrote sarcastically, the War Department could have saved itself much trouble and expense if it had sent "brave ranchmen," rather than the troops, into the field against the Indians. "If their evidence in the Few Tails case is worth anything," the newspaper stated, "the names of Daniel Boone and Kit Carson will no longer occupy a front seat in history. We got the fighters."[44]

The defense considered subpoenaing Captain Baldwin to repeat his testimony, which he had given at Plenty Horses's trial, about a state of war existing at the time of the two killings. It abandoned the idea, however, after learning that Baldwin could not say whether the same condition of war existed off the reservation. The defense might have called up Sumner to testify on this point. He was familiar with conditions in Meade County because Camp Cheyenne, where troops from Fort Meade had been stationed for nine months, was within its boundaries. But Sumner was on leave at the time of the trial. Besides, he may not have helped the defense's case, considering the sympathetic attitude he had exhibited toward Plenty Horses at the Sioux Falls trial.[45]

In addition to the local press, Thomas H. Russell, a member of the 1874 Gordon party to the Black Hills and an early settler at Deadwood, also covered the trial. Because of the intense national interest in the case, Russell managed to obtain a reporting assignment from the *Chicago Herald*. While the trial was attracting "universal attention," the *Record* reported that the people of the Black Hills cared "less about it" because acquittal was "expected as a matter of course." Nonetheless, as the *Record* itself had earlier reported, the trial was being conducted in a "packed courtroom," presumably composed mostly of local people. They may not have cared, but they certainly were interested in the trial. The Sturgis newspaper editorially scolded the Sioux Falls papers for their "slobbering sentiment" toward the Indians. It suggested that the court officials in the Few Tails case could "draw an example" from Judge Shiras's directed acquittal of Plenty Horses and could "square accounts."[46]

The trial came to an end on 2 July when Judge Thomas, declining to follow Shiras's example, put the matter to the jury. In his instructions, the judge admonished the jurymen to eschew racial prejudice in reaching a decision. The "twelve good men and true" acquitted the defendants so quickly that the *Record* described their promptness as "something of a surprise, even to the defendants and their friends." Of the verdict, the newspaper commented: "Thus ends one of the greatest farces that Meade County has ever experienced. Probably not one man in a thousand has thought for a moment that these men should even have been arrested—much less placed on trial. But the outside pressure has been such that nothing would do but to haul them up, keep them in jail for months, and finally bring them before a court of justice—for what? Simply killing an Indian that, with others, was engaged in stealing horses. . . . The jury took three ballots, the first and second stood eleven for acquittal."[47]

The *Sturgis Advertiser,* seemingly ashamed of the trial's outcome, buried its report of the acquittal on an inside page. "The prosecution was vigorously conducted," it wrote, "but with the memory of the release of Plenty Horses, the murderer of Lt. Casey, fresh in their minds, it was not expected a jury would be obtained who would convict the slayers of Few Tails." The *Times* at Deadwood predicted the eastern press would claim that, "no matter what the circumstances," the "slaying of an Indian by a white man" would not "be punished by a western jury." It protested the suggestion, stating the jury was justified in its verdict.[48]

As predicted, newspapers outside the Black Hills generally characterized the outcome as racially motivated. The tendency to recognize a difference between the two murder cases was considerably stronger outside the Hills. As the Black Hillers saw it, the Few Tails case was decided with the acquittal of Plenty Horses. Perhaps the Meade County state's attorney, who had prosecuted the Few Tails case under pressure from the army and Sterling, sized up the situation accurately when he asserted, "A white man cannot be convicted for the killing of an Indian [in Meade County]." It cost the county under fifteen hundred dollars to prosecute the case and the federal government slightly over three hundred dollars. "All will concede," said the *Record,* "that this is a pretty cheap way to get out of what promised at one time to be an expensive piece of business."[49]

★ 10 ★

THE SIOUX SOLDIERS

G arrison life at Fort Meade was rather routine after the Indian campaign of 1890–91 and would remain so for the rest of the century, with periods of unusual activity. Retirements, promotions, transfers, and reports of training marches dominated the monthly post reports.

Although life at Fort Meade was relatively uneventful during this period, the effects of two armywide activities were felt at the post to some degree. Of little impact was the significant army reorganization of 1891, which abolished geographical divisions and replaced them with a system of departments whose commanders reported directly to army headquarters in Washington. Miles's Division of the Missouri became the Department of the Missouri, with headquarters still in Chicago but with jurisdiction reduced by the removal of the Departments of Dakota and the Platte. The old Department of Dakota was renamed the Department of Dakota and Lakes and was expanded to include Wisconsin and Iowa. Department headquarters remained at Fort Snelling, and Fort Meade continued under its jurisdiction.[1]

Of greater impact on the fort was the army's decision to embark on an experiment to speed the assimilation of Indians into American culture by enlisting whole companies of Indians as regular army soldiers, rather than individually as scouts. The secretary of war had authorized Miles to enlist up to twenty companies of sixty-man Indian troops in November 1890. They were to have served during the emergency arising from the Messiah campaign. Total army strength at the time was only 27,000, and Schofield had sent Miles all the troops he could spare from other departments. Miles, however, had been too busy directing the troops ringing the Sioux reservations to organize the Indian recruitment effort; it was also an inauspicious moment to recruit Indians into military service.[2]

In March 1891, however, less than three months after the Sioux cam-

143

paign had ended at Wounded Knee, an order was issued to implement the new policy by authorizing the enlistment of up to two thousand Indians into the regular service. For years the frontier army had been allowed to employ Indians as scouts, but as civilians and not as regular army soldiers. The change in policy was due to concerns within the Indian Office and the War Department that the young Indians on the various reservations should be kept "beneficially" occupied. The government believed that Indians would be less of a threat to the peace of the frontier if they could be gainfully employed. Employment opportunities for them on— and off—the reservations were virtually nonexistent.[3]

Promoters of Wild West shows, such as Buffalo Bill Cody and Colonel Alvaren Allen, offered some Indians seasonal jobs at meager wages to add color to their productions, but the commissioner of Indian affairs was opposed to the seeming exploitation of the Indians in this manner. He expressed his opposition to the show appearances in his annual reports for both 1890 and 1891. Although these shows gave the Indians an opportunity to earn a little money, the commissioner believed they also brought them into association with "some of the worst elements of society." Also according to the commissioner, "Their representations of feats of savage daring, showing border life as it formerly existed, vividly depicting scenes of rapine, murder and robbery, for which they are enthusiastically applauded, is demoralizing in an extreme degree." He further complained that their travels throughout the country with these shows fostered "the roving spirit so common among them" and encouraged "idleness and a distaste for steady occupation." Also, their families often suffered during their absences. "They frequently return home bankrupt in purse," the commissioner reported, "wrecked morally and physically and, in such cases, their influence and example among other Indians is the worst possible."[4]

Even though some of his commanders opposed bringing Indians into the regular army, Schofield strongly favored the idea. Indian men, he pointed out, considered soldiering an especially worthy occupation. He insisted that the proposal be given "a full, fair and persistent trial." The secretaries of war and the interior endorsed the plan, and the president approved it. General Order No. 28 of 9 March 1891 set the Indian recruitment campaign into motion, authorizing all cavalry and infantry regiments west of the Mississippi River (except those composed of black soldiers) to enlist one company of Indians. Maximum unit strength was placed at fifty-five. Eligibility was restricted to physically fit male Indians eighteen to thirty-five years of age, who would serve for five years at the same pay and privileges as white soldiers. The enlistment of up to ten married Indians per unit was also authorized.[5]

These all-Indian units, commanded by white officers, were designated Company I if infantry and Troop L if cavalry. These were two of the four companies (I and K, infantry; L and M, cavalry) that had been skeletonized, or dropped, from regimental rolls in 1890 under Schofield's army reorganization. Unlike the black soldiers, who were segregated on the regimental level, the Indians were segregated on the company level and assigned to white regiments.

One of the leading advocates of the experiment was First Lieutenant Hugh L. Scott of the Seventh Cavalry. When the Indians were suitably armed and mounted, Scott believed, they were "the best light horsemen the world has ever seen." Despite his friendship with the Southern Cheyennes, however, Scott was unable to persuade many to enlist because they were relatively well off on their Oklahoma reservation. The Sioux in South Dakota, on the other hand, enlisted in large numbers. Scott attributed the difference to the fact that the Sioux "had no food, no horses, no blankets, nor clothing and were willing to do anything that would bring them food and shelter." Scott eventually managed to fill Troop L of his own regiment with recruits from Comanche and Kiowa reservations in Oklahoma. The Seventh Cavalry was stationed at Fort Sill, Oklahoma, when its all-Indian troop was formed.[6]

There were approximately nineteen thousand Indians, almost all Sioux, on the South Dakota reservations when the army began recruiting for its all-Indian units. Of these, over ten thousand were on the Pine Ridge and Rosebud reservations, where most of the Indians involved in the troubles of the 1890–91 campaign were enrolled. The enlistment of Sioux seemed to hold promise because of their traditional warrior culture. It was believed that the discipline of army life and the skills the Indians could develop as soldiers would hasten their assimilation into the white culture, and at first it appeared it would work out that way.[7]

Six regular army Indian units were recruited among the Sioux of the

Dakotas. Company I, Twenty-second Infantry, was organized among the Standing Rock Sioux, whose reservation extended into both states, and served at Fort Yates (just across the border in North Dakota) from June 1891 to April 1893. Company I, Sixteenth Infantry, was recruited from among the Brulé Sioux of the Rosebud Reservation in December 1891, and its members were discharged at Fort Douglas, Utah, in May 1894. Sioux recruited at the Yankton Agency in September and October 1891 for Company I, Twenty-first Infantry, served at Forts Randall and Sidney before being discharged at Fort Omaha in December 1894. Oglalas from the Pine Ridge Reservation, where the Ghost Dance troubles had ended in January, were recruited in June 1891 for Company I, Second Infantry, and were discharged in May 1894 at Fort Omaha, Department of the Platte.[8]

Lieutenant Edward E. Dravo of the Sixth Cavalry recruited fifty-five Brulé Sioux on the Rosebud Reservation in the spring of 1891 for Troop L of his regiment, then stationed at Fort Niobrara, Nebraska. Captain Jesse M. Lee, who inspected the unit that fall, had high praise for it, reporting that the experiment was doing more for the "progress and civilization" of the Indians than had been accomplished in all previous years. The Indian soldiers performed the same fatigue duties and drill as their white counterparts at the fort. They also made periodic practice marches on the Rosebud Reservation to demonstrate their soldierly skills. In the summer of 1892, these Indian soldiers participated with their regiment in restoring peace to Johnson County, Wyoming, following the range war between ranchers and homesteaders.[9]

Sioux soldiers recruited on the Cheyenne River Reservation included some of Hump's young men and a few survivors of Big Foot's band. These recruits were principally from the Miniconjou, Two Kettle, Sans Arc, and Blackfoot subdivisions of the Sioux. They formed Troop L of the Third Cavalry and were assigned to Fort Bennett, but with the abandonment of that fort in October 1891 the troop was transferred to Fort Meade. The all-Indian troop, arriving at Sturgis by rail on 8 November, marched un-mounted down Main Street to its new station. First Lieutenant G. H. Macdonald, First Cavalry, commanded the troop because all three Third Cavalry officers assigned to it were on detached service at the time. The First Sergeant was James Chasing Hawk, recruited at Leslie, South Dakota, by Macdonald on 21 October 1891.[10] Macdonald reported, on his arrival at Fort Meade, that his Indian charges objected to being "walking

The all-Sioux Troop L, Third Cavalry, was almost at its full authorized strength of fifty-five soldiers when it posed for this photograph in front of its quarters at Fort Meade. The troop was recruited on the Cheyenne River Reservation of South Dakota in 1891 and was transferred from Fort Bennett to Fort Meade that fall. Most of the soldiers were mustered out of service in 1894. It was commanded by First Lieutenant J. C. Byron during most of its tour of duty at Fort Meade. (Courtesy of Old Fort Meade Museum Association.)

soldiers." He pointed out that they were "splendid horsemen" and that they had enlisted as cavalrymen, not as foot soldiers. He also revealingly said of them:

> They show greater respect for their officers than the white soldiers do. . . . they do not learn to drill as quickly as whites, but they are much easier to handle and keep splendid discipline. . . . The greatest advantage obtained by making a soldier of an Indian is that it seems to civilize him. When these men were enlisted they were as dirty as the dirtiest Indians. . . . Three of them had been wounded at Wounded Knee. Now money could not hire them to resist the whites. They are as loyal as can be. We give all the commands in English and require the men to ask for articles they want in the mess rooms in English. That way we are teaching them the English language.[11]

Eight troops of the Eighth Cavalry, temporarily commanded by Sumner, constituted the garrison at Fort Meade on the arrival of the Indian troop. The Third Cavalry troop was thereafter carried as an attached unit on the monthly post roster. The Eighth Cavalry's own Troop L was then stationed at Fort Keogh and was largely composed of Northern Cheyenne Indians who had served as "Casey's Scouts" during the troubles on the Pine Ridge Reservation the previous winter. Ironically, these scouts took a pay cut when they joined the regular army. As scouts, furnishing their own horses and tack, they had been paid forty cents per day above the pay of a cavalry private. As enlisted soldiers, with the army providing their horses and tack, they received only thirteen dollars a month, the basic pay of a private.[12] Indian scouts had also enlisted for six-month periods, more attractive to them than the longer enlistment required of regular soldiers. Therefore, the number of scouts authorized for the entire army was reduced from 1,000 to only 150 as a means of increasing Indian enlistments into the regular army.[13]

Although the Indian soldiers had reputations as excellent horsemen, the Sioux troop at Fort Meade had difficulty breaking army horses. Lieutenant Macdonald requested that they be excused from this duty, pointing out that American horses were larger than the ponies his Indians were accustomed to. Eight members of his troop had been kicked by horses, Macdonald reported, two of them badly enough to require hospitalization. Macdonald remained in command of the Indian troop until 31 December, when he returned to his home station.[14] By the time of Macdonald's departure, the army had succeeded in enlisting 759 men into its Indian units. Second Lieutenant Byron of Troop A, Eighth Cavalry, who had formerly commanded the regiment's detachment of Indian scouts, took over the Indian troop.[15]

Dr. McGillycuddy visited the Indian troop at Fort Meade in January 1892. The irony of having Indian soldiers at a post established fourteen years earlier to protect the Black Hills settlers from the Indians was not lost on him. After watching the troop drill under Lieutenant Byron, McGillycuddy observed, "It was a strange sight to see Indians who had earlier been chased by the Third Cavalry wearing caps bearing its Troop L insignia." The former agent found the Indian soldiers generally well satisfied with army life. He did report, however, that the married Indians were unhappy about being separated from their wives, who were still at the Cheyenne River Agency.[16]

Byron got into trouble with Sumner early in 1892, and it almost cost him his assignment. Eighteen of the Indians in Troop L were married, thus exceeding by eight the maximum permitted, and their wives had not accompanied them to Fort Meade. The separation brought on at least one divorce when the wife of a transferred trooper learned that her husband had "turned his attention to another." To safeguard other marriages, Byron proposed that a detachment of his Indians be permitted to go to Cherry Creek on the Cheyenne River Reservation and return with the wives of the married men. At the time of their transfer, Macdonald had promised his troopers that they could bring their families to Fort Meade, and Byron felt obligated to make good on the pledge.[17] Instead of going through Sumner, Byron wrote directly to a friend at department headquarters for the authority to move the families of his married troopers. He explained that the men were homesick, and he predicted their morale would be greatly improved with their families on the post. Sumner was in favor of the plan, but he was offended that Byron had gone over his head. He ordered the lieutenant to resign the command of the Indian troop. Byron reluctantly did so, pointing out, however, that he had been ordered to resign and that he was acting against his personal wishes. Sumner assigned First Lieutenant Stephen L. Slocum of Troop C, Eighth Cavalry, to the Indian troop as Byron's replacement.[18] Before the change could be implemented, Lieutenant Colonel Caleb Carlton of the Fourth Cavalry was promoted to the colonelcy of the Eighth (the long-absent Brisbin had died in January, creating the vacancy). Carlton assumed the command from Sumner before Byron's letter of resignation was acted on. Carlton recognized the value of the lieutenant's experience with the Indians, both as scouts and as soldiers, and restored him to the command of the unit.[19]

Some old log buildings along Bear Butte Creek, formerly occupied by laundresses, were fixed up for the Indian families. These huts were about a half mile north of the barracks buildings, and the Indians moved into them in the summer of 1892. The post surgeon, describing the huts in his monthly report of sanitary conditions, termed them "neat and clean," with each hut divided into two twelve-by-twelve-foot rooms. He noted, "So far their surroundings are good."[20]

What the army had not realized when it authorized permitting Indian families on the military reserve was that Sioux families are generally extended families. They were not limited to wives and children but included grandparents and frequently other relatives also. There were soon more nonenlisted Indians at some military reserves than seemed justified by the number of married Indian soldiers. This became a factor in the army's subsequent decision to abandon its experiment with Indian troops.[21]

All but three members of Troop L, Third Cavalry, at Fort Meade were full-bloods, including all the noncoms. Bishop William H. Hare said of the latter: "They seem proud of their positions and exercise firmness and tact in exercising authority over the privates, who treat them with respect." Thirty-two of the Indian troopers were between eighteen and twenty-four years of age. Several were over the maximum allowed age of thirty-five. The average height of the Indian soldiers was five feet, seven and a half inches, slightly shorter than the average height of the white soldiers.[22]

Bishop Hare of the Episcopal Diocese for South Dakota, headquartered in Sioux Falls, frequently conducted church services at Fort Meade when his travels brought him to the Black Hills. Bishop Hare had a special fondness for Fort Meade; the troops stationed there in 1888 had provided about two-thirds of the funds needed to purchase the lots for the first Episcopal church in Sturgis. Dr. Ira Sanderson, the contract surgeon at Fort Meade at the time, had been the first warden of the church. The bandmaster of the Eighth Cavalry was in charge of music at the church, and his band frequently entertained at church activities. Many of the Indian troopers had become Episcopalians on the Cheyenne River Reservation, and they usually turned out in large numbers whenever Bishop Hare conducted services at the post. The whites, the *Episcopal Church News* reported, were "deeply impressed, not only by the number of Indians present (there not being a spare seat in the Chapel) but by the reverent and hearty way they joined in the service." Reverend A. B. Clark of the Rosebud Mission, sent by Bishop Hare to conduct services at the fort, reported that the Indian troopers turned out for his services too. "All expressed joy and gratitude for the service in their own tongue," Clark reported. "Only about five from this troop of soldiers can understand English well, though many are trying to learn. They seem generally pleased with their situation and speak warmly of the kindness of the officers in command."[23]

The Indians also made a reputation for themselves in baseball games with Eighth Cavalry teams, taking quickly to the national game. Confidence that service in the army would improve the lives of the Troop L Indians was expressed by the *Sturgis Weekly Record*. They not only would be taught "order, punctuality, cleanliness and respect for authority" but also would be educated in English and "the white man's ways." Moreover, the *Record* predicted, the program would end the Indians' distrust of the whites and their inability to distinguish between their true friends and those who would exploit them. Such distrust, the publisher contended, had been "the direct or indirect cause of most of our Indian wars."[24]

Relations between the white and the Indian cavalrymen on the post were described as friendly, with the two races mingling freely at the canteen and in the barracks. One of the veteran white soldiers of the Eighth, whose opinion of all this has been lost to us, was Sergeant Albert Knapp of Troop B, who had won the Medal of Honor for "bravery in scouts and actions against Indians" while serving in the campaign against the Apaches in Arizona in 1868. He became the only Medal of Honor winner buried in the post cemetery when he died at the fort in 1897.[25]

The Indian troop at the fort included a translator and eight others who had attended the Indian School at Carlisle, Pennsylvania. Chaplain Vattman served as the post superintendent of schools and conducted classes in English for the Indian troopers. Father Vattman found the Indians reserved in their English classes until they were reasonably certain of making no mistakes.[26]

A highlight of Troop L's tour at Fort Meade came in October 1892, when it was selected, along with the Indian troop of the Sixth Cavalry at Fort Niobrara, to participate in the army component at the upcoming Columbian Exposition in Chicago. The army wanted the public to see how the Indians had progressed in the service. It was considered an honor that these two units were to be included in the show, particularly since their ranks were filled by so many Sioux who had recently been at war with the army. The Indian troop at Fort Meade left for Chicago by train from Sturgis on 15 October and returned ten days later.[27]

The saloons and moonshiners in nearby Sturgis were seen as bad influences on the Indian as well as the white soldiers at Fort Meade. South Dakota was then a Prohibition state, but beer was sold in saloons. Whiskey was dispensed on the sly. The town's mayor was credited with running the largest saloon. Lieutenant Byron asked to be appointed as a special agent with the same authority as Indian agents to arrest anyone selling liquor to Indians. Schofield endorsed the proposal, recommending that it be broadened to include the commanders of all Indian units. Such appointments, he wrote, would greatly aid these commanders in dealing with "evil doers" who attempted "to debauch the Indian soldiers."[28] The Interior Department opposed the plan, however, and Byron was instructed to pass his complaints on to the U.S. marshal in Deadwood. He did so, providing the marshal with the names of the offenders in Sturgis. Subsequent prosecutions slowed, but failed to halt, the illegal traffic. State voters repealed Prohibition in 1897. The fact that Indian soldiers, like their white counterparts, could buy beer at the post canteen also presented a problem when they visited reservations. Intoxicating beverages were prohibited on reservations, and agents complained that these visiting soldiers were setting a bad example for the other Indians. Agent McLaughlin at Standing Rock claimed that the soldiers recruited there were the "most worthless Indians on the reservation." Indian soldiers had not lost their tribal benefits by enlisting, and those stationed near their reservations frequently returned to draw their annuities, to the chagrin of the agents.[29]

Sumner, temporarily commanding again while Carlton was on leave, reported in 1894 that only 89 of the 336 soldiers at the fort were nondrinkers. Carlton's daughter later wrote of the army's treatment of chronic drunkards in her recollections of life at Fort Meade. These men were, according to her memoirs, given the choice of taking a dishonorable discharge or submitting to injections of a drug that made them ill whenever they drank liquor.[30]

The Eighth Cavalry's all-Indian troop remained at Fort Keogh during the period that Troop L of the Third Cavalry was stationed at Fort Meade. Sumner, when he had commanded the regiment and the post, thought it would be best if all the troops there were of the same regiment. So he had proposed that the designations of the two Indian troops, but not the men themselves, be switched. That meant assigning the Indians at Fort Meade to the Eighth Cavalry and the Eighth's Indian troopers at Fort Keogh to the Third Cavalry. Carlton endorsed the proposal when he succeeded to the command. He pointed out that the officers of the Eighth Cavalry would likely take more interest in the Indian troop if it was part of their regiment. "This would cause no expense," Carlton wrote to higher head-quarters, "and it would only be necessary to change the numbers on the men's cap."[31] Two years after Sumner's suggestion, Carlton was still trying to get it adopted.

The cavalry troop at Fort Meade was almost at full strength and mak-ing "remarkable progress as soldiers"—so much so that a second white officer, Second Lieutenant A. E. Williams, was assigned to it. Although Williams was from the Third Cavalry, like the Indian troopers them-selves, the command of the unit remained with Lieutenant Byron.[32] Carl-ton had high regard for Byron's work with the Indians, reporting that they had attained a high degree of competence under him. One mounted noncommissioned officer and three privates from the Indian troop were included in the daily guard mount, and often one of them was selected as the "cleanest man of the entire guard."[33] Byron was promoted to first lieutenant in February 1893 and assigned to the Second Cavalry. How-ever, he remained at Fort Meade on a special-duty status as the command-ing officer of the Indian troop.

Meanwhile, the army was beginning to have doubts about Indian troops. The secretary of war complained that Indian recruiting was not progressing, particularly for infantry companies. The Indian infantry company at Fort Sully, for instance, was down to only twenty-four mem-bers. Armywide, many Indian soldiers were becoming disillusioned with military life and were taking early discharges. Regulations permitted sol-diers to petition for discharge after three years of service. Moreover, the army had experienced increasing difficulties with discipline, which often became a problem when Indian soldiers were stationed near their home reservations. Members of the Eighth Cavalry's Troop L at Fort Keogh had asked to be discharged late in 1892, when interviewed by a visiting inspector. And whole companies of Indian infantrymen at Forts Yates and Sidney petitioned for early discharges in 1893.[34]

The trend toward sharp reductions in the ranks of the Indian units extended to Fort Meade after Byron was reassigned as a professor of military science at a Virginia school in February 1894. He obtained a transfer back to the Eighth Cavalry in May but remained on special duty in Virginia. He was replaced as the commanding officer of Fort Meade's Indian troop by First Lieutenant William F. Flynn of Troop E, Eighth Cavalry. Flynn served in that capacity from 20 April to 6 October 1894 on a special-duty status. Then the command evolved to Williams, who was less popular than Byron with the Indians, and their performance as soldiers deteriorated.[35]

Carlton, who felt Byron had been especially adapted for duty with the Indians, believed few of them would have taken their discharges if he had been kept with them. At the end of 1893, when Byron had still been in command, Troop L's roster had included one first sergeant, five sergeants, four corporals, two trumpeters, one farrier, a blacksmith, one saddler, a wagoner, and thirty-six privates, for a total strength of fifty-two—only three below the maximum authorized strength. By October 1894, the number of Indians who had taken early discharges dropped the troop strength to thirty-two, including eight who were on furlough and expected to be discharged soon.[36]

In February 1895, there were only three privates remaining in Troop L—and all of them were absent without leave. They were discharged in March, and the troop was dropped from the garrison rolls. All of the troop's members were out of the army before the expiration of their five-year enlistments. With no troops to command, Lieutenant Williams was placed on special duty with Troops B and D, Eighth Cavalry. He returned to his home regiment when Troop L was dropped from the post report in April.[37]

The Eighth Cavalry's Troop L at Fort Keogh, commanded by First Lieutenant William D. McAnaney, was disbanded on 4 May 1895. It was the end of the unit organized in 1889 as "Casey's Scouts" and brought into the regular army two years later. The number of Indian soldiers remaining in the regular army was down to fewer than two hundred by 1896. The army's experiment with these troops came to an end when fifty-three Indians of Troop L, Seventh Cavalry, were discharged on 31 May 1897. A total of 1,071 Indians had been enlisted or reenlisted in eight troops of cavalry and nineteen companies of infantry since the program had begun six years earlier.[38] The secretary of war, in appraising the experiment, asserted that the Indian companies had never been substantially success-ful as soldiers. This was so, he stated, despite "strenuous and intelligent efforts on the part of the officers" to make the experiment succeed.[39]

The Seventh Cavalry's Lieutenant Scott, who had played a key role in implementing the experiment not only within his own regiment but army-wide, gave a different reason for the failure. "The truth was that the army was angry at General John M. Schofield for mustering out the white men of the two [skeletonized] troops in each regiment," Scott reported, "and did not want the experiment to succeed. Innumerable obstacles were thrown in my way by unthinking officers, and support in Washington was withheld by a change of the Secretary of War."[40] Scott's experience with the Indians, gained while serving at western posts including Fort Meade, had convinced him that the program had real merit and potential. His own Troop L had been a success, he immodestly but accurately reported, only as long as he had stayed with it. "But its officers could not be changed around as in white troops," he contended. The observation was supported by what had happened to Troop L, Third Cavalry, after Lieutenant By-ron's departure. "Since all the other troops were a disappointment," Scott explained, "the experiment of enlisting Indians was regarded as a fail-ure." Scott claimed that the Indians who had served in the Seventh Cavalry's Troop L later became leaders on their reservations as a result of the training they had received as soldiers.[41] In any event, the experiment was over, and it became just another chapter in the records of the frontier military.

ABANDONMENT AVERTED

Disbanding the all-Indian unit reduced the Fort Meade garrison to the field staff, the band, and eight troops of the Eighth Cavalry. The former Indian Troop L rejoined M as a skeletonized (inactive) unit, and the remaining two troops of the regiment (A and C) were stationed at Fort Yates. Troop A returned to Fort Meade in November 1897, and the garrison comprised the entire regiment, except for Troop C, until the outbreak of the Spanish-American War. By the end of the experiment with Indian soldiers, Fort Meade was the only active fort in South Dakota. The last of the Missouri River posts in the state, Randall and Sully, had been abandoned in 1892 and 1894, respectively. Fort Meade also came perilously close to abandonment during this period.

As early as 1893, Schofield had advised against spending any more money on Fort Meade than was necessary to maintain the existing buildings and garrison. The secretary of war S. B. Elkins, believing that the Indian wars were over and that the western frontier had disappeared, saw no further need for large numbers of troops in the West. Instead, he proposed a gradual abandonment of small forts and the establishment of regimental posts in each of the larger states that were then without such posts.[1]

Fort Meade's existence was also threatened by a continuing problem with the water supply. The water level of McMillan Springs, which supplied the post, dropped so severely during periods of drought that a supplemental supply had to be pumped from Bear Butte Creek. But since sewage from Sturgis was still entering the creek above the pumping station, the quartermaster furnished a wagon to bring drinking water from town. The town was supplied by the Sturgis Water Works Company, a private firm owned by Joseph J. Davenport, who piped water from a series of dams the company had built on Alkali Creek. A survey of the officers of the post disclosed that most of them were getting their drinking water from Davenport. They also reported that this water was superior in quality to that available on the post.[2]

Sumner, one of Davenport's customers, revealed that he had gone to considerable expense to obtain Sturgis water because of its superior quality. Ordinarily, he stated, the army was not very concerned about water because its soldiers were used to drinking all kinds without harm. "But when it comes to using water taken from holes in the ground directly below the sewerage of a town as large as Sturgis, . . . there can be no doubt of the danger of drinking it," Sumner wrote. "Therefore I prefer to be on the safe side." If he were still in command of the post, Sumner went on, he would lose no time in hooking Fort Meade up to the Sturgis water lines. "I believe this will have to be done at an early date," Sumner concluded, "or the Post abandoned."[3] The problem was not solved until several years later when an artesian well was dug near the post sawmill.

Schofield made his last official visit to Fort Meade as the army's top commander on 6 June 1895, before retiring in September. He was accompanied by Brigadier General John J. Coppinger, the newly appointed commander of the Department of the Platte, and they conferred with Carlton about the future of the post. Their visit was closely followed by that of Secretary of War Daniel S. Lamont, who, along with the army's quartermaster general, arrived at the post for a one-day inspection on 22 June. The result of these visits was a decision to retain Fort Meade as an active post and to transfer it to Coppinger's department. Coppinger believed the post should be maintained for an indefinite period, but he described the wooden buildings of the fort as in an advanced state of decay. He wrote, "These buildings ought to be gradually replaced by others of brick or stone with fireproof roofs and modern improvements."[4]

Carlton agreed, pointing out that it would be cheaper to replace the buildings than to repair them. The department quartermaster wrote that the old barracks should be replaced or the post abandoned. He proposed an appropriation of nearly $200,000 for modern barracks, quarters, stables, roads, and drainage if Fort Meade was "to be retained as a permanent post."[5]

The army then decided it was time to make a decision on which of three forts in the region—Meade, Robinson, or Niobrara—should be considered for abandonment. Coppinger determined that Fort Niobrara was "less important and desirable as a military station than the other two." He described Fort Meade as "well adapted to a cavalry command" and as having a healthy climate that gave the garrison the lowest sick rate among all the posts in his department. Further, Coppinger pointed out that Fort Meade was well situated in regard to the Sioux reservations. These were, he wrote, factors that appeared to him "to be decisive in favor of its maintenance for an indefinite period."[6]

General Miles, who had succeeded Schofield as the head of the army, supported Coppinger in the matter. He stressed that Fort Meade was situated in the region where trouble with the Indians, if it came again, would most likely originate. Miles, recommending the repair rather than the replacement of the Fort Meade buildings, advised the secretary of war that the post should be designated a permanent installation. What funds could be spared, he stated, should be used to keep the buildings in good repair. The fort's primary mission, Miles emphasized, was still "to protect the settlers in South Dakota, Wyoming and Montana in case of an uprising among the Sioux Indians."[7]

Miles justified his position with a seven-point statement detailing his reasoning. The chief reason was the post's strategic location, which he described as the best in the Northwest. Miles claimed the Sioux reservations contained "twenty-five percent of the uncivilized Indians in the United States." Moreover, he pointed out that the Sioux had "always regarded, and still" regarded, the Black Hills as sacred. The general noted, "It was only after a most desperate struggle that they were compelled to relinquish this ground as part of their reservation, and they still long to regain it." He concluded: "Would it, then, be safe to remove the protection that Fort Meade affords to the people of these Hills? Certainly it is but natural to suppose that at the first outbreak of trouble they would attempt to regain what they still regard as their sacred heritage, perpetrating, if necessary, upon the present inhabitants a second Custer massacre."[8]

These were the same arguments advanced for establishing the Black Hills post twenty years earlier. Miles urged that an appropriation of $100,000 be provided "to place Fort Meade in good condition," since there was "no prospect of it being proper to abandon it."[9] Pettigrew introduced the appropriation bill, increasing the request by $50,000. In reporting the bill, the Senate Committee on Military Affairs stated: "There are reasons enough for the maintenance of a strong military garrison at Fort Meade, and in order to protect our soldiers from the inclemencies of a rigorous climate suitable buildings should be provided."[10] Congress, however, appropriated only $30,000, which was used to construct two sandstone quarters buildings, using stone taken from a quarry north of Sturgis.[11]

Carlton was promoted to brigadier general on 28 June 1897 and retired two days later. The commander's daughter, writing about her father's years at Fort Meade, recalled:

When my father first took command of the post he was surprised to find that the previous commanding officer, a devout Catholic, had allowed the sisters of the Roman Catholic Church in Sturgis to sit at the pay table with the Paymaster. As each man was paid, he passed them and the Sisters would ask for a contribution to their work. Sometimes they would say, "Why, Sergeant, only five dollars? Here is Corporal Healy who has given us ten dollars and he is only a Corporal while you are a Sergeant." My father put a stop to this when the Sisters took to going through the barracks. My father had the Adjutant write to the priest that the barracks were no place for women—they were the bedroom, dressing room and sitting room of fifty or more men and the Sisters must keep out.[12]

Carlton is now best remembered at Sturgis as the officer who began the custom of playing "The Star-Spangled Banner" at military ceremonies long before the song became the national anthem. At his wife's suggestion, Carlton ordered that it be the last number played whenever the band performed at military formations or special entertainments on the post. Programs printed for these events requested that all people within hearing rise when the number was played and that all men not under arms remove their hats. "During the practice marches, as well as in garrison," according to Carlton's daughter, "this custom was followed and the same behavior required of all civilians within the lines."[13] Carlton believed that he was "probably the first officer of the United States Army to order this air played at all band practices and to require all persons present to rise and pay it proper respect."[14] After his retirement, he continued his cam-

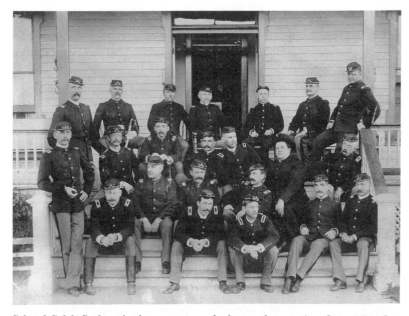

Colonel Caleb Carlton, back row center, who began the practice of requiring that "The Star-Spangled Banner" be played at retreat ceremonies, with some of the officers of the Eighth Cavalry, which he commanded at Fort Meade. They are, back row from right, Captain Norton Strong, M.C., Captain A. G. Hennisee, Major J. Morris Brown, M.C., Carlton, Major Almon B. Wells, Captain Edward Luff, and First Lieutenant (and Adjutant) Joseph J. Gaston. Center, Captain A. W. Sprole, Chaplain Edward J. Vattman, Second Lieutenant Farrand Sayre, Second Lieutenant E. W. Evans, Captain J. A. Johnston, and First Lieutenant Andrew G. Hammond. Front, Captain H. F. Kendall, Second Lieutenant R. L. Livermore, First Lieutenant D. C. Cabell, First Lieutenant W. F. Flynn, Captain E. A. Godwin, First Lieutenant Charles W. Farber, First Lieutenant J. C. Byron, First Lieutenant R. J. Duff, and First Lieutenant Quincy O'Maher Gillmore. (Courtesy of the Library of Congress.)

paign to have the piece selected as the national anthem. The *New York Times* publicized his efforts, and the movement gradually gained momentum; Carlton urged the governor of Pennsylvania to promote the custom among that state's militia. Not long afterward, Carlton met with the secretary of war about the matter. The song subsequently became the official military retreat number. Carlton prided himself on the fact that wherever he was in command, he "tried to enforce respect for our national flag." He did so by requiring all to rise and remove their hats when the colors passed them.[15]

President Woodrow Wilson made the custom mandatory for all military services in 1916. In 1919, at its national convention in Minneapolis, the American Legion adopted "The Star-Spangled Banner" as its official song. Congress designated the tune as the national anthem on 31 March 1931, and it became official with the signature of President Herbert Hoover. "I never hear it played that I do not think how pleased my father would be," Carlton's daughter commented after his death.[16]

Carlton was succeeded as the commanding officer of the Eighth Cavalry by Colonel John M. Bacon, who arrived at the post in August 1897. In the meantime, the Eighth's lieutenant colonel, Thomas McGregor, was in command of the regiment and the post. Bacon came to the Eighth after being promoted from the lieutenant colonelcy of the Seventh Cavalry, where he had served since 1884. Bacon's service at Fort Meade lasted only eight months; at the onset of the Spanish-American War in April 1898, he became brigadier general of volunteers in the Department of Dakota and Lakes and moved to Fort Snelling. McGregor again took command in his absence.[17]

At the outbreak of the war, Congress more than doubled the maximum authorized strength of the regular army, to nearly sixty thousand officers and enlisted men. The increase permitted rebuilding the skeletonized companies, as well as filling out other understrength units. Regimental strengths, including all grades, commissioned and enlisted, were set at 1,225 for cavalry and 1,326 for infantry. In addition, the volunteer force was gradually increased until it reached a peak of 216,000 by war's end in August. Recruits for Troops L and M of the Eighth arrived at Fort Meade in May.

Although most of the Eighth Cavalry remained at Fort Meade throughout the brief war, the garrison was reduced by the transfer of five of its troops to other stations. Troops I and F changed stations to Forts Robinson and Sill, respectively, in April. The following month Troop B was transferred to Fort Washakie in Wyoming and Troop K to the Tongue River Agency in Montana. Troop G changed station to Fort Niobrara, saved from abandonment by the war, in June. However, troops L and M were reactivated and brought up to full strength by August.[18]

On 28 April, the War Department authorized the mobilization of three regiments of volunteer cavalry "to be composed exclusively of frontiersmen possessing special qualifications as horsemen and marksmen." One regiment was organized as the Third U.S. Volunteer Cavalry by South Dakota Attorney General Melvin Grigsby. Men were recruited from the ranges of South Dakota, Nebraska, Wyoming, and Montana, and they became known as "Grigsby's Cowboys." The force was mustered into federal service in May, along with the First South Dakota Volunteer Infantry of the state militia.[19] Some of the officers of the Eighth Cavalry at Fort Meade mustered in the men of the volunteer regiments. Others were placed on detached service for the purpose of purchasing horses for the volunteer cavalry units. Four officers of the Eighth, two captains and two first lieutenants, obtained extended leaves of absence so that they could accept commissions in the volunteer forces at higher ranks. They reverted to their prewar ranks when they returned to the Eighth after the war.[20]

Fort Meade was the staging area for the Black Hills battalion of "Grigsby's Cowboys." Commanded by Major L. H. French, it consisted of four troops: A, C, and D, recruited in the northern Black Hills, and K, from Milford, Nebraska. Troop A, from Lead, was headed by the seemingly ubiquitous Seth Bullock; Troop C, from Spearfish, was commanded by George E. Hair; and Troop D, from Sturgis, was led by John E. Hammon. Hammon had been a sergeant in Company G, Seventh Cavalry, at the Battle of the Little Bighorn. He had gone into ranching in Meade County after his fifteen years of army service, taking his discharge while the Seventh was still at Fort Meade.[21]

Seven officers and 203 enlisted men of the Black Hills battalion arrived at Fort Meade between 9 and 12 May, camping on the target range while efforts were made to enlist more recruits and to purchase horses. On the twenty-third, 9 officers and 227 men of the battalion left the fort for Chickamauga, Georgia, to train for service in Cuba. First Lieutenant M. E. Wells was left behind with 15 enlisted men to take possession of horses for the battalion when purchased. A rush order went out for over six hundred horses, and Wells's detachment left for Georgia with most of them in June. Two hundred thirty-nine of the newly purchased horses were distributed among the Eighth Cavalry troops still at the post, most of the horses going to the reconstituted Troops L and M.[22] Jack Hale of Tilford and J. B. Gammon of Beulah, Wyoming, prominent ranchers of the region, supplied most of the mounts for the fort. "The distribution of over $65,000 right around Sturgis for horses is just another evidence that we are always 'strictly in it,'" commented the *Record* in Sturgis.[23]

The people of Sturgis naturally took a special interest in Troop D of the Black Hills battalion because of its local men. A Fourth of July solicitation by the Women's Relief Corps of Sturgis raised thirty-nine dollars, which was sent to Captain Hammon in Georgia for his men. "The camp is in bad shape," reported one of Hammon's men, home on sick leave, "and the sudden transition of people used to the pure fresh ozone of the Black Hills to the malarial swamps down in that country is disastrous." Nevertheless, when the war was over, Hammon returned with seventy-nine of the eighty-one men recruited for the company. One man had died in the Georgia camp of spinal meningitis, and another man had been transferred. The war ended before "Grigsby's Cowboys" could embark for Cuba, and the members were mustered out in September.[24]

McGregor had been promoted to the colonelcy of the Ninth Cavalry, then in Cuba, in July. Major C.C.C. Carr commanded the Eighth Cavalry for the remainder of its stay at Fort Meade. Carr had worked his way up the ranks from private to captain in the First Cavalry before joining the Eighth in 1891. In October, he led the remaining troops of the regiment out of Fort Meade to join the occupation forces in Cuba. Fourteen railway coaches moved the troops to Huntsville, Alabama, where the regiment assembled for Cuba.[25]

Replacing the Eighth at Fort Meade was the First Cavalry, which had been in the thick of the fighting in Cuba. This was one of the oldest regiments in the army, having been organized in 1833 as a force of dragoons. "The old First Cavalry," the *Record* reported shortly after the regiment's arrival at Fort Meade, "had been mixed up in every Indian war in the far West from Mexico to the Canada line. . . . It has a record to be proud of."[26]

The first units of the First to reach Fort Meade were Troops G and M, totaling 107 men, under Major Allen Smith. They arrived by rail during a snowstorm in early October as the Eighth was vacating the post. The drastic change in climate from what the troopers had experienced in Cuba was a hardship. These were the only troops on the post, the smallest garrison in the installation's twenty-year history, until January 1899 when Troops H and I of the regiment arrived with an additional 183 men.[27]

The garrison was depleted in February when the army issued orders allowing soldiers who had enlisted for two years during the Spanish-American War mobilization to take early discharges. Seventy-five men of the First took the opportunity. Despite the reduced size of the garrison, the few troops remaining quickly entered into a flurry of off-duty activities. The Fort Meade Theatrical and Vaudeville Company was performing at the Sturgis Opera House by March. The post also had an active dancing club that scheduled periodic masquerade balls.[28]

Colonel Abraham K. Arnold, a much-decorated hero of the Civil War, was the First Cavalry's commander. Major Smith served as the post commander until Arnold arrived on 13 May 1899. The *Record* welcomed him with the observation that the fort had been without a regimental headquarters since the departure of the Eighth the previous October. "Now we feel at home again," the paper stated as Arnold brought the headquarters of the First to the post with him.[29]

Two other developments provided assurances that Sturgis would continue to reap economic benefits from the fort. Foremost was the army's decision to designate Fort Meade as a permanent post, enlarge its garrison, and expand its facilities. The resolutions of the state legislature urging these steps, which had almost become a ritual at each session, had at last been heeded. Probably more of an influence in the decision was the high regard the army's top commanders had for the post's strategic location, which had been a decisive factor in avoiding abandonment at a time when small posts were disappearing in favor of larger ones in the metropolitan sectors of the country. The army's rapid buildup for the war in Cuba had also temporarily ended talk of post closings.

The assistant secretary of war visited Fort Meade in November 1899, indicating the new importance the government placed on the post. He was pleased to find improvements of the facility well under way. Moreover, the post exchange system, which had replaced the trader's stores at army posts in 1889, was abolished by Congress in March 1899. The act eliminating the post exchange system also prohibited the sale of liquor on all military reservations. Although post canteens would later be reinstated, their temporary closings were a big boost to merchants in nearby communities.[30]

Prohibition in South Dakota had been repealed in 1897, and the Sturgis saloonkeepers were well prepared to serve the soldiers who could no longer get liquor at the post. The town's economic fortunes had fluctuated with the size of the garrison and the extent of its off-post spending since the joint beginning of the community and the fort—and would continue to do so well into the twentieth century.[31]

☆ 12 ☆

THE NEW FORT MEADE

A "new" Fort Meade began taking shape on the site of the old shortly after the turn of the century. More than one million dollars was spent on improvements at the post during the first decade of the new century; most went to replacing the original wooden quarters and stables with stone and brick structures and to improving the road and water systems. Nearly half of the extensive rebuilding program was completed during the 1900–1907 period and the remainder by 1911.[1]

Instrumental in getting Congress to provide the funds for this accelerated building program were the South Dakota congressional delegation and the Sturgis Commercial Club. The latter published six hundred copies of a pamphlet quoting General Miles's reasons why the fort should become a permanent post. It included a map of the surrounding country, showing the fort's position in relation to the settlements and the nearby Indian reservations. Copies were furnished to South Dakota's senators and representatives for distribution to members of both houses of Congress. The rest of the pamphlets were distributed where they would "do the most good." Getting the government to spend sizable sums on the post was seen as "the only way" that Fort Meade could be declared a permanent post.[2]

Senator Pettigrew's efforts on behalf of Fort Meade were an issue in the senator's 1900 reelection campaign. The *Sturgis Weekly Record,* whose publisher was the son of the state's other U.S. senator, Gideon C. Moody, accused Pettigrew of being "anti-military." It implied he had not done much to get troops assigned to the post and charged him with feeling that "one officer and two private soldiers" at the fort were "sufficient for the whole state of South Dakota." U.S. senators were still elected by state legislatures at the time, and the *Record* urged that Pettigrew be denied a second term.[3]

The *Sioux Falls Argus Leader* came to Pettigrew's defense, pointing out that his influence had "contributed almost entirely to the maintenance and improvement of Fort Meade."[4] Although that may have been overstating the case, Pettigrew had clearly been instrumental in getting funds and troops for the fort throughout his service in Congress, both as territorial delegate and as U.S. senator. The *Record,* staunchly Republican, was piqued at Pettigrew for deserting the GOP for the Populist movement that year. Its campaign to defeat him was obviously based more on political considerations than on any neglect of Fort Meade by Pettigrew.

The *Record*'s disenchantment with Pettigrew was apparent in the manner in which it covered his campaign. When Pettigrew campaigned in Meade County, for instance, the *Record* sarcastically reported: "The senator drove through Sturgis to his post of Fort Meade that he built and has kept going all these years, according to the claims made for him." The newspaper also mockingly suggested that Fort Meade be renamed "Fort Pettigrew" to accommodate the senator's ego. The GOP-dominated legislature, sharing the *Record*'s displeasure with Pettigrew, elected Republican Robert J. Gamble to replace him.[5]

Fortunately for the future of Fort Meade, General Miles headed the newly created Army Reorganization Board, whose responsibilities included deciding which posts should be permanent or temporary. The war with Spain had been expensive, and the "Filipino Insurgency" had put added pressure on the national treasury. Congress was in a cost-cutting mood, setting army strength at a maximum of one hundred thousand men in 1901 and insisting that the War Department reassess its organizational structure in the light of changing military needs. With the Indian wars over, frontier posts became a questionable expense.

General Miles, a longtime supporter of Fort Meade, announced in December that the board had reaffirmed the post's status as a permanent installation. The fort's abandonment, so greatly feared by Sturgis residents, was thus again averted. Fort Robinson was also designated a permanent post, but Fort Niobrara was again placed on the list of temporary posts. It was finally abandoned in 1906.[6]

Fort Meade's garrison had been reduced to three troops of the First Cavalry after Troop M was reassigned to duty in Yellowstone National Park in 1899. It was further reduced when Troop I left for the Philippines in July 1900 and Troop G followed in May 1901. Troop H would remain at the post until October 1901, when it was sent to Fort Keogh.[7]

Rebuilding the garrison to regimental strength took place when the Thirteenth Cavalry, organized under the act of 2 February 1901, began forming at the fort that May. It was the first regiment stationed at Fort Meade that was organized there and did not come from someplace else. Recruiters throughout the country were instructed to assign enlistees to it. By the end of May, Troops A, B, and C had been filled. Troops D and E were added in June, and the remaining seven troops of the regiment were filled out by the end of July.[8]

Lieutenant Colonel Edward M. Hayes, Fourth Cavalry, was promoted to the colonelcy of the new regiment in February 1901. He commanded the regiment and the post until 26 January 1903, when he retired. The command was then rotated among Lieutenant Colonel T. W. Jones, Majors Levi P. Hunt and Charles W. Taylor, and Captain Ervin L. Phillips during the remainder of the Thirteenth's service at the post.

Several Sturgis contractors were among the successful bidders for supplying the new regiment and constructing its facilities. One of them was William Grams, the builder of the Meade County courthouse, who erected the one-hundred-foot-high iron flagpole on the east end of the parade grounds in 1901. He was also awarded contracts for building some of the sandstone quarters and the new guardhouse. Other successful local bidders included Nic Schummer, another prominent Sturgis builder; H. O. Anderson, who supplied the plumbing and heating fixtures for many of the new buildings; and Samuel A. Oliver of the Sturgis Electric Works Company, who provided electricity to the fort and the wiring for its buildings. Dominic Keffeler of rural Meade County got a contract for tearing down one of the old wooden barracks buildings to make room for a sandstone replacement.[9] In addition, the local economy benefited from the closing of post canteens. Although many within the army opposed the policy, the *Sturgis Weekly Record* hailed it as "a wise one." Under the headline "The Canteen Beer Joint Gone," the newspaper commented, "It's time the thing quits." The paper reported that many "staggering drunks" emerged from the canteen, where six glasses of beer cost a quarter. It also disclosed the existence of a "hog wagon" that was in use after paydays expressly to carry drunken soldiers from the canteen beer joint to their

The original wooden buildings of the fort were replaced with sandstone structures in the first decade of the twentieth century. These were the enlisted men's barracks. The structure in the middle, with a cupola on the roof, was the headquarters building, which now houses the Old Fort Meade Museum. (Courtesy of Old Fort Meade Museum Association.)

quarters. "[The closing of] the official drunk shop," the newspaper editorialized, "will not hurt the military branch of the service as badly as its admirers think."[10]

Post commanders took a different view of the matter. They reported that closing the canteens had resulted in increases in desertions, arrests, and acts of lawlessness as the soldiers were forced off the post to drink. In Sturgis, four drunken soldiers of the Thirteenth Cavalry caused a disturbance in Bob Tallent's restaurant late one night, and Tallent shot a private from Troop B when the soldier resisted the night watchman's attempt to arrest him. The other three soldiers were jailed. The wounded man recovered in the post hospital, and Tallent was not charged.[11]

Secretary of War Elihu Root, bowing to the wishes of the army, implored Congress to rescind the law prohibiting the canteens. "The old fight against the canteen," the *Record* predicted, "will be waged with the usual bitterness by the temperance people all over the country." The temperance movement gained support from an unexpected source. Brigadier

General A. S. Daggett, on his retirement in 1901, attacked "the evils of the army canteens." He charged them with encouraging debt as well as drinking, since soldiers were allowed to charge their drinks when they ran out of money between paydays. He pointed out that many of the army's recruits came from rural districts and had had little exposure to saloons and drinking. These recruits, he claimed, arrived at their assigned stations to find saloons in the form of canteens sanctioned by the government. "He entered the service free from drink and debt," Daggett said of the recruit. "He is discharged with both fixed upon him." Nevertheless, the temperance advocates, along with the business interests also favoring the ban, lost the fight: Congress reauthorized the canteens.[12]

In addition to reaping benefits from Fort Meade's building activity and the enlarging of its garrison, Sturgis area residents also profited from the demand for horses. The army contracted for a large number of horses for delivery at Fort Meade, principally for forming the Thirteenth Cavalry, throughout the spring and summer of 1901. Horses not needed were sent to other posts, including Keogh in Montana and Leavenworth in Kansas. Among the successful contractors were Charles Martin, Clark Anderson, and Harry Bunting, all of Sturgis, and Abe Jones, who ran a big horse ranch in the Slim Buttes country north of the fort. The purchase price averaged $106 per head.[13]

Horse prices were raised by competition from representatives of the British army, who were then in the country buying mounts for troops in South Africa. Normally, the army insisted on broken horses, but it made an exception for those purchased for the newly formed Thirteenth Cavalry. It employed a small force of riders at the post to get the horses in shape "for the raw recruits." Anderson and Bunting bought unbroken horses, 15.1 to 16 hands high, from area ranchers for eighty-five dollars and hired men to break the horses. Horses that failed the army's inspection were sold back to their owners for the original price plus "a reasonable fee for breaking."[14]

Horse purchases in the Department of Dakota and Lakes, purchases that had reached a high of 1,200 during the Spanish-American War, dropped to 162 in 1900. By June 1901, however, the army had offered contracts for 683 head at Fort Meade alone. They were filled by range horses brought to Sturgis from ranches in Nebraska, Wyoming, Montana, and North Dakota, as well as from western South Dakota.

Jack Hale of Tilford and Abe Jones were charged in 1901 with failing to fulfill their contracts for supplying horses to Fort Meade. A board of inspectors sent to the post from Omaha rejected horses that the two Sturgis area contractors had supplied in 1896 and 1900, respectively, as failing to meet contract specifications. Replacement horses were purchased at higher prices on the eastern horse market. The government sued the two Sturgis area contractors and their bondsmen to recover the difference between the contracted prices and the cost of the replacements. The disputes centered on a preference among the contracting officers for horses that were Kentucky-bred rather than raised on the western ranges.[15]

Army witnesses were brought from as far away as the Philippines, Kentucky, Chicago, St. Louis, and Omaha when Hale's case came to trial in Deadwood in September 1901. A directed verdict favored Hale and his bondsmen. The judge ruled that replacements should have been sought on the local market rather than in Chicago if Hale's horses were unsatisfactory. Had the case gone the other way, the *Record* editorialized, it would have meant "the War Department felt the Northwest could not raise suitable Cavalry horses." The paper pointed out that the purchase of over six hundred acceptable horses at Fort Meade in 1901 refuted "the theory so fondly held" that the West had "no cavalry mounts." The newspaper further charged there was a bias among army horse buyers for Kentucky-raised horses—"horses with arched necks, horses that are pretty, but which a western horse could drive to death on any march from one day to twenty years." According to the *Record,* the inspector who came to Fort Meade wanted "Kentucky horses or none." The paper further claimed that many Kentucky-bred horses were purchased in the East at fancy prices and shipped to Fort Meade. "Some died, some went wrong and none could stand hardship."[16]

Major Samuel L. Woodward was the contracting officer for the horses purchased at Fort Meade in 1901–2, and Jones was again among the successful bidders. Woodward admitted to originally sharing the prejudice of some army officers against range horses. But after buying nearly seven hundred of them for the Thirteenth Cavalry, he wrote that the ranchers of the region were raising "as fine a class of horses for cavalry purposes" as could be found "anywhere in the world." Woodward noted, "They are of good size and form, hardy, free from disease, especially of the eyes, feet, throat, and lungs; tractable, and very amenable to discipline and training." Woodward favored horses that were four or five years old and broken to saddle. Those he purchased in the Black Hills cost about 25 percent less than those bought at eastern markets. If he had to buy horses for his own use, Woodward added, he would "be very glad to select them from these range horses." He further stated: "Nine months ago there were issued to each of two troops of the 13th Cavalry, now at this post [Fort Meade], eighty-four of these horses. The men were generally untrained recruits. The troops have since marched an average of five hundred miles upon expeditions, besides drills, and have not lost a horse, nor are there any which are subject to condemnation. The officers report there have never been any cases of serious sickness among them, and they are generally tractable and well-trained. This record cannot be surpassed."[17]

General Robert S. Baden-Powell, the chief of cavalry for the British army, found American cavalry horses to be superior to those of the British when he compared the two during a visit to the United States in 1903. But he believed the physique of the English cavalryman was superior to that of his American counterpart. "Your cavalry horses, on the other hand," the visitor declared, "are perfection and their like cannot be equalled in any other country."[18]

New, detailed specifications for the selection of cavalry horses were issued in 1904. The preferred horse was a gelding, four to eight years old, fifteen to fifteen and a half hands high, and weighing from 950 to 1,000 pounds. The regulations specified: "[The cavalry horse] must be sound, well bred, of a superior class, and have quality; gentle and of a kind disposition; thoroughly broken to the saddle, with light and elastic mouth, easy gaits, and free and prompt action at the walk, trot and gallop; free from vicious habits, without material blemish or defects, and otherwise conform to the following description. . . . Each horse will be subjected to rigid inspection and any animal that does not meet the above requirements should be rejected."[19]

Fort Meade had a polo team in 1902, and it defeated a Tenth Cavalry

172

team from Fort Robinson on neutral ground at Hot Springs, South Dakota, about equidistant from the two posts. A return match was held at Fort Meade, perhaps marking the first time the sport was seen there. Fort Meade also had a basketball team that winter. And the Thirteenth Cavalry Social and Dramatic Club provided a series of entertainments that were open to the public. A five-man Sibley tent–pitching contest by troops from the post was part of the annual Fourth of July celebration in Sturgis that year. Hunting was another favorite pastime of the soldiers, and it was reportedly encouraged by the regimental and post commander. "With Colonel Hayes," the *Record* reported, "a man does not have to ask twice for hunt leaves." The colonel, the paper explained, believed "good hunters make good scouts."[20]

Fire destroyed the barracks of Troop L, Thirteenth Cavalry, on 1 May 1902, forcing seventy enlisted men out of the burning structure. They lived in tents on the parade grounds until 4 May. Then the troop marched to Fort Yates for a temporary change of station. It did not rejoin the Fort Meade garrison until October.[21]

In the spring of 1903, the Thirteenth Cavalry changed station with the Sixth Cavalry, then on duty in the Philippines. Eight troops of the regiment, along with the headquarters and the band, left the post during February and March. Troop L hosted a farewell ball at the post before its departure. Thirty-one recruits for the Thirteenth Cavalry arrived at the post from San Francisco in April, only to be shipped back with the last squadron on its way to the Philippines. The *Record* described the moves as "all right for railroads, but unhandy for taxpayers."[22]

Troops E and H were the last to leave, departing in May when an advance detachment of the Sixth Cavalry arrived. The incoming detachment comprised the headquarters, the band, and Troops A and C, totaling 11 officers and 103 enlisted men, with Colonel Allen Smith in command. The remainder of the regiment arrived in September and October. A packtrain of sixty-five mules was assigned to the fort the following fall, and John E. Hammond was employed as trainmaster at a salary of one hundred dollars a month.[23]

Fears that Fort Meade's days were numbered were rekindled when General Miles made a startling observation in his recommendations for improvements in the structure of the army. The cavalry had become

173

obsolete, Miles reported, and he predicted its horses would be replaced by "the automobile, the bicycle and the motor cycle" in the next war. So he proposed that the cavalry branch be reduced to the minimum and that priority attention be given to the construction of "military roads of strategic importance."[24]

Nonetheless, there was no immediate threat to Fort Meade or its garrison. The accelerated construction program at the fort made it unlikely the army would soon abandon the post. In fact, the army was still advertising in the Black Hills for cavalry horses for use in the Philippines in June 1905. "The Black Hills country produces the best horses on the face of the earth for Cavalry purposes," the *Record* boasted.[25] Moreover, the region's horses were popular among the post officers who played polo. One of them, Lieutenant J. S. Jones, Sixth Cavalry, advertised an offer to provide area breeders with a list of those officers who desired ponies.

The post polo team competed in regional competition in Colorado in September. It also took part in a tournament at Hot Springs in October, together with teams from Forts Robinson, Riley, and Leavenworth and from Sheridan, Wyoming. The Chicago and Northwestern Railroad, which had acquired the old Fremont, Elkhorn, and Missouri Valley line serving Sturgis, offered special low-rate fares for round-trip tickets to the Hot Springs tournament from anywhere in the Hills.[26]

Colonel William Stanton became the Sixth Cavalry and the post commander in April 1905, replacing Colonel Smith, but his service at Fort Meade lasted only one year. He retired the following March and was succeeded by Colonel Alexander Rodgers, Fifteenth Cavalry, who had formerly served as a major in the Sixth.

The Sixth participated in large-scale maneuvers, involving troops from five states, at Pole Mountain, Wyoming, in the summer of 1906. One officer and seventy-five enlisted men were left behind to maintain the fort. The rest of the regiment and its horses traveled by rail to Chadron, Nebraska, leaving on 27 July. The Sixth then marched overland to Fort Robinson, where it joined local troops for the march to Fort D. A. Russell near Cheyenne, Wyoming, where the participating troops were assembled. It took thirteen days for the regiment to march from Fort Robinson to the "Camp of Instruction" near Pole Mountain. A sergeant from Troop A, writing about the trek in the *Record,* stated he had traveled through much wasteland during his soldiering. He noted, "None could compare with what we encountered on this journey." The march home in September backtracked over the same ground, which the sergeant described as "the most desolate country. Nothing to see but the worst of prairie."[27]

That fall, the monotony of routine garrison duty and practice marches was broken as troops from the fort found themselves in action once again.

☆ 13 ☆

THE ABSENTEE UTES

Troops from Fort Meade became involved in the last campaign against Indians on the northern plains, late in the fall of 1906. This time the adversary was not any of the traditional tribes of the plains but rather the Utes from distant Utah. Over four hundred of them, led by Chiefs Soccioff, Appah, and Red Cap, had left the Uintah Reservation in July, unhappy about conditions on the reservation. Deciding to cast their lot with the northern tribes, they embarked on a remarkable odyssey that took them hundreds of miles from home before they met the troops from Fort Meade.[1]

The Utes of the White River band were displeased with the way the government had allotted their lands in severalty and resented the opening of part of their reservation to white settlement. They did not want to live in close proximity to whites and decided to seek a new home for themselves in the north country of the Sioux. Few whites lived there, they believed, and Indians could live as in the old days. The government had granted citizenship to Indians in 1905, and the Utes felt that freed them to live wherever they chose.

With a large pony herd, about fifty head of cattle, and a few wagons, the Indians moved by travois through a corner of Colorado into Wyoming in July and headed toward Sioux country. The reservation agent, whom they blamed for the loss of their lands, caught up with them in Wyoming but failed to persuade them to return. The commissioner of Indian affairs sent word that the citizenship on which they based their independence carried burdens as well as privileges. They would have to support themselves, and they would be subject to punishment by the local authorities for any depredations they committed. Nonetheless, the Utes refused to turn back.

Traveling through Wyoming, the band frequently crossed private ranch land and reportedly killed game without regard to state hunting laws. The governor of Wyoming, fearing trouble between the Indians and the citizenry, appealed for troops to force the Utes to return to Utah. The government sent Chief Inspector James McLaughlin of the Indian Office, the former Sioux agent at the Standing Rock Agency, to parley with the Utes. He found them camped northwest of Newcastle, Wyoming, and persuaded forty-six of them to turn back. But the majority were defiant and insisted on continuing their flight, announcing they would fight rather than be forced back.

Repeated unconfirmed rumors of depredations by the Utes, rumors that turned out to be false, and continuous pleas from the governor for troops to remove them finally brought action from Washington. The president turned the matter over to the War Department on 18 October, and Major General Adolphus W. Greely, the Northern District commander, was directed to send troops after the Utes.[2]

Units were sent in pursuit from Forts Meade, Robinson, Keogh, and Mackenzie. It was far more troops than required, but the secretary of war, William Taft, explained that his purpose in sending so large a force "was to overawe [the Indians] and persuade them to return quietly to their homes." Otherwise, he pointed out, they would have to be "disarmed and compelled to do so."[3]

Late in October the Utes were camped on the Little Powder River about forty miles north of Gillette, Wyoming. It was believed they were heading for the Crow or the Northern Cheyenne reservation in Montana, since the Sioux had not offered them refuge. General Greely sent orders to Colonel Rodgers at Fort Meade to pursue the Indians with six troops of his Sixth Cavalry and to use the city of Belle Fourche as a base. Rodgers was directed to bring the Indians to Fort Meade as prisoners until the government decided what to do with them.

Colonel Rodgers and his troopers left Fort Meade on 26 October. The command carried field rations for fifteen days and was accompanied by a packtrain with 129 mules, six wagons, and an ambulance. Twenty-five civilian employees, mostly packers, were also included in the entourage. White Bull, a Miniconjou Sioux, and Henry Fielder, an interpreter, both from the Cheyenne River Reservation, traveled with the troops in the hope they would be helpful in dealing with the Utes. Meanwhile, closing in on the Indians were six other troops, including two troops each of the

177

Sixth and Tenth cavalries from Forts Keogh and Robinson, respectively, and two companies of infantry from Fort Mackenzie near Sheridan, Wyoming.

Captain Carter P. Johnson of the Tenth Cavalry reached the Ute camp first but failed to convince the Indians that they should surrender. With only two troops at his disposal, the captain felt powerless to compel them. The Utes continued north and crossed the line into Montana before realizing that additional troops were closing in. Recognizing the hopelessness of their situation, the Utes surrendered. Surrounded now, the Indians parleyed again with Captain Johnson, who had White Bull and Fielder with him, and agreed to be escorted to the Black Hills. A storm delayed their departure until 6 November, when the march to the Hills began. Troop A of the Sixth Cavalry was detailed as the close escort for the band, with the rest of the command following a short distance behind.

At Belle Fourche, a two-day conference was held with General Greely, who had been sent out as a personal representative of the secretary of war and who agreed that the Utes could send a delegation to Washington to air their grievances before the president and the commissioner of Indian affairs. With this assurance, the Indians agreed to go peaceably to Fort Meade. The Utes considered Captain Johnson of the Tenth Cavalry a man of honor and stated that they would be satisfied if their future was "trusted to him." So it was agreed that he would be the intermediary in negotiations between the band and the government. Four thousand pounds of provisions were sent to Belle Fourche from Fort Meade for the travel-weary Utes and their military escort. In addition to the Sixth Cavalry, the command trailing the Utes included Johnson's two Tenth Cavalry troops. When the weather cleared, the march to Fort Meade was continued. At Belle Fourche, schools were closed so that the children could watch the Utes march through the community. The procession, strung out for two miles, was described as "a most interesting and unusual sight."[4]

Rodgers's command returned to Fort Meade with the prisoners on 24 November, having marched 150 miles since leaving the post the previous month. The Indians were placed at a wooded campsite on Alkali Creek on the western edge of the military reservation, within two miles of the troops at the post. Captain George L. Byram, Sixth Cavalry, was detailed as the officer in charge of the Utes, and Sergeant Walter Baker of

Troop A was placed in charge of the camp guard. The Utes, carried on the post rolls as prisoners of war, were given unlimited freedom within the camp, but they could not leave without permission. A census taken in the Indian camp in January 1907 showed 371 Utes: 146 men, 121 women, 93 children under twelve years of age, and 11 youths over twelve. The census also revealed that there had been one birth and one death at the camp since its establishment in November.[5]

The Utes attracted considerable attention among the residents of Sturgis during their quasi-confinement at Fort Meade. Many townspeople visited the Indian encampment and traded with the prisoners, some also getting their photographs taken with the Indians. The *Omaha World Herald,* seeking to confirm reports that the Utes were destitute, wired Colonel Rodgers about the situation. He replied that they were not destitute and that the government was furnishing them with clothes. He also reported the Utes were being fed from the Fort Meade commissary and they had been furnished with "an abundant supply of tentage, blankets and fuel," so there was "no possibility of their suffering."[6]

The secretary of war assured the governor of South Dakota that the prisoners would be cared for by the federal government and would not be a burden on the state. The Fort Meade quartermaster distributed slightly over eleven hundred dollars' worth of clothing to the Utes in December to prepare them for the Dakota winter. Funds expended for their care were deducted from the trust funds held in the U.S. treasury for the Ute tribe and distributed periodically on a pro rata basis. In government correspondence, the Fort Meade captives were referred to as the "Absentee Utes."[7]

In January, Captain Johnson accompanied a delegation of the Utes to Washington, where they met with President Theodore Roosevelt and Indian Commissioner F. E. Leupp. Roosevelt advised the Indians to return to their Utah reservation, where they had relatives and land rights. They showed no inclination to do that, however, and Roosevelt asked them how they expected to support themselves in South Dakota. "Our father, the government, is good," was their answer. "We trust the government to take care of us."[8] The president advised them not to rely on the government's generosity but to find some way to support themselves. Finally, it was agreed that an effort would be made to lease some Sioux land on the Cheyenne River Reservation for the Utes. White Bull had assured the Utes that they would be welcome there, and Captain Johnson was instructed to negotiate the lease.

Rodgers was in Washington on leave of absence at the time and also attended the meetings between the president and the Indians. While in the capital, Rodgers learned that his Sixth Cavalry would be reassigned to the Philippines at intervals during the year. Word that the Sixth would be leaving Fort Meade rekindled fears that the post was scheduled for closing, despite the government's growing investment in it. State Senator Henry Perkins, who was also the president of the Sturgis Commercial Club, steered a joint resolution through the legislature memorializing Congress to designate the fort a brigade post. The resolution also petitioned the government to provide additional buildings for the fort, pointing out that Fort Meade was the only post in South Dakota and was strategically located in reference to the Indian reservations.[9] These were old, but still valid, arguments for maintaining the post. "Troops from this post recently captured the roving Indians in Montana and now have them quartered at Fort Meade," the resolution reminded lawmakers. In addition, it cited Fort Meade's healthy climate and the convenient transportation facilities for military movements and noted that over $600,000 had been spent rebuilding the post during the previous six years.[10]

The army had no intention at the time of abandoning Fort Meade. But the threat had been raised so often that the people of Sturgis, and their elected officials, were becoming anxious. The issue created a voluminous file of correspondence between the Sturgis Commercial Club, the city officials, and the South Dakota congressional delegation. The state legislature added a sizable file of memorials and resolutions to Congress on proposals for the post. Legislators from Sturgis and Meade County were invariably the moving forces behind these measures. These coordinated campaigns were undoubtedly factors in keeping Fort Meade open and garrisoned at a time when most frontier posts had already been relegated to the history books. The strategy was simple but effective: persuade the government to spend a lot of money on buildings, and it would find the troops to occupy them!

Another attempt to get the Utes at Fort Meade to return to their reservation took place in March, when their former agent, Captain C. G. Hall of the Fifth Cavalry, arrived from Utah to consult with them. The

Utes seemed "to dislike him very much," the *Record* noted. "The Indians do not want to go back to Utah, and claim that if they have to go, they will fight. Just at present they are very restless." The newspaper also reported that troops at the post were making a practice march with full belts of ammunition in case "the renegades" attempted something. The paper added, "They seem to be getting ugly." Nothing came of the threat, however, and by the end of the month the Utes and the troopers were playing each other in baseball. The game was described as "very exciting and interesting," with the Utes providing musical accompaniment.[11]

Meanwhile, Captain Johnson completed arrangements with the Office of Indian Affairs by which the Utes would lease four townships of the Cheyenne River Reservation from the Sioux. The leased land was in the Thunder Butte district of the reservation, some 150 miles northeast of Fort Meade. Thomas Downs, a special Indian agent at the Cheyenne River Agency, came to the fort in May to meet with the Utes and explain the terms of their lease. The five-year lease, effective 1 July 1907, was granted for a fee of four and a half cents an acre, to be financed from the Utes' annuity funds.

Early in June, Captain Johnson returned to Fort Meade from Fort Robinson, where his regiment was stationed, to accompany the Utes to their new home. He found that many of their horses had died during the winter and that there was a shortage of wagons to transport the band and its equipage. Eight Utes had also died, and there had been five births at the camp since January, making a total of 368 persons to be moved. The dead had been buried in unmarked graves on a hill above the Indian camp. The burial site was near the Utes' ceremonial grounds where they had conducted the Bear Dance, a festival of spring, when the sun had melted the winter's snow. A number of friends from Sturgis and the fort who had established cordial relations with the band over the winter were allowed to witness the ceremony.[12]

Sergeant Baker had become a friend of the Indians during his guard service with them, and Johnson recommended him for a civilian job at Thunder Butte so that he could remain with the Utes. Downs offered the sergeant the job of "additional farmer" at the agency at a salary of sixty dollars a month, providing he could obtain a discharge from the army. Although his enlistment had not expired, Baker succeeded in getting discharged so that he could go with the Indians to their new location. He would later have reason to regret taking the early discharge.

White Bull also came from his home at Cherry Creek to guide the Utes to their leased lands. Before leaving, the Utes formed a commission to represent the band in its dealings with the reservation officials. They elected a chief named Yellowstone as the chairman of the commission. Johnson extracted a promise from the Utes that they would lay their complaints before the "proper authorities rather than taking matters into their own hands" on the reservation.[13]

On 10 June, Johnson had the Indians break camp and proceed to Chase's ranch ten miles east of Fort Meade for a rendezvous with an escort detachment from the post. The commanding officer there provided two wagons to supplement those of the Utes. But these still were not enough to carry all the equipment and provide transportation for those without horses, compelling many of the women and children to walk. The lengthy caravan aroused the interest of ranch families along the route, who would recall the procession of the Utes for years thereafter.

Under the headline "The Utes Are Gone," the *Record* reported, "The Indian village on Alkali is no more." Their departure, the newspaper commented, "if not a matter of regret," was "not a cause of rejoicing." The *Record* described the Utes as friendly, good-natured, and free spenders of whatever sums of money came into their hands. The newspaper noted, "They added spice and picturesque variety to our street scenes."[14]

At Chase's ranch, a sergeant and six privates of the Sixth Cavalry from the fort, reporting for duty to Captain Johnson, arrived with seven six-mule wagons driven by civilian teamsters. The wagons carried enough rations to feed the Utes until 30 June, the date of their scheduled transfer to Indian Office jurisdiction, and to feed the escort detachment until its return to the fort. First Lieutenant Duncan Elliott, Eighth Cavalry, was detailed to assist in the movement and arrived at Chase's on 11 June, having been delayed by a washout on the railroad bringing him to Fort Meade.

In addition to the Utes, the entourage included ten cavalry horses, about five hundred Indian ponies, and a dozen head of cattle. The latter were the survivors of the herd of fifty that had left Utah with the Indians the previous summer. Johnson, reporting on the hardships of the move, disclosed that the Utes organized a shuttle system during the march. "Those who had horses used them generously to aid their friends who had none," he revealed, "and as soon as camp was reached each day they would double back to the previous camp and bring on the luggage of those left behind. For several days, this method of travel rendered our progress very slow."[15]

Heavy summer rains had caused extensive flooding in Meade County and also slowed the progress of the Ute column. Sergeant Henry Rosseau of Troop B, Sixth Cavalry, had drowned that May when he had attempted to ford a rain-swollen creek while returning to the post from a three-day march. The troop's first sergeant was later awarded a certificate of merit for twice entering the stream at the risk of his own life in a futile attempt to save Rosseau as his horse was swept away.[16]

Johnson's command was delayed for five days at the Belle Fourche River while waiting for floodwaters to recede. On 23 June, Johnson was further delayed by having to return three of the borrowed wagons to Fort Meade, as he had promised to do by that date. Johnson had loaded these wagons with "extra Indian luggage, old and decrepit women and little children" as fast as the wagons were emptied by the issuance of rations. The return of the wagons to the fort forced many women and children to walk. However, Sioux from the reservation came to the rescue of the fatigued travelers by bringing sixteen light wagons.[17]

By 30 June the travelers were at Goose Creek in the center of the reservation, some thirty miles from the Thunder Butte station and forty-five miles from the agency headquarters. Johnson left his charges there on 1 July and rode into the agency, where Downs assumed jurisdiction over the Utes by signing a receipt for 367 of them. Two Utes had died on the arduous journey (one was a twenty-year-old male named Run-A-Piece, whose death was attributed to general tuberculosis), and there had been one birth on the way. Johnson stayed with his former charges until they were settled on their leased lands. The site they chose for their village was at the point that Thunder Butte Creek entered the Moreau River. Johnson remained with them until 6 July and then returned to his home station in Nebraska via Fort Meade.[18]

Shortly after the Utes left Fort Meade, Secretary of War William Howard Taft made an official visit to the post. The leading citizens of Sturgis rolled out the red carpet for the future president and took full advantage of the opportunity to lobby him hard for an enlargement of the post. The town was "profusely decorated with flags and bunting," and a platform was erected on the corner of First and Main streets, where Taft was welcomed to the community. Taft's train arrived on the afternoon of 17 June with "all the whistles and bells in town" announcing its arrival. He was accompanied by the South Dakota congressional delegation and Governor Coe Crawford, as well as by the army chief of staff and U.S. Marshal Seth Bullock. A special train carried area newspapermen and dignitaries to Sturgis for the big event. Taft and his party went immediately to the post and then returned to town for the public ceremony on Main Street. Mayor and State Senator Perkins, on behalf of the citizens of Sturgis and Meade County, presented Taft with a hair bridle and an engraved silver bit that carried the secretary's initials. Taft expressed surprise at seeing such a large turnout for "an ordinary cabinet officer."[19]

"My visit here is to inspect Fort Meade and to consider the advisability of making it a full regimental post," Taft confided. He had high praise for the climate of the region but pointed out that the day when the post had been needed to protect the settlements from Indians was happily past. "To the pioneer the soldier meant more than he does now," he commented. "When civilization was being established in the west the soldier was indispensable. He is indispensable still, but he is not now needed to protect your homes from an old enemy."[20]

Taft's remarks must have been somewhat alarming to Perkins and other town boosters. Taft had implied that he felt Fort Meade might be expendable, since the threat of Indian attacks no longer existed. The secretary was escorted back to Fort Meade after the public ceremony for a review of the Sixth Cavalry. Colonel Rodgers hosted a banquet for the visiting dignitaries at his quarters, and Taft's party left for the East by train that same evening. Before the departure, the *Record* attempted to get Taft to commit himself on the future of Fort Meade, but with little success. "I cannot say in advance of my report," Taft told the newspaper, "but I think Fort Meade is a beautiful place. It has a magnificent setting and is designed by nature for an army post." From this statement, the *Record* hopefully concluded, "It may be assumed that the secretary will make Fort Meade a full regimental post."[21]

In July, it was announced that the Fourth Cavalry, then in the Philippines, would replace the Sixth Cavalry at Fort Meade. Three troops each of the First and Second Squadrons of the Sixth left the fort in September. Troops D and F remained behind under Captain Byram, who became the post commander. He had no sooner assumed the command than he received a letter from a member of the Ute commission at Cheyenne River, asking that Captain Johnson "come here at once." The Utes wanted "to have another talk with him."[22]

The Utes at Thunder Butte had been unhappy almost from the time of their arrival. Agent Downs, carrying out the wishes of the president and the secretary of the interior, had insisted that the Utes work and that they send their children to boarding schools. They adamantly refused, and in an effort to force their compliance, Downs had cut their rations in half. Byram forwarded the letter from the Ute commission to department headquarters, and Johnson was directed to hasten to the reservation to meet with the troubled Utes.

Meanwhile, acting on false information that the Utes were planning an uprising, Downs sent a detachment of Indian police to Thunder Butte to keep close watch on them and organized a group of volunteers for "emergency duty." He reported the Sioux in the area were moving to other sectors of the reservation because they didn't want "to be mixed up in trouble."[23] Downs asked for three troops of cavalry from Fort Meade to disarm the Utes and to remove their leaders from the reservation.

Byram had only two troops under his command at Fort Meade, and rather than deplete the garrison there, the War Department sent one squadron of the Second Cavalry from Fort Des Moines, Iowa, to the scene. In addition, the entire garrison of Fort Robinson and "as much of the Fort Meade command" as could be spared were ordered to be prepared to intercept the Utes if they should attempt to leave the reservation.[24]

With President Roosevelt's specific instructions, Captain Johnson was sent as the government emissary to the Utes. He was told to inform the Utes, in the president's name, that the government did not "intend to support" the Utes "in idleness" simply because they did not wish to work. He was also instructed to tell the Indians that if they did not accept the work and school dictates, they would "probably face a winter of suffering," since their rations would be "cut off entirely." However, Downs was directed to avoid any measure of coercion in his handling of the situation. The Utes were to be left "free to make their own choice and either go to work and earn their living, or remain idle and accept the consequences without complaint."[25]

Johnson, after talks with the Utes, was critical of Downs's harsh treatment of them. He reported they planned no uprising but objected to leaving their families to accept off-reservation employment and to sending their children to boarding schools away from their leased lands. Johnson stated, "A hundred pounds of flour and a little patience is a more potent factor in the solution of this problem than one hundred soldiers."[26] Downs was as critical of Johnson as the captain was of him. He claimed the secret of Johnson's popularity with the Indians was that he had never required them to work or send their children to school until ordered to do so by the president. In fact, Downs charged, Johnson "never denied them any request."[27]

Despite the admonition against coercion, Downs continued to appeal for more troops. Second Cavalry and Sixteenth Infantry troops from Forts Des Moines and Crook, the latter near Omaha, Nebraska, were rushed to the region until nearly one thousand soldiers were assembled there. They were supported by a packtrain from Fort Meade, which left Sturgis by rail on 7 November and reported for duty with the Second Cavalry at Gettysburg, east of the reservation.

Following orders, Captain Johnson assured the concerned Utes that the troops were there simply to maintain law and order. Johnson advised against trying to disarm the Indians, pointing out that this would be interpreted as an act of the government's distrust of their goodwill. Besides, their weapons were not modern and were useful to the Indians in killing game to supplement their rations. However, if the Utes resorted to violence and the troops were forced to respond, the Indian commissioner expressed the hope that "the collision" would be "short, sharp and decisive."[28]

That the soldiers intended to keep the Utes under close surveillance for a long time soon became obvious to the Indians, who could see two cavalry troops busily building dugout shelters at Thunder Butte. Bowing to the inevitable, about 130 Utes, led by Red Cap, agreed to relocate at Rapid City in November. The Utes were settled at a camp on a one-thousand-

acre tract of land owned by the Indian school. By this time they had no
stock other than their horse herd. The school superintendent felt confident he could control the Utes, especially with Fort Meade so close by in
the event of trouble. The army favored the relocation because maintaining troops on the isolated Cheyenne River Reservation was expensive and
inconvenient. Pick-and-shovel jobs on the railroad at Rapid City were
obtained for able-bodied Utes, and others were put to work cutting firewood for the Indian school. The enrollment of the Ute children in the
school ended the need for recruiting Indian children from Montana to fill
out the classes.

The 226 Utes who elected not to go to Rapid City voted in December to
remain at Thunder Butte for the winter. When spring came, they agreed,
they would return to their home reservation in Utah. Until then, the men
were given employment gathering firewood for the reservation schools.
Captain Johnson also obtained a special appropriation for supplies to
carry them through the winter. The number of troops at Thunder Butte
was reduced, and no further trouble was experienced with the Utes there.
In retrospect, Downs decided that Baker, the former sergeant, had been
chiefly responsible for spreading "exaggerated stories" of a planned Ute
revolt, and he was fired, despite having given up his army career for his
reservation job.[29]

The First and Third Squadrons of the Fourth Cavalry, composed of
Troops A, B, C, D, I, K, L, and M, had arrived at Fort Meade from the
Philippines in October and November. The Second Squadron was as-
signed to Fort Snelling. Troops D and F of the Sixth Cavalry then left Fort
Meade to rejoin the rest of the regiment en route to the Philippines,
leaving only the eight troops of the Fourth Cavalry at the post. Captain
James B. Hughes commanded the two squadrons and the post during the
temporary absence of the regimental commander, who had gone with the
Second Squadron to Fort Snelling.

On 31 December, Captain Hughes reported that two Utes from Rapid
City had appeared at the post asking for Captain Johnson. They complained that the railroad had no more work for them, they had not been
paid, and their families were cold. They wanted Johnson to "settle matters."[30] Johnson, back at his home station at Fort Robinson, was again
summoned to placate the unhappy Utes. Meanwhile, Captain Hughes

received orders to send the two Utes back to Rapid City, using post wagons if necessary. If shelter and food were given them, he was advised, it would only encourage the rest of the Utes to return to the post.

Captain Johnson found the complaints of the Utes valid when he reached Rapid City. The railroad had suspended improvements on its tracks, and no other employment could be found for the Indians. The superintendent of the Indian school had discontinued issuing rations to the Utes while they were working, and he did not have the funds to feed them when they became unemployed. The disappointed Indians decided that they, like those at Thunder Butte, would return to Utah in the spring. The government then came forth with the rations required to get them through the winter.

Captain Johnson reported that the Indian school pasture where the Utes were grazing their fifty-head horse herd was in poor condition. He pointed out that the horses would be needed for the Utes' return trip to Utah, and he succeeded in getting funds to buy hay for them. Johnson was placed on detached service as a special inspecting officer for the Indian Office and was directed to visit the Utes at Rapid City and Thunder Butte at least once a month. In June, Captain Johnson brought the Utes at Thunder Butte to Rapid City to join their brethren for the long trip back to Utah. Coming with him was the Ute woman that White Bull had married. She and White Bull had been unable to communicate with each other, so it had been decided it would be best for her to return home with her people. The marriage was the only one between members of the two tribes during the seventeen months the "absentee Utes" were in South Dakota.[31]

The Department of the Interior allocated nearly $10,000 to Captain Johnson for expenses in moving the Utes back to Utah. He bought extra wagons and harness at Rapid City and left in July for the eleven-hundred-mile overland trek to the Uintah Reservation. The movement involved 350 Utes, 21 fewer than listed in the 1907 census at Fort Meade. The loss counted those who had died at Fort Meade, Thunder Butte, and Rapid City, as well as those born during the band's stay in South Dakota.

Johnson's caravan, traveling by way of the Pine Ridge Reservation and Forts Robinson and D. A. Russell, reached the Uintah Agency at Fort Duchesne on 22 October. Since the "absentee Utes" had not intended to return when they had left their homes, they had disposed of their reservation property before departing. Consequently, they were destitute when they got back. Their agent was authorized to spend up to seventy-five thousand dollars of the tribe's trust funds to prevent want and suffering among them. The expense was charged against each individual's share of those trust funds—just as the cost of the clothing they had received at Fort Meade had been.[32]

The trek to South Dakota and back had been a long and painful experience for the disillusioned Utes, and they were worse off when they returned than when they had left. For his long and effective service with them, Captain Johnson received a special Interior Department commendation and was soon promoted to major.

The presence of the Utes in South Dakota had brought out the last significant call-up of troops to quiet trouble with Indians. The Utes' return to Utah marked the end of Indian service for troops at Fort Meade. The need for which the fort had been founded had also ended. The post's future, despite regarrisoning by eight troops of the Fourth Cavalry, was uncertain.

★ 14 ★

SEMI-ABANDONMENT

Rumors that Fort Meade was about to be abandoned were rampant in the Black Hills in the spring of 1911. The post was virtually cleared of troops when the Mexican Revolution broke out and twenty thousand American troops were rushed to the border. The first to arrive at Fort Sam Houston, Texas, the rendezvous point for the assembling border units, were six troops of the Fourth Cavalry from Fort Meade, under Colonel E. Z. Steever. The other two troops of the regiment at Fort Meade were dispatched to New Mexico. The last of these units left the post in March. "It may be some time before troops are stationed here again," the *Sturgis Weekly Record* prophetically lamented.[1]

City officials, ever fearful of the post's closing and the economic consequences on Sturgis, acted quickly to avert the threat. They barraged the state's congressional delegation with appeals for replacement troops for the fort despite the more urgent need along the Mexican border. They were able to persuade Senator Robert J. Gamble to introduce a bill appropriating $200,000 for post improvements and for expansion of the military reservation. The measure failed to win congressional approval, however, principally because of opposition from army headquarters.

General Leonard Wood, the army chief of staff, presented Secretary of War Henry Stimson with a reorganization plan that called for closing small and isolated posts, abolishing the army's geographical departments, and creating brigade-sized garrisons throughout the country. "It is General Wood's idea," the *Record* reported, "that a mobile army should be concentrated in eight or ten centers instead of being distributed generally throughout the United States as at present."[2] Wood listed Fort Meade, with the older Fort Snelling, as among the posts that would be abandoned under his reorganization.

Congressmen E. W. Martin of Deadwood and Charles Burke of Pierre carried their concerns about Fort Meade's future to President Taft. The president, who would run for reelection in 1912, was aware of the political consequences that widespread closings of posts would have on his campaign, as well as on those of other Republican candidates. The South Dakotans had no trouble persuading him to shelve Wood's reorganization plan for the time being. Exercising his authority as commander in chief, Taft directed Wood to arrange for the regarrisoning of Fort Meade.[3] The general dutifully complied.

"I am assured that cavalry to the full capacity of the post will be placed at Fort Meade," Martin wired Mayor W. E. Ladd at Sturgis. "There is no serious prospect of an abandonment of the post, but the matter will need some further attention."[4] In a follow-up letter, Martin outlined the reasons for his optimism: the government had expended over one million dollars in improving the Fort Meade facilities during the previous six years, including a water system that cost more than one hundred thousand dollars. Moreover, the president was opposed to the post's abandonment. The congressman believed that Fort Meade's proximity to the Sioux reservations, where trouble could break out at any time, was sufficient justification for continuing the post. "Upon the merits of the case," Martin asserted, "I expect that Fort Meade will be retained as a department of the permanent military establishment."[5]

True to the president's promise, replacement troops arrived at Fort Meade in late December. The first arrivals were Troops I and K, Twelfth Cavalry, which came from Fort Huachuca, Arizona, under the command of Lieutenant Colonel Horatio G. Sickel, who had earlier served at Fort Meade with the Seventh Cavalry. The assignment of these troops to Fort Meade, however, became embroiled in the presidential political campaign then beginning to take form. "Are troops to be kept at Fort Meade, S. D., merely until the presidential election and then withdrawn and the post abandoned?" asked the *Sioux City Journal*. Wood, with Stimson, was scheduled to appear before the military affairs committee, and the *Journal* predicted they would be asked some embarrassing questions on Fort Meade. The newspaper's Washington correspondent wrote, "In committee circles there is a well defined suspicion that the present activity of the administration to do something for Fort Meade is political and temporary, and that President Taft has caused troops to be sent there at the insis-

191

In 1913, these soldiers of Company M, Nineteenth Infantry, pitched their pup tents within the shadow of Bear Butte. This was near where Camp J. G. Sturgis had been established in 1878 for the first units assigned to garrison Fort Meade, then being built a short distance southwest of this site. (Courtesy of Old Fort Meade Museum Association.)

tence of Representatives Martin and Burke to lull public feeling at this time, when the political situation is ticklish, but there is no real purpose to have the troops to long remain there."[6]

At any rate, two more troops of the Twelfth Cavalry (L and M) arrived at Fort Meade from Fort Apache, Arizona, on 11 January 1912. The rest of the regiment, commanded by Colonel C. H. Murray, was assigned to Fort Robinson. In June, the Fort Meade garrison was fully restored with the arrival from the Philippines of Companies I, K, L, and M of the Nineteenth Infantry, with its headquarters and band. Colonel Willard F. Waltz, the commanding officer of the infantry regiment, assumed the command of the post from Sickel.[7]

Lieutenant F. B. Edwards, Twelfth Cavalry, was credited with bringing an army horse buyer to the fort in October. "It has been a long, hard fight to get the necessary orders for a purchasing officer to be sent here," the *Record* observed. "It is hoped every horse breeder and every person interested in the development of the Black Hills will use every effort to make the showing as good as possible."[8] Horses for the army's remount station were purchased at Hermosa and Belle Fourche as well as at Fort Meade that month.

National attention was focused on the hotly contested presidential race. Taft, as expected, had been renominated by the Republican party. But the Republicans had been split by the defection of Theodore Roosevelt, who became the presidential candidate of the Progressive, or "Bull Moose," party. Although most of the South Dakota congressional delegation supported Taft, the state went for Roosevelt. The bitter Republican split enabled Democrat Woodrow Wilson to win the presidency. South Dakota Senator Gamble had been defeated in the Republican primary, but Congressmen Martin and Burke, who had worked closely with him in fighting against the closing of Fort Meade, were reelected.

Suspicions that Fort Meade's garrison would be removed or reduced after the presidential election were confirmed shortly after President Wilson took office. The post lost half its troops in February 1913 when the infantry soldiers were transferred to Galveston, Texas. Their departure left only the four troops of the Twelfth Cavalry at the post.[9] The South Dakota legislature was then in session, so State Senator John D. Hale of Meade County gained approval of a joint resolution that asked Congress to designate Fort Meade as a brigade post. The resolution was almost a word-for-word repetition of the one Senator Perkins had introduced at the 1907 session.

Although no additional regular army troops were assigned to Fort Meade in 1913, the Fourth Regiment, South Dakota National Guard, took its summer field training there in July. More than five hundred state militiamen from the regiment's twelve companies participated in eight-day maneuvers on a rotation basis.

While the guardsmen were at Fort Meade, two soldiers from Troop K, Twelfth Cavalry, got into a fracas at a bawdy house on the outskirts of Sturgis. The two-story operation on the north side of Bear Butte Creek, just three blocks from Main Street, was run by "Poker Alice" Tubbs. The cigar-chewing madam, whose attire invariably included a khaki army shirt and campaign hat, was as notorious for her skill at faro and poker as

The army's version of a chuck wagon carried kitchen supplies to a training site of the Nineteenth Infantry during field exercises in 1913 along the northern boundary of the Fort Meade military reservation. Bear Butte, which first attracted military attention to the Black Hills region, is in the background. (Courtesy of Old Fort Meade Museum Association.)

for the girls in her upstairs cubicles. She had a full house—in her upstairs rooms if not in the card game below—when the trouble broke out.

The Troop K soldiers, denied admission because of the crowd of guardsmen already inside, vented their resentment by cutting the telephone and power lines to the house and pelting the house with rocks. A number of shots were fired, and when the smoke cleared, the two soldiers were down with bullet wounds. One of the soldiers, a sergeant, died at the post hospital, but the other, a private, recovered. Tubbs and six of the inmates of her house were immediately arrested and confined in the county jail. The *Record,* reporting it had made a careful examination of the incident, absolved the guardsmen of any involvement in the fracas. It was "but justice," the newspaper stated, to point out that "none of them were responsible for the trouble, or in anyway participated in the assault upon the place."[10]

Tubbs was charged only with keeping a house of ill fame and was fined.

"Poker Alice" Tubbs and friends, including "Grasshopper Jim" Fredricks, right, who founded the notorious "Scooptown" near Bear Butte in the summer of 1878 to provide liquor and women for the soldiers assigned to establish Fort Meade. Poker Alice, who was seldom seen without an army shirt and a campaign hat, operated a house of ill repute in Sturgis City, one mile east of the fort. She had been a poker dealer in nearby Deadwood before moving to Sturgis City. Poker Alice fatally shot a soldier who had become abusive when refused admittance to her place because she already had "a full house." (Courtesy of Old Fort Meade Museum Association.)

Those arrested with her were each fined fifteen dollars for frequenting her place. The identity of the person who killed the sergeant and wounded the private was never established, although it was generally believed in Sturgis that Tubbs was responsible. Later reminiscing about her colorful life and career, Tubbs confessed to once having had occasion "to shoot a repeating rifle with deadly effect."[11] Nobody in Sturgis had any doubts about when that had happened.

Fort Meade was temporarily cleared of troops when the Third Squadron of the Twelfth Cavalry was sent on border duty in New Mexico in May 1914. The four troops left Sturgis in two trains for Fort Wingate, leaving behind wives and families and a caretaker force of two officers and fourteen enlisted men. Troop K returned to the post in October, while the other three troops of the squadron were detailed to strike duty in Colorado. These returned to the fort in November. There the squadron remained until March 1916, when the fort was emptied again for border patrol service in New Mexico. The Twelfth joined General John J. Pershing's forces pursuing the Mexican revolutionary Pancho Villa, who was raiding both sides of the border.[12]

"Fort Meade is again without troops," the *Record* observed, "and is in the hands of about twenty caretakers."[13] Captain Louis S. D. Rucker, Jr., a retired army officer, returned to active duty as the post commander, serving only until 15 September when Major Leo Foster, another retired officer, replaced him.

To the dismay of the Sturgis business community, no replacement regular army troops were assigned to Fort Meade. There were periodic changes among the personnel attached to the quartermaster caretaker force, but no new units were posted to the fort. Meanwhile, the government decided to establish a number of camps throughout the country to train military recruits and volunteers for periods of six weeks to three months. A vigorous campaign was launched in the Black Hills to have Fort Meade designated as one of these sites. L. O. Shirley of Hot Springs, a reservist and member of the Federal Training Camps Association, spearheaded the drive. He pointed out that the government had spent a lot of money to rebuild Fort Meade, then standing virtually empty, and urged its utilization. Moreover, he proposed that the commercial clubs of the region adopt resolutions supporting the plan, claiming that every community would "be benefited" by the influx of trainees.[14]

Directors of the Sturgis Business Club were quick to act on the suggestion, calling a special meeting for the purpose. One of the fruits of their labor was a resolution of support by the Black Hills Association of Commercial Club Secretaries. Adopted at Lead on 27 December 1916, the resolution described Fort Meade as "one of the best equipped posts in the west with over $2,000,000 worth of permanent improvements." B. J. Glattly, of the Hot Springs Commercial Club, was appointed to work with Shirley in promoting the training site.[15] Another result of this campaign was the unanimous approval by the state legislature in January 1917 of Joint Resolution No. 6. Introduced by Meade County's Senator Hale, the resolution memorialized Congress to use the Black Hills post for training purposes. When that failed, an effort was made to have Fort Meade designated as a mustering-out station for the Fourth South Dakota Infantry. This militia regiment, called up to active duty in June, had served on border duty in Texas before being "defederalized" the following March. Fort Meade was not chosen, however, because of its isolation. Instead, the state's militiamen were mustered out at Fort Crook, near Omaha, Nebraska.[16]

No sooner were the South Dakota National Guardsmen back home than the country entered the war against Germany, and they were again mobilized. The Fourth Regiment's Company I at Rapid City, with a medical unit, was mobilized at Fort Meade. The guardsmen spent four months there as the companies were rebuilt to full strength. Most of Company I's new recruits came from Rapid City and the northern Hills towns.[17]

Ernest Cole, who wrote the weekly "Fort Meade Notes" column for the *Record* during this period, reported a Company I dance in June and a Red Cross benefit dance hosted by the medical corpsmen in August. The guardsmen left the post in late September for further training at Camp Greene in North Carolina. The platform of the Sturgis depot was crowded with friends and relatives of the departing guardsmen when they left.[18]

The *Record* reported in September 1918 that a large number of draft registrants found physically unfit for general duty would be sent to Fort Meade for limited-service assignments. They were sent to Fort Omaha instead, and Fort Meade remained virtually unmanned. The *Weekly Review* in Philip, South Dakota, editorially asked, "Why Is Fort Meade Abandoned?" The paper pointed out that there were thousands of acres of the Fort Meade reservation suitable for an artillery range. The newspaper charged that the government, instead of using what it already owned, was "paying big prices elsewhere for such land." It remarked that the government had implored the citizenry to economize and "waste not" on behalf of the war effort. "If waste is sinful at this time," the newspaper charged, "certainly it is so in the Fort Meade case."[19]

Fort Meade did serve as a recruiting station during World War I. The post commander doubled as the recruiting officer. The Central Division commander visited the post in October and announced that the fort would become a training school for small detachments of Signal Corps troops. From July 1918 to the end of the war in November, however, the Fort Meade garrison numbered only one or two officers and six quartermaster and six medical detachment enlisted men.[20] Major Foster was relieved as the post commander at Fort Meade in May 1919. He was replaced with a succession of officers, ranging from first lieutenant to lieutenant colonel.[21]

General Wood visited the Black Hills in July 1919 and made a brief stop at Fort Meade. But his visit was more political than military in purpose. Wood had been removed as the army chief of staff after President Wilson took office because his policies conflicted with those of the president. The general had been openly critical of the Wilson administration's slowness in preparing for war, and the president had retaliated by denying him an overseas command during the war. At war's end, Wood had been encouraged to seek the Republican nomination for president. On his 1919 visit to Fort Meade he was accompanied by Governor Peter Norbeck and Seth Bullock, who were promoting Wood's candidacy within the state. Norbeck had his eye on a U.S. Senate seat, and Bullock, a veteran Black Hills politician, was an influential supporter of both men.[22]

Wood returned to the Black Hills in March 1920 as an announced Republican candidate for the presidency. The day before the primary election he again visited Fort Meade briefly with the mayor of Sturgis. After a quick tour of the post, garrisoned by only one officer and thirteen enlisted men, they returned to Sturgis, where Wood addressed a political rally at the Meade County courthouse. Wood's short visits to Fort Meade in 1919 and 1920 may have been designed to placate voters in the region who remembered that he had once favored the post's abandonment, and if so, the tactic worked. In the election, Wood carried Meade County handily and the rest of the state narrowly. He was undoubtedly aided substantially by the popularity of Norbeck, who won the Republican nomination for the Senate and the subsequent general election, and by the considerable influence of Bullock. Despite Wood's primary victories, however, the Republican presidential nomination went to Warren G. Harding.[23]

Neither the government nor the Sturgis boosters seemed to know what to do with Fort Meade after World War I ended. One Sturgis booster who was determined to see the fort's facilities put to good use was the pastor of the First Presbyterian Church, the Reverend Carroll D. Erskine, who was elected to the state senate in 1920. Erskine had taken a leave of absence from his church at the outbreak of the war to serve as the secretary of the Young Men's Christian Association at an army camp in Texas. He was subsequently commissioned as a chaplain and was assigned to greet wounded servicemen as they returned home. On his own return, and his election to the state legislature, the popular pastor decided to do something about unmanned Fort Meade. At the 1921 session he introduced a resolution asking Congress to transfer Fort Meade to the Public Health Service for use as a "soldiers' hospital."[24]

The *Lead Daily Call,* commenting on the resolution, pointed out the unoccupied Fort Meade structures were "well built, mostly of brick and stone, and no successful businessman would think of permitting them to lie unused."[25] John W. Weeks, appointed secretary of war in 1921, expressed no objection, so an amendment authorizing the transfer was attached to the army appropriations bill that passed the Senate in June. The amendment was eliminated by the conference committee, however, when it was determined that Weeks had the authority to make the transfer under existing legislation. Then, to everybody's surprise, the secretary changed his mind and announced he intended to regarrison Fort Meade with a regiment of cavalry.[26]

Congressman William Williamson of the state's Third Congressional District, which encompassed Fort Meade, reported that the work of the congressional delegation had paid off. He explained the delegation had threatened to have Fort Meade transferred to some other government agency unless the War Department garrisoned it with troops. "We now have the assurance that this will be done and indications are that in the not very distant future the fort will be occupied," Williamson disclosed. He was determined that the fort "not stand empty" as it had the past ten years and promised its transfer to some other department if troops were not promptly assigned there.[27]

But there still were no regular army soldiers stationed at the post by September, except for the small caretaker force. So Erskine renewed his campaign to have the facility converted to hospital use. When the two-year-old American Legion held its state convention in Rapid City that month, Erskine as the chairman of the legion's legislative committee, proposed a resolution supporting his plan. An eloquent speaker, Erskine addressed the convention and in a moving speech about the country's obligation to its war wounded, easily won adoption of the resolution.[28]

Congressman Williamson also renewed his efforts to get congressional

199

action on the issue. But Weeks insisted that the army planned to regarrison the post, terming it one of the best in the country, and he "absolutely refused to turn it over to the Public Health Service." The delay in assigning troops there, he explained, was occasioned by the postwar reduction in the army's authorized strength and the continued need for a troop presence on the Mexican border. However, Weeks assured Williamson, troops would be posted to Fort Meade as soon as they could be spared from the border.[29]

Meanwhile, the campaign to convert the facility to a veterans' hospital was gaining momentum within South Dakota and neighboring states. L. D. Milne of Sturgis journeyed to Wyoming in the spring of 1922 to urge the legion posts there to get behind the movement. The *Newcastle News-Record,* supporting the proposal, editorialized that it made sense to use abandoned army posts in the West for hospital purposes. It pointed out these posts were located in healthy climes and that it would be cheaper to renovate their buildings for hospital use than to pay for the care of disabled veterans in civilian hospitals. Moreover, the newspaper charged, private institutions that had contracted to care for invalid war veterans were making a profit of three hundred dollars a year on each veteran. "These dollar grabbers give as little care and attention as they can and get by." The *News-Record* asked:

Why not take these wards from the care of these unscrupulous money hounds and place them away from the humidity, congestion, malaria and pest ridden conditions into our unused government posts? Why not make each of these unused forts a hospital unit and do our duty to our returned crippled warriors as we should? . . . The soldier would profit by living in healthy conditions, breathing pure air under western skies, he would for the same expenditure of money fare many times as well, the taxpayer would profit by building a greater loyalty and more satisfied people. . . . It looks as though this is true economy which if followed generally would mean plenty of money to pay bonuses and other obligations. LET's GO.[30]

Unhappy with the War Department's delay in assigning troops to Fort Meade, Congressman Williamson again tried to force the issue. A bill was introduced that authorized the U.S. Veterans Bureau to spend seventeen million dollars for constructing hospital and outpatient facilities for veterans. Williamson tacked on an amendment that permitted the president to transfer Fort Meade to the Veterans Bureau for hospital purposes. Prospects brightened when President Harding authorized a veterans hospital in the Tenth Public Health District, which included the two Dakotas, Minnesota, and Montana. The District American Legion Auxiliary endorsed the proposed Fort Meade transfer at its 1922 annual meeting at Pierre in May. Seventy-five posts also were on record in favor of the Fort Meade hospital when the state legion convention was held at Sioux Falls in June. But a supporting resolution was dropped when the state commander was informed: "Fort Meade is not available from the War Department as it will be garrisoned by a regiment of cavalry."[31]

Further, the War Department successfully blocked Williamson's efforts to legislate the transfer. It was vague, however, about the exact time that troops would be returned to Fort Meade. As late as June 1923, it was still "studying" the matter.[32] But it did approve the use of the idle fort by the National Guard. The state's militiamen held their annual field training there in the summer of 1922. The guardsmen, chiefly members of the 147th Field Artillery Regiment, came in three separate contingents between 11 June and 25 July.

The citizens of Sturgis, ecstatic about having troops at the fort again, however briefly, rolled out the red carpet for them. A banquet for the guard officers, headed by State Adjutant General E. A. Beckwith, was held in the clubrooms of Erskine's church when the first contingent arrived at the post. The officers were profuse in their praise of the community's hospitality toward their men. They were also "equally loud in praise of Fort Meade as the ideal spot in location, equipment and environment for the training of the citizen soldier."[33]

A delegation of city officials and leading businessmen greeted the guard contingents as they arrived at the fort. In return, the 147th band, from Mitchell, conducted free concerts for the public on the parade grounds every night during the encampment. Fort Meade ranked high as a training site for the guardsmen, according to the *Aberdeen American-News,* because it had "the advantage of beauty spots in the Black Hills, besides electric lights, shower baths and other conveniences."[34]

Captain Hardy J. Story, Third Infantry, whose regiment was stationed at Fort Snelling, was in command of the small detachment of regular army caretaker troops at Fort Meade during this period. Despite their fondness for Fort Meade, the guardsmen took their annual field training in 1923 on the banks of the Missouri River north of Pierre. At the completion of their training, a vote was taken on where they would prefer to go for their 1924 summer encampment: Sparta, Wisconsin; Pierre; or the Black Hills. The vote was overwhelmingly for the latter.[35]

The *Sturgis Weekly Record,* miffed about the army's failure to honor its commitment to regarrison Fort Meade with regular army troops, predicted the post would "remain unoccupied indefinitely." In a two-column, boxed, front-page article, the newspaper pointed out that "one of the best equipped cavalry posts" in the country had stood virtually vacant for over ten years. It added, "There is every reason why Fort Meade should be utilized, if not as a fort, as a U.S. Veterans Bureau Hospital." The article, a masterpiece of parochial boosterism, contained a litany of reasons why Fort Meade was ideal for hospital purposes. The paper emphasized the healthful climate of the region and claimed army records showed that soldiers previously serving at Fort Meade had been the healthiest in the country. Further, it stated that Black Hills winters were moderate, with no more than five major storms each year. It also claimed the post's water supply was superior and pointed out the post already had a well-equipped, sixty-bed hospital that was not in use. In addition, the article concluded: "Fort Meade is within the Black Hills district which has been named the Switzerland of America and is visited by tourists from all over the world for its health-giving climate and scenic beauties. . . . The problem of caring for the disabled ex-serviceman is evident and Fort Meade as a U.S. Veterans Bureau Hospital is the solution."[36]

Repeated assurances from the War Department that the fort would be regarrisoned "within six months" put an end to the campaign to convert the facility into a hospital—for the time being. But the citizens of Sturgis were skeptical about the matter, considering all the previous pledges, and they repeatedly badgered their elected representatives in Washington to speed the process along. In December, Senator Thomas Sterling informed the *Record* that the War Department was sending an inspector to the fort to examine the buildings and determine what repairs were needed before troops were posted there. He also reported the army planned to move troops overland to Fort Meade. He added: "They can't do that in temperatures 20 to 30 degrees below zero, hence the limit as to time. . . . I think the assurance given by the Department are [sic] as definite as can reasonably be expected."[37]

Finally, in the spring of 1924, Captain H. C. Kliber of the Quartermaster Corps at Omaha arrived at the post to prepare the quarters buildings for troops. He soon had twenty men, hired locally, at work installing new furnaces in the quarters and cleaning up the other buildings in preparation for occupancy by 1 April. The Sturgis firm of Garlick and Borge received the contract for hauling almost two million pounds of supplies to the fort. A contract for nine carloads of feed for the cavalry horses due to arrive was awarded to the Tri-State Milling Company at Sturgis. There were limited refrigeration facilities at the post, so the Curnow Market, another Sturgis firm, was given the contract for providing fresh meat and meat products, except for beef. The Armour Packing Co. was the successful bidder for the beef contract. Regarrisoning the fort, noted the *Black Hills Press,* gave "the farmers in this vicinity a ready market for much of their surplus hay and grain." The paper added: "It is also a good market for butter, eggs and vegetables. It means a lot to the prosperity of Sturgis and the surrounding country."[38]

During this activity, Secretary Weeks informed Senator Sterling that there would be a delay in the arrival of the troops at the post. They were coming from a hot climate, he explained. "It was not advisable to send them to Fort Meade until the weather moderated. They will reach South Dakota sometime in May." The salubrious Black Hills weather that the *Record* had been so boastful about was not very cooperative that particular spring. Nevertheless, in mid-April an advance detachment of the Fourth Cavalry from Fort Sam Houston arrived at Fort Meade to begin the regiment's second tour of duty there.[39]

The First Squadron of the Fourth, consisting of Troops A, B, and C, reached Sturgis on 6 May under the command of Lieutenant Colonel C. E. Hathaway. Its delayed arrival did not spare the two hundred officers and men from the fickleness of Black Hills weather. The troops, "fresh from the burning sands of Texas," arrived in the midst of a blinding snowstorm. The troopers walked from the Sturgis depot to the post, undoubtedly grumbling about their change of station despite their pleasant earlier tour in the Black Hills. Their horses arrived two days later.[40] The Second and Third Squadrons of the regiment remained in Texas until 1925, when they were transferred to Fort D. A. Russell in Wyoming. Congressman Williamson, visiting the post in July, reported that efforts to have these squadrons brought to Fort Meade were hampered by a shortage of quarters for officers and married enlisted men.

The First Squadron quickly resumed routine garrison duties, punctuated by periodic practice marches to points in the Black Hills and surrounding prairies. It fielded a baseball team that competed on weekends with Hills teams, both on and off the post. Its band presented a number of concerts at the post and also in the neighboring towns. The Fort Meade polo team competed against two other teams, including one composed of members of the National Guard's 147th Field Artillery, at a tournament in Pierre that fall. The team returned to the post with the first-place trophy. The sport became so popular among the officers at the post that area ranchers began raising polo ponies for them. Relations between the cavalrymen of the Fourth and the civilian populace generally reflected the same spirit of amiability and cooperation that had marked their earlier associations. But it was not all sweetness and light.[41]

The Ku Klux Klan was active throughout the Black Hills in the mid-1920s, shielding its racism with acts of charity among the poor of the region. Occasionally its members burned crosses on the hills around Sturgis to flaunt the Klan's presence. On the night of 6 August 1924, a fiery cross was seen on a hill between Sturgis and the fort. Acting on their own, soldiers from the fort showed their disdain for the Klan and its hooded followers in rather dramatic fashion. They set up two Browning automatic rifles, taken from the post without authorization, on an opposite hill and poured a heavy barrage of bullets into the burning cross. The noisy staccato of firepower late at night so close to the town aroused the entire populace. Although it was suspected that a large number of soldiers had participated in the firing, only two men were arrested for creating the disturbance. They were turned over to the military authorities, court-martialed for their unauthorized use of the army weapons, and sentenced to six months in the guardhouse with partial loss of pay.[42]

Among the visitors at the post at the time was Jean MacArthur, whose husband, Douglas MacArthur, was soon to become the commanding general of the Department of the Philippines. She spent the summer with friends at the post and returned at Christmas, remaining until the spring of 1926. Although her famous husband never served at Fort Meade, Mrs. MacArthur later recalled with pleasure her happy times at the "charming old fort" and her "delightful friends" in Sturgis.[43]

In 1927, the long-sought goal of Sturgis boosters to have Fort Meade restored as a regimental post was finally realized. The Fourth Cavalry's two squadrons at Fort D. A. Russell, along with headquarters, were ordered to Fort Meade to join the First Squadron. These troops arrived at Fort Meade in late June after an overland march of nearly two weeks. Sixteen carloads of their equipment shipped by rail reached the post ahead of them. After being separated for three years, the entire regiment was together again. It had taken some doing, particularly by the people of Sturgis, whose prosperity depended so greatly on the fort, and by the state's congressional delegation. But the fort was once again fully manned. The much-discussed plan to convert the facility to a veterans' hospital was shelved. It was an idea, though, that would surface again.[44]

★ 15 ★

THE HORSES GO

President Calvin Coolidge vacationed in the Black Hills in the summer of 1927, and Fourth Cavalry troops from Fort Meade were assigned to guard duty. Coolidge established his summer White House at the Game Lodge in Custer State Park, and an executive office was set up for him in the Rapid City High School. At the Game Lodge, Fort Meade soldiers with loaded guns kept the roadway, which arched in front of the lodge porch, closed to all except the president's immediate party. The military guard was composed chiefly of members of Troop C, Fourth Cavalry, although it also included a select group of soldiers from other troops of the regiment.

Among the presidential guard were a number of Indian soldiers. "Quite a change in half a century when white soldiers were sent into this country to protect the whites from the Indians," observed one Hills newspaper. "Now the Indians are sent to protect the President of the United States from the whites."[1] One of these Indian guards was Private Daniel Brokenleg, an Oglala Sioux from Pine Ridge, who was then serving in Troop A. All soldiers guarding the president subsequently received copies of a letter of commendation that Coolidge sent to the regiment and also received special medallions identifying them as members of the Presidential Guard.[2]

Coolidge never visited Fort Meade or Sturgis during his Black Hills stay. But a large number of Sturgis citizens crowded along the tracks to witness the presidential train passing through town en route to the Tri-State Rodeo at Belle Fourche in July. The Coolidge train passed through Sturgis again in August when the president went to Deadwood under military escort for the annual Days of '76 Rodeo.

Coolidge spent three months in the Hills and, accompanied by Fourth Cavalry escorts, made a side trip to Yellowstone National Park. He spent several days fishing and sight-seeing there before returning to the Black Hills. It was from his temporary office in the Rapid City High School that Coolidge announced he would not be a candidate for reelection in 1928. The president was impressed with Colonel Osmun Latrobe, the commander of the Fourth Cavalry, during his Black Hills vacation. On his return to Washington, Coolidge had Latrobe transferred there as his military attaché. Latrobe left for his new assignment after seeing his daughter married at the post chapel.[3]

Troop C returned to Custer State Park in December to dismantle the government airplane hangar that had been erected for President Coolidge's visit. It managed to salvage 90 percent of the hangar lumber for use at the fort. Also in December the Fourth Cavalry provided a chaplain, the band, a bugler, a color guard, and a firing squad for the funeral of a civilian at a church in Whitewood. It was not usual for regular army troops to extend military honors for off-post funerals, but in this case the deceased was John Burri, the former chief trumpeter with the Seventh Cavalry. Burri had taken his discharge at Fort Meade in 1885 and had been a member of the fort's original garrison, so an exception was made for him.[4]

In February 1928 the army reorganized its cavalry regiments to include only a headquarters, a band, a machine-gun troop, and two two-troop squadrons. Troops A and B formed the First Squadron and E and F the Second Squadron of the Fourth Cavalry. Periodic practice marches, some quite extensive, throughout the Hills and surrounding plains broke the monotony of routine garrison life for the Fort Meade soldiers. The Fourth's Troop F, known as the Black Horse Troop because of its matched black horses, became famous throughout the region. It participated in numerous parades and also performed precision riding drills at area celebrations.

The First Squadron's Troop A became the regiment's show unit in 1932 and conducted mounted and dismounted sham battles at area rodeos. These exhibitions were usually accompanied with the martial music of the Fourth Cavalry band. The band, in addition to conducting public concerts at the post, was also a popular attraction at special events throughout the Hills.

In 1933 Fort Meade became the headquarters for the Civilian Conser-

Guard mount, involving the officers of the day, sentinels, and the regimental band, was a daily routine on the parade grounds of Fort Meade each morning. The Fourth Cavalry served two tours of duty at the post—in 1907–11 and 1924–43—longer than any other unit during the sixty-six-year history of the fort. (Courtesy of Old Fort Meade Museum Association.)

vation Corps (ccc) program in South Dakota. Officers of the Fourth Cavalry staffed the Sub-District Headquarters Company at the post, while reserve officers were called up to command the field camps scattered throughout the state. Thirty-three camps were established in South Dakota, and the enrollees worked on a wide range of public-benefit projects. These projects were generally carried out under the supervision of the Forest Service, the Bureau of Reclamation, the Soil Conservation Service (scs), or the Works Progress Administration (wpa).

The first contingent of ccc enrollees arrived at Fort Meade on 29 April 1933, when ninety-four young men reported for service. Formed into Company 789—the first organized in the Black Hills—they were conditioned by army calisthenics and were sent in mid-May to work on Black Hills National Forest projects. By 5 July, more than seventeen hundred enrollees had been processed at the fort for duty at the Black Hills camps. The Sub-District Headquarters Company provided basic support services, including administration, supply, communications, and transportation functions.

At first, the post facilities were used to quarter and feed the enrollees. In 1934, separate facilities were built on the west edge of the military reservation. The site became known as Camp Fechner, named for National CCC Administrator Robert Fechner. Ten barracks buildings, mess halls, bathhouses, and shops were constructed southwest of the fort's main gate by the corpsmen, working under the supervision of civilian instructors. The camp's capacity was two hundred, but many more recruits were processed there before being sent to the field camps. The corpsmen, who ranged in age from seventeen to twenty-one, were paid thirty dollars per month.[5]

Company 2765, a Soil Conservation Service unit, was subsequently assigned to Camp Fechner and engaged in timber stand improvement, road construction, dam building, and soil erosion control work. Educational facilities at the camp included a school building, a library, a reading room, and a carpentry shop equipped with power tools and a diesel tractor for instructional purposes. Such subjects as carpentry, lathework, elementary English, penmanship, reading, high school English, dramatics, business, and job guidance were taught by instructors hired through the WPA.

Corpsmen promoted water conservation practices throughout the region by presenting demonstrations on contouring pasture land to preserve moisture and by constructing stock dams. They also planted trees in shelterbelts to prevent wind erosion. Like many of the cavalrymen at the fort, a number of the CCC youths who had served at Camp Fechner settled in the Black Hills after their enlistments were up.[6]

Fourth Cavalry troops took part in the summer of 1934 in the attempted assault on the world's record for highest balloon flight into the stratosphere. They constructed a tent city at the launch site—a natural bowl, encircled by high cliffs, twelve miles southwest of Rapid City. The deeply sheltered site, selected to avoid surface winds during the inflation of the balloon, was popularly known as the "Stratobowl." It housed support personnel for the flight—a joint venture of the National Geographic Society and the U.S. Army Air Corps—and was occupied by more than one hundred soldiers and civilian technicians. Among the military personnel assigned there, the site became known as the "Stratocamp."[7]

Captain Orvil A. Anderson of the Army Air Corps directed the work of the Fort Meade soldiers. Under his supervision the camp developed from an almost deserted basin into a bustling little village. Within a few weeks it had a drainage system, sawdust-paved streets, a waterworks, two electric lighting systems, a sewage-disposal plant, parking spaces, a traffic officer, a hospital, and an ambulance. There was even a fire department with a full-size hose wagon, two professional firefighters, a dozen fire extinguishers, and a volunteer corps, providing a safeguard against accidents in handling quantities of explosive gas. No smoking was permitted in the neighborhood of the hydrogen cylinders. Three telephone lines and two radio stations kept the Stratocamp in communication with the outside world. A special weather station was set up at the camp through the combined efforts of the U.S. Weather Bureau, the Signal Corps, and the Army Air Corps.

Forty-two army trucks, driven by national guardsmen, hauled fifteen hundred heavy steel cylinders, each containing 190 cubic feet of hydrogen, from the railroad at Rapid City to the Stratocamp. Busloads of troopers from Fort Meade were brought to the camp to help inflate the balloon. Three soldiers were assigned to each of the thirty-six tethering ropes mooring the balloon to the ground. It took six hours to inflate the balloon with more than 210 thousand cubic feet of gas. Although the cavalrymen had no previous experience with balloons, they "quickly mastered the novel job."[8]

Besides Captain Anderson, who was the ground crew officer and alternate pilot, the crew consisted of Major William E. Keppner, the pilot, and Captain Albert W. Stevens, the observer, both also from the U.S. Army Air Corps. They rode in the gondola, dubbed "Explorer," which was packed with scientific instruments. The balloon lifted off from the Stratocamp on the morning of 28 July. It reached an altitude of 60,613 feet—just 624 feet short of the world record for balloons—before a rip in the bag sent it plummeting earthward. The crew members parachuted down some of the instruments that had recorded valuable atmospheric data before themselves bailing out at five thousand feet.

The gondola crashed on a farm near Holdrege, Nebraska, almost ten hours after lift-off. Few instruments were salvaged from the wreckage. The flight was not a total failure, however, in the view of Captain Stevens. He wrote, "The army approved the flight, and lent freely of its men, both from the Air Corps and from the cavalry unit at Fort Meade, and considered that the time spent was valuable training for army personnel."⁹

A second attempt at the altitude record was made from the Stratocamp in November 1935. Again, cavalrymen from Fort Meade were involved in the flight preparations. Troops of the regiment, then commanded by Colonel Robert Beck, were trucked to the camp. Their duties included conducting support activities for the launch, policing the roads, and controlling the crowds of spectators, estimated at over twenty-five thousand, attracted to the scene by the national publicity centered on the event. Two hundred soldiers inflated the balloon, described as "the largest sphere, by far, ever constructed" up to that time, with 3.7 million cubic feet of gas. However, rather than being filled with explosive hydrogen, the balloon was expanded with helium, a nonexplosive, invisible gas. The danger of accidental explosion was thus reduced considerably from the 1934 undertaking.¹⁰

The gondola, named "Explorer II," was 9 feet in diameter and hung 315 feet below the top of the balloon. In addition to carrying a two-man crew, the gondola contained about a ton of delicate instruments for collecting data in the stratosphere. The flight crew this time consisted only of Captains Anderson, the pilot, and Stevens, the observer. The balloon lifted off at 7:01 A.M. on 11 November and rose to an altitude of 72,395 feet, or 13.71 miles—a record that remained unbroken for twenty-two years!

At 3:14 P.M. on the day of the launch, the balloon came to a controlled landing near White Lake, South Dakota, 225 air miles east of Rapid City. Troops from Fort Meade were rushed by truck to the landing site to keep souvenir hunters away from the gondola until it could be removed. Later, John J. Pershing, the retired general of the army and a trustee of the cosponsoring National Geographic Society, presented Captains Anderson and Stevens with the society's highest medal for scientific achievement in recognition of their record-setting flight.

Fourth Cavalry troopers from Fort Meade served as the military escort for another president in the fall of 1936. They guarded President Franklin D. Roosevelt when he came to the Black Hills for the unveiling of the Jefferson figure on Mount Rushmore.

Colonel R. C. Rodgers was named the commander of the Fourth in January 1938. In July 1938, the regiment marched across country to Pole Mountain, Wyoming, to participate in an army exercise that involved several thousand regular army and National Guard troops. The Fourth was assigned to repel a mock enemy invading force during the maneuvers, which were scheduled to last a full week. But a squadron of the regiment ended the drill in one day by riding over a mountain spur thought to be a natural barrier for mounted troops, especially with machine-gun packs, and galloping down on the enemy's camp. As one of the Fourth's officers described the surprise attack: "The wild gallop ended only when the Squadron drew up in front of the invader's command post and captured the commanding general, his entire headquarters staff and the headquarters regiment. That was enough! The umpires gave up on the hopeless task of trying to rearrange the exercise and the whole affair was terminated forthwith. Thus, even at that late date, the old horse cavalry proved its value in combat."[11]

After a few days of rest for man and horse, the Fourth started the long return march to Fort Meade. The distance of about 375 miles was covered in two weeks, and there were several days when the troops did not march. A scout car was sent ahead to announce the pending return of the regiment. Consequently, the troopers were greeted by their wives and children assembled along the road as they reached the fort. The troopers had marched about 850 miles on the round-trip. "That, in my opinion" stated one of the Fourth's officers, "is a considerable horseback ride in any time or country. We shall not see its like again, and a romantic period in military life passed into history, to the profound and lasting regret of all old cavalrymen."[12]

In November 1939 most of the Fourth was trucked to Camp Joseph Robinson, near Little Rock, Arkansas, for a prolonged period of training that would result in a change of structure for the regiment. Left behind, in addition to the families of the departed soldiers, was a force of about 120 caretakers under Major L. A. Pulling. Among them were quartermaster and band detachments and part of the medical corps. The local newspaper, commenting on the move, stated, "Not since the return of the First Squadron to Fort Meade in 1924, and the Second Squadron return in the summer of 1927, has Sturgis been so devoid of soldiers."[13]

The void was partially filled when the limited national emergency program sent the South Dakota National Guard to Fort Meade for five days of intensive training in late November. The guardsmen lived in the barracks of the departed cavalrymen while there. A Reserve Officers Training School was established at Fort Meade the following spring, and this also helped to strengthen the post garrison.

During this period the War Department decided to create a Corps Cavalry Reconnaissance Regiment by converting the Fourth and Sixth cavalries into half-horse, half-mechanized units. One squadron, designated "portee," was made up of three rifle troops equipped with horses for off-road reconnaissance missions and with trucks. The second squadron consisted of two troops equipped with speedy scout cars and one troop of motorcycles. Reorganizing the Fourth, though ridding the command of half its horses, brought an extra four hundred enlisted men into the regiment.[14]

The long absence of the Fourth from Fort Meade again brought rumors in Sturgis that the post was soon to be abandoned. The country was getting closer to direct involvement in the war in Europe, and the mobilization of American manpower through the draft was nearing implementation. Orders were issued shifting troops from small, isolated posts to larger stations at centers of population. The shifts were designed to speed the mobilization and training of the enlarged military establishment. But to the citizens of Sturgis, they portended the eventual abandonment of Fort Meade.

Fort Meade's future became a key issue in the 1940 mayoral campaign in Sturgis. Harry Atwater, out of office since 1938, sought reelection by opposing his Democrat successor, John T. Milek, the publisher of the *Black Hills Press* and former Meade County state's attorney. Atwater, a Republican leader and longtime aggressive promoter of Fort Meade, accused Milek of being unfriendly with the post commander and his staff, thereby jeopardizing the town's economic base. Atwater informed the voters that his goals were to reestablish good relations with the post commander and his staff and to work closely with the South Dakota congressional delegation in securing the return of the Fourth Cavalry to the fort. Further, Atwater promised, he would push for improved housing for post personnel, something that would require "the expenditure of a large amount of money."[15] Atwater won the election and acted promptly to keep his campaign promises. The long-successful policy of getting the government to spend more money on the fort every time its continued existence was threatened was once again brought into play. With Atwater's and the city council's consent, all WPA employees allotted to Sturgis were used on post improvement projects. These included constructing a hay storage shed and retaining walls, renovating twenty-five officers' quarters, veneering many of the buildings with cut stone, hard-surfacing the roads on the post, laying sidewalks, enlarging the water system and target ranges, and erecting fourteen miles of fencing. Photographs of these improvements were sent by the chamber of commerce to the South Dakota congressional delegation for use "in presenting Fort Meade in a favorable light before the military authorities."[16]

The chamber of commerce set up a special Fort Meade Committee headed by Jarvis Davenport, a major supporter of the state's Republican congressional delegation. Senator Chan Gurney and Congressman Francis Case held important positions on the Senate military affairs committee and the House subcommittee for army appropriations. They could be relied on to help keep Fort Meade from being closed. Davenport and Mayor Atwater were the guiding forces in fostering good relations between the town, the fort, and the politicians in Washington.[17]

Congressman Case pointedly reminded the War Department that Fort Meade could handle a considerable increase in troop numbers by utilizing the CCC barracks of Camp Fechner. Senator Gurney also worked behind the scenes in the interests of his Sturgis constituents. He assured Atwater and the Sturgis Chamber of Commerce that there were "no plans to change the home of the Fourth Cavalry from Fort Meade."[18]

After participating in maneuvers along the Arkansas-Texas border that spring, the Fourth Cavalry returned to Fort Meade in late May. The Sturgis depot was swarming with people as the first two troops arrived by special train with the remaining horses after a seven-month absence. Big crowds also lined the streets as the newly mechanized troops, moving overland, hit town a few days later. The Fourth, designated a Corps Cavalry Reconnaissance Regiment, arrived with "40 scout cars, 230 horses, 32 trailers, 97 motorcycles, 47 trucks and 38 radios."[19] The community hosted a well-attended "welcome home" picnic for the soldiers. Colonel and Mrs. Rodgers, along with the regiment's staff officers and their wives, were feted by Sturgis businessmen at a barbecue at Mayor Atwater's cabin on Little Elk Creek. The Sturgis business community, led by Davenport, was acutely aware of Fort Meade's contribution to the town's economy and cooperated fully in events designed to keep the post occupied.[20]

For its part, the Fourth contributed its mechanized units to area celebrations, at which its armored scout cars, mounted with .30- and .50-caliber machine guns, attracted great interest. In addition, the Fourth Cavalry band performed in area parades and also conducted public concerts at the fort. The regiment's officers appeared before local service clubs to explain the role of the mechanized cavalry in the army's program of modernization. One of them, speaking at a Rotary Club meeting, reported, "The necessity of instructing truck drivers, radio operators and motorcycle riders in their new tasks made the Arkansas stay an eventful one."[21]

On 17 July, Fort Meade was almost emptied of troops again as the Fourth traveled to Camp Ripley, Minnesota, for summer maneuvers. About one hundred men were left behind to take delivery of some new tractor units, for hauling horse semitrailers, that had failed to arrive before the troops departed. It was August before the expected tractor units for the Fourth reached the fort. A thirty-three-man detachment convoyed twenty-one of the units, each pulling trailers carrying eight horses, to Camp Ripley. Also taking part in the Fort Ripley maneuvers were South Dakota National Guard troops, including Company F, 109th Engineer Battalion, from Sturgis, which was scheduled for federalization. The maneuvers ended shortly after the arrival of the tractor units, and the regiment returned to Fort Meade.

Returning to the fort with the Fourth were 60 reserve officers assigned to a year of training with the regiment. Housing was needed for them and for the recruits arriving to bring the regiment up to authorized strength. "Fort Meade barracks are now filled to capacity and the overflow of recruits are being housed in tents at the post," the *Tribune* reported in September. Mayor Atwater hastened to Washington, where he sought the aid of the congressional delegation in getting more housing approved for the post. Before returning home, the mayor wired Davenport the good news: orders had been issued for the construction of fifty units of housing for noncommissioned officers at the fort, and barracks would be provided for 906 enlisted men. At full strength, the Fourth would have 68 officers, 1 warrant officer, and 1,284 enlisted men. Its mechanized troops would be equipped with 405 .30- and .50-caliber machine guns, 259 .45-caliber submachine guns, 88 scout cars, and 171 motorcycles.[22] A large tract of pasture land about twenty-five miles northeast of the fort was leased to provide a gunnery range for these troops. Small-arms firing continued at the long-established practice range just north of the fort.

The Fourth lost its commander in September when Colonel Rodgers was transferred to Fort Riley, where he was shortly promoted to brigadier general. He was succeeded by Colonel Howell M. Estes, Sixth Cavalry, who had served with the Fourth twenty-five years earlier. A $325,000 building program at Fort Meade got under way shortly after Colonel Estes arrived in October. It included the construction of a number of "temporary but substantial" structures required for the enlarged garrison. The principal additions were barracks buildings, motor-repair shops, a canteen and telephone building, a warehouse, dayrooms, a recreation hall, a post exchange, a new thirty-bed ward for the hospital, and a permanent ammunition magazine of brick. Five miles of post roads were also hard-surfaced.

Ever alert for opportunities to improve relations between the post and the town, Mayor Atwater appointed an official city committee "to cooperate with Fort Meade." He named Davenport and Erskine, among others, to the committee. Colonel Estes and Senator Gurney were the committee's guests at a dinner in Sturgis in late October. The senator had come to inspect the building activity at Fort Meade and to discuss the need for off-post housing in the community. At the dinner, Colonel Estes apologized for the fact that it was often necessary to send the troops away from Fort Meade for training purposes. He expressed his appreciation of the town's "fine interest" in the post and asked cooperation in providing wholesome recreation for the new recruits who would soon be arriving. Entertaining soldiers from Fort Meade was nothing new for Sturgis; it had been doing so for over sixty years. But the entertainment was not always wholesome.[23]

Early in January 1941 the first group of area inductees under the Selective Service Act arrived at Fort Meade. The six men, inducted at

Rapid City, were soon followed by hundreds of others inducted at Fort Snelling and elsewhere. The area induction center was moved from Rapid City to Sturgis that month when the city offered free quarters in the city auditorium on Main Street for the two officers and three enlisted men assigned to the center. A recreation room for inductees awaiting their assignments was provided across the street from the auditorium. The Sturgis Induction Center lasted only until 1 March; area inductees were thereafter sent to centers at Sioux Falls, Omaha, or Fort Snelling. But the Main Street recreation room was retained for the free use of the troops at Fort Meade, including the newly arriving trainees.

It was also in January 1941 that Sturgis was awarded the $121,000 Fort Meade Defense Housing Project, financing the construction of thirty-five off-post housing units in Sturgis on a cost-plus basis that averaged $3,445 per unit. The land for the housing complex, subsequently named "Comanche Court" for the famous Seventh Cavalry horse formerly at Fort Meade, was purchased from Davenport. Rental of the units was restricted to federal employees, and preference was given to officers assigned to Fort Meade. The project, like the building activity at the fort, provided employment for a large number of area craftsmen and laborers. Occupancy of the units began in mid-June.

At Fort Meade, where the horse and mechanized units of the Fourth were busy breaking in the first inductees, the training activities were further diversified by the formation of a "snow troop." It was composed of one hundred officers and men selected from the various troops. Its members were issued special cold-weather clothing and equipment for "pioneering expeditions," or camp-outs, to training sites in the snow-clad northern Hills.[24]

Lieutenant Colonel John B. Coulter, the Fourth's executive officer since 1938, took over the command of the regiment and the post when Estes was transferred in March. Fort Meade's garrison at the time consisted of the following: Troops A, B, and C, with horses; the mechanized troops, E, F, and G; and headquarters, service, band, quartermaster, Signal Corps, ordnance, medical, and finance detachments. Coulter, who would be promoted to full colonel in July, invited the public to the fort for an Army Day review of the regiment in April. "It was the first time for the public to see

217

the regiment at approximate full strength," noted the *Black Hills Press*. There were then about one thousand men in the garrison. Despite inclement weather, a large crowd of spectators turned out for the review.[25]

In August, the Fourth left for Louisiana to take part in "the biggest-ever war games" held in peacetime. A detachment of post caretakers and inductees was left behind under the command of Lieutenant Colonel Benners B. Vail. While the Fourth was gone, an officer from the remount station at Fort Robinson, Nebraska, came to the Hills to buy horses. "Few people realize the need for horses in the army," he told a reporter. "They have heard so much about mechanization that they sometimes think the horse units are not needed. But each branch is important and one must not be sacrificed for the other."[26] Nevertheless, the day of the horse cavalry at Fort Meade was nearing its end.

Returning to the fort in October, the Fourth was greeted by another rousing homecoming in Sturgis. Main Street was blocked off, and two bands played as the regiment's horses, scout cars, and motorcycles paraded through town. The patriotic fervor of the townspeople who lined the curbs as the cavalcade passed by had been fanned by the draft and the federalization of the local National Guard unit. But the citizens had long considered the troops at Fort Meade as "our boys," and their interest in them was not entirely mercenary. Many close and lasting friendships had developed between the citizenry and the troops, and a number of local girls had married soldiers from the post, as had girls from other Black Hills communities.

Older men who were among the first inductees received at Fort Meade were nearing the completion of their year of training in November and were given early discharges. Replacements for them arrived from Fort Riley. Colonel Coulter, promoted only four months earlier, was unexpectedly elevated to the rank of brigadier general in November and assigned to the Second Cavalry Division at Fort Riley. He was succeeded as the post and regimental commander by Colonel Joseph M. Tully, who had been executive officer of the Third Cavalry Brigade at the Kansas fort.

By month's end, the "Guardhouse Jamboree," an all-soldier talent show, was being presented to packed houses at the post theater and in the Sturgis Auditorium. Featured between acts were numbers by the Fourth Cavalry band and glee club. There was also a contest at the fort early in

December to determine the Fourth's "best bugler." It was won by Private Hobart Reasoner, Troop A, from Ashland, Nebraska. Garrison life, though quickened somewhat by the departure of the older inductees and the arrival of their replacements, was pretty much back to normal.[27]

Making a surprise visit to Fort Meade in the first week of December was the Seventh Corps area commander with his G-2 (intelligence) officer. The Fourth's troopers were immediately sent into the field in the vicinity of the fort for a series of winter exercises under his observation. Consequently, there were not many troops at the post on the historic Sunday morning when the electrifying news came that the Japanese had bombed Pearl Harbor. The declaration of war that quickly followed the attack brought the troops rushing back to the fort.

Although situated far in the country's interior, Fort Meade immediately activated steps to prevent sabotage. A twenty-four-hour guard was placed at the post reservoir and water pumps. The public was warned to stay away from the vicinity of the reservoir and firing ranges as the facility went on a wartime footing. The discharge of twenty-eight-year-old inductees was promptly ended. Those previously released were given the option of returning to their old units at their discharged rank or of being assigned to other units as privates again. Camp Fechner had been scheduled for abandonment, since many of its enrollees had gone into the military service, but was temporarily saved from that fate when its mission was shifted from conservation projects to national defense work at Fort Meade.

Company 2765 members were put to work fencing the military reservation for better security and enlarging its firing ranges. Camp Fechner remained in use until the summer of 1942. Then Captain Ronald Ringsrud, a reservist who had served as the camp commander since 20 January 1941, closed the camp and shipped its equipment to district headquarters in Omaha.[28]

Meanwhile, Rapid City—denied the military post that had become Fort Meade sixty-three years earlier—was chosen as the site for a newly authorized air base. Construction of the Rapid City Air Base, only the state's second military installation, began at a site nine miles east of the city early in 1942.

In April 1942 the horse troops of the Fourth Cavalry were sent to

Omaha to appear in an Army Day parade. Orders had been received for a complete mechanization of the regiment, so en route home, all the cavalrymen except those of Troop C turned in their horses at the Fort Robinson remount station. The *Sturgis Tribune* reported, "Many a tough trooper had a lump in his throat as he turned his horse into the stable for the last time."[29] Troops A and B of the First Squadron were issued M-5 light tanks on their return to Fort Meade. The only horse unit then remaining at the post was Troop C of the First Squadron, and it replaced Troop A as the show unit of the regiment. It gave a demonstration on loading and unloading the horses in their giant semitrailers during an open house at the fort on Memorial Day. The horse troop made its last Black Hills public appearance during a parade in Rapid City on the Fourth of July. "There were few sights as stirring as a troop of cavalry clattering down the pavement," the local newspaper said of the parade.[30]

The mechanized units of the regiment went by train to the South in the summer of 1942 for the big army maneuvers in Arkansas, Tennessee, and Louisiana, but Troop C remained behind. It was redesignated in the fall as the horse troop of the Tenth Cavalry Reconnaissance Squadron and transferred to Camp Hale, Colorado. Thus closed a colorful era in the long and varied history of Dakota's last horse cavalry post. More mounted cavalry units had been stationed at Fort Meade throughout its eventful history than at any other branch of the army. And many of them had played significant roles in the military history of the western frontier.

At Camp Hale, Troop C became part of an army experiment in combining horse and ski troops into a reconnaissance force capable of coordinated winter action in mountainous terrain. When that proved to be impractical, the former Fourth Cavalry soldiers were transferred to Camp Carson, Colorado, and "cadred out" to other units.[31]

It was November before the Fourth Cavalry, part of the newly designated Seventh Service Command, came back to Fort Meade after the wartime maneuvers in the South. Security at the post, as at all U.S. military installations during the war, was tightened. There was much less public access to the post than before the war, although weekly dances were still held. Young women attending the dances were required to have invitation cards to get past the guards at the gate. The cards, which were nontransferable, were placed in the hands of "well-known and competent people" in each of the Hills towns for distribution to those who requested them (Mayor Atwater's wife distributed the invitations in Sturgis). The names of the card purveyors were published in the local newspaper, and only "girls of good reputation and unquestioned loyalty" were encouraged to apply.[32]

The service center established in the post's recreation building, where the dances were held, was staffed by three hostesses and also included a Red Cross office. Music for the dances was provided by the Fourth Cavalry band most of the time, but occasionally the newly established band at the Rapid City Air Base played. In addition, uso and Masonic service centers, which provided recreational activities, including dances, for the soldiers, were opened at Main Street locations in Sturgis. Relations between the community and the post, generally good in peacetime, were even better in wartime. The patriotic fervor that gripped the country at the time was especially pronounced in Sturgis, whose citizens considered Fort Meade's garrison as "family."

Wartime restrictions on publicity about troop movements delayed a public announcement of the Fourth Cavalry's departure from Fort Meade in January 1943 for war service. But, of course, the whole town knew. It was impossible to move an entire mechanized regiment through a small community like Sturgis without attracting attention. It was not until the following week, however, that the local newspapers could report that Fort Meade's garrison was once again down to a caretaker force.

On the eve of the Fourth's departure, Mayor Atwater presented a silver staff ring, used to attach streamers to the regimental colors, on behalf of the citizens of Sturgis at a brief ceremony on the post. After the cavalry-men had reached their destination—the Mojave desert in California, where they underwent a period of intense training before leaving for England—the Sturgis Tribune reported their departure. It also disclosed that the farewell ceremony at the fort had been attended by a representa-tive group of local businessmen. "It is with much regret that Sturgis witnessed the departure of the Fourth Cavalry," the newspaper com-mented. "Their long residence here had made them a part of the commu-nity."[33]

Mayor Atwater's gift to the Fourth from the people of Sturgis was presented in recognition of the fact that the regiment had served longer at

Fort Meade than any other unit. Although the service was not continuous, it amounted to over twenty-two years. The ring presented by Atwater brought the total number of meritorious rings awarded to the regimental staff to sixty-three, including seven earned in Indian campaigns, thirty-seven in Civil War battles, and eighteen in the Philippines. The regiment's reputation was further enhanced by earning eight more rings for distinguished service during World War II, including participation in the invasions of Sicily and Normandy, and additional honors in the Korean and Vietnam conflicts. The regimental motto, *Paratus et Fidelis* (Prepared and Loyal), well describes the Fourth's long record of service to the country at Fort Meade and elsewhere.[34]

THE LAST YEARS

The departure of the Fourth Cavalry marked the end of an era in Fort Meade's history. The regiment was the last of a long string of noted horse cavalry units to serve there, and its mechanization reflected the changes adopted by the army as it waged modern warfare. Appropriately, the unit replacing the Fourth at Fort Meade reflected this "new army." The Eighty-Eighth Glider Infantry Regiment, formerly part of the first airborne battalion to be organized in the United States, reached the post by train in February 1943 from Fort Bragg, North Carolina. Colonel Joseph Hinton was the regimental commander. Members of this regiment were trained to speedily load troops and equipment into cargo aircraft for fast transport to target areas.[1]

The Eighty-Eighth was part of the First Airborne Infantry Brigade, commanded by Brigadier General Leo Donovan, who established his headquarters at Fort Meade. His command also included glider and parachute troops stationed at Alliance, Nebraska. "He will do considerable commuting between here and Alliance," the *Tribune* said of Donovan.[2] The number of men in Donovan's command at Fort Meade varied from twelve hundred to fifteen hundred and were trained in infantry tactics including forced night marches, although they also had mock gliders and a tower north of the fort for practice parachute drops. The paratroopers at Fort Meade were taken to Alliance for their jump training, and the glider pilots received their flight training there as well.

In the summer of 1943 the brigade spent ten days in combined maneuvers at Fort Robinson. The Fort Meade garrison was enlarged in July when a detachment of thirty-six Women's Army Corps (WAC) volunteers arrived from Fort Oglethorpe, Georgia. In addition to clerical and stenographic chores, the women soldiers were assigned as chauffeurs and truck drivers and in radio repair. They were also welcomed participants at the dances held every Wednesday and Sunday night on the post, with music provided by the Eighty-Eighth's band.

The commanding general of an airborne infantry command being assembled at Camp McCall, North Carolina, came to Fort Meade in October to determine the Eighty-Eighth's combat readiness. He reviewed the troops on parade and announced that they would soon leave the fort to become part of his command. The Eighty-Eighth, under Donovan, left Fort Meade in November and trained at Camp McCall before going to England to take part in the Normandy invasion.

The only companies remaining at Fort Meade after the departure of the glider troops were the 1744th Service Command Unit, which constituted the station complement (caretakers); the Signal Corps detachment, which operated the Post Photo Laboratory; the WAC detachment; and the 620th Engineer General Service Company, which occupied part of abandoned Camp Fechner. Although few people in the Black Hills knew it, the 620th was unique. There were only three outfits like it in the Seventh Service Command and very few others of similar character in the entire army.

Formed under a confidential War Department order issued 3 October 1942, the 620th was activated at Fort Meade on 1 November of that year. What made the company unique was that, except for its officers and a cadre of noncommissioned officers, it was filled entirely with men who were suspected of subversive activity or disloyalty.[3] With an authorized strength of five officers and 127 enlisted men, the 620th's ranks were filled with draftees, many of them aliens, whose loyalty to the United States was considered questionable. These men were assigned, through the Military Intelligence Service of the War Department's general staff in Washington, from army units all over the country. Other "special" organizations—like the 620th—within the Seventh Service Command were stationed at Fort Leonard Wood, Missouri, and Camp Carson, Colorado.

Hard evidence of subversion or disloyalty was not necessary for an assignment to one of these special units. Mere suspicion was sufficient. All members of these companies had two things in common: "There was no proof that they had committed any subversive acts after their induction, for if they had they would have been court-martialed; and, second, all of them had intelligence field files alleging that they said or did something subversive prior to their induction."[4] Most of the men assigned to these organizations were considered nonconformists, or men who refused to fight against any of the nations at war with the United States. They were drafted despite their political views about the war. It was feared that exempting them would provide a convenient excuse for avoiding wartime service. So although these men were accepted into the service, the army decided it would be best to segregate them, keep them within the continental United States, and assign them duties of a harmless character.

At Fort Meade, members of the 620th made camouflage nets, planted trees, painted barracks, collected garbage, and performed similar menial duties. All their work projects were nonsensitive in nature, and they received little military training. Moreover, they were issued no arms. The men of the 620th, like all other soldiers stationed at Fort Meade, were permitted to leave the post during their off-duty hours. Unlike the rest of the garrison, which was garbed in green fatigues, members of the 620th wore blue fatigues like those issued to prisoners of war but without the letters POW on the backs of their shirts. When they were in their dress uniforms, however, there was nothing to distinguish them from the rest of the garrison. So very few outside the army knew of their special status.

In the summer of 1943, the government suspected that something sinister was afoot when a group of men from the 620th rented a cabin in Spearfish Canyon. It had the cabin tapped in the expectation that some sort of sabotage or espionage was being planned. The summer-long surveillance, however, failed to produce any incriminating evidence against members of the company. Other members of the 620th banded together to rent an apartment in Deadwood, where they enjoyed the hospitality of that wide-open town during their off-duty hours. Most members of the company were native-born American citizens of foreign descent. They were primarily of German or Italian origin, although there was also a smattering of Danes, Finns, Hungarians, Yugoslavians, and White Russians in the company.

There was little work on the post for the 620th after the glider troopers left. So the next month the novel company was transferred to Camp Hale. The citizens of Sturgis, had they known the 620th was filled with soldiers the army considered undesirables, would have been shocked, since they had treated these men as freely and as generously as they had the other soldiers from the fort. Ironically, aside from the station complement, the

620th was the last company-sized army unit stationed at Fort Meade before the post's abandonment as a military installation. It was a strange ending for a garrison that had included many of the army's most highly regarded and decorated outfits during its long years of service.[5]

After the departure of the 620th from Fort Meade, the Sturgis Chamber of Commerce launched another aggressive campaign for new troops. It hired R. B. (Dick) Williams, a teacher in the local school system since 1932, as its first full-time secretary for the summer months. Williams, an energetic go-getter with a knack for inspiring patriotism and arousing enthusiasm for local history, knew where to go for help. He appealed to the South Dakota congressional delegation, which had done so much in keeping the post garrisoned in the past. But this time the army reported it had no units it could assign to Fort Meade for training. "Trained men were going overseas," Congressman Case reported. "To save manpower, new men were assigned to large divisional centers."[6] The War Department suggested that Fort Meade be turned over to the Veterans Administration (VA) for hospital and domiciliary purposes—the same proposal it had thwarted in the 1920s when the Reverend Mr. Erskine had suggested it.

But conditions had changed, and the War Department, more concerned with getting masses of men into combat than operating small training posts, was willing to abandon Fort Meade. Case was skeptical about the prospects for getting another VA hospital for South Dakota, however, since one was already located at Hot Springs in the southern Black Hills and another had been authorized for Sioux Falls in the eastern part of the state. It was at this crucial time that the VA came to Congress with a request for thirty-six million dollars for the construction of nine special hospitals throughout the country for the care of veterans. There was a growing need, the VA asserted, for hospitals for neuropsychiatric patients. "These are not mental cases," Case reported. "They are nervous cases produced by modern war. Many of them recover rapidly under proper environment. It is considered bad treatment to mix them with regular hospital or domiciliary cases."[7]

Case, ever alert to opportunities for bringing federal projects into his district, asked the VA administrator to consider Fort Meade for conversion to one of these special hospitals. An inspector was sent to Fort Meade from the VA hospital at Sheridan, Wyoming, to check out the facilities of the virtually empty army post. He reported that they were ideal for the suggested purpose. The VA administrator notified Case he would make a formal application for the transfer of the facility from the War Department to his agency, providing the plan met the approval of the local community. Case relayed the information to Sturgis, and Williams organized a community meeting of businessmen and city, county, and school officials and other townspeople to discuss the proposal.

On 10 February 1944 the *Tribune* noted, "Once again Representative Case has come through for South Dakota, the Black Hills and especially for our little town of Sturgis." Reporting on the community meeting, it disclosed those in attendance had been unanimous in their support of the hospital proposal. "This change would be very beneficial to Sturgis," the newspaper asserted. "It would assure permanent operation of Fort Meade."[8] The newspaper listed the post's location and climate and the existence of barracks that could be converted into hospital wards and staff quarters as factors in favor of the conversion, and it described the abandoned fort as "particularly suited to occupational therapy such as gardening, dairying, etc."[9]

In March, the VA certified to the surgeon general that Fort Meade was suitable for the rehabilitation of veterans requiring psychiatric treatment. The War Department declared the fort surplus, and the secretary of war ordered its transfer before 15 April. The small force of army caretakers remaining at the post was then reassigned by the Seventh Service Command headquarters in Omaha. Before departing, Colonel Polk J. Atkinson, the post commander, presented citations of meritorious service to civilian War Department employees with the longest service. One of them was John J. Keysor, who had served in the Eighth Cavalry from 1892 to 1898. He had joined the civilian force as a night watchman in 1917, and since 1918 he had been a clerk in the quartermaster's office.[10]

President Roosevelt approved the interagency transfer in May, and it was carried out under the provisions of an act of Congress adopted on 22 June 1944. Case guided the legislation through the House, and Gurney through the Senate, and it was implemented 11 September. Case also saw to it that $300,000 was appropriated for the conversion project. It was expected the converted 725-bed hospital would be filled to capacity in five or six months. James E. McMurrer was named as the acting hospital manager, and Grover H. Dodd was hired to supervise the conversion building activity. Because of the shortage of skilled civilian craftsmen due to the war, however, the conversion work did not get under way until 13 October. The small number of civilian workers that McMurrer and Dodd were able to hire in the area was insufficient to move the conversion project along as fast as desired. Consequently, in November, over one hundred German prisoners of war from Fort Robinson were brought to Fort Meade to establish a branch camp and help with the conversion.

The POWs, most of them former members of the German army's elite Afrika Korps, were guarded by a detachment of American soldiers from the main camp at Fort Robinson, commanded by Captain Henry N. Sawicki. At Fort Robinson, which had received its first German POWs in June 1943, the prisoners had been principally engaged in helping farmers harvest their crops. Employers of POW labor were required to pay the government the same rate per unit of work as civilian labor would have cost had it been available.

In November 1944, when the Fort Meade POW branch camp was established, there were seventy-four thousand POWs working on agricultural projects throughout the United States. Another seventy thousand were engaged in an assortment of menial chores, such as collecting garbage on military reservations. Major General C. H. Danielson, commanding the Seventh Service Command, had approved the establishment of the branch camp at Fort Meade. He was proud of the work the POWs in the camps within his command had accomplished. He wrote: "Last year the prisoners there harvested 3,685 acres of beets—enough to supply sugar to a city of one million for one year. In addition, they harvested 141,000 bushels of potatoes, 15,000 bushels of small grain and other crops for a total marketable value of $1,092,945. For this labor, the employees paid the United States more than $50,000. As a matter of fact, I can safely say that from an overall viewpoint, our prisoner troubles have been infinitesimal in comparison to the amount of useful work obtained."[11]

Thus, within six months after being abandoned as a military post, Fort Meade was again home to a detachment of U.S. troops—this time as security guards for the German POWs. The army's reoccupation of the fort was carried out under a contract with the VA. Two barracks buildings at the west end of the fort were enclosed by a fence as a compound for the prisoners, who were put to work on the conversion projects; for his labor, each prisoner was paid eighty cents a day in canteen coupons. These were used to buy such "extras" as tobacco, soap, writing paper, beer, and soft drinks. The arrangement was not without controversy, however. Some of the civilian laborers on the project resented working side by side with POWs and walked off their jobs.[12]

The issue came to a head when several civilian workers who had been fired complained that the POWs had taken their jobs. A six-man committee, which included Dick Williams of the chamber of commerce and Frank Hunn, the publisher of the *Sturgis Tribune,* was appointed to investigate the complaints. A meeting was held in the city auditorium with the VA officials and the civilian workers who either had been fired or had quit. Dodd claimed the fired workers had been discharged for failing to do "a day's work for a day's pay." McMurrer explained, "There is still plenty of work for anyone who wants to do a day's work." He reported that some men had applied for skilled work for which they were not qualified and had refused to take other work. Plasterers and sheet metal workers, he said, were especially needed.[13]

The committee sided with the hospital officials and determined that the prisoners had to be used or the project would be unacceptably delayed. It extracted a pledge from the VA officials that the prisoners would be replaced as fast as the Sturgis Manpower Commission could provide the skilled workers needed. Meanwhile, the civilian laborers were reminded that they "owed loyalty to this vital project and should produce a day's work for a day's pay." Hunn, reporting the committee's findings, editorialized: "Men who work on the project have personally told me they don't like to work with PWs [*sic*], that if they could be kept in separate groups, it would be okay, but they [the prisoners] are working all over the project. In justice to the management, who say this is necessary because of lack of free labor, we believe that if enough labor were available these PWs would be absolutely kept in groups away from our labor. After all, they are our enemies."[14]

Besides doing general carpentry work, the German prisoners performed masonry and bricklaying tasks on the conversion project. They also laid some sidewalks in front of the quarters buildings and left a lasting reminder of their presence by inscribing "POW 1944" in the cement on a number of walks. There was no further trouble between the prisoners and the civilian laborers, but the two groups were kept apart as much as work conditions permitted. The prisoners never left the post unless sent to town to pick up supplies under armed guard. So there was very little contact between them and the townspeople. At Christmas, the first at Fort Meade under VA ownership, a special mass at the chapel attracted thirty-six prisoners. The POW chorus also sang at the service.

In February 1945, the *Tribune* reported that "a miracle of reconstruction" had been accomplished by the workers at the fort under McMurrer and Dodd.[15] The conversion of the buildings was almost complete, and the hiring of hospital attendants was well under way. The assignment of the medical staff awaited the selection of an army physician as manager of the new hospital. Formal dedication of the hospital was held during observance of Army Day on 6 April, with Williams serving as the master of ceremonies. It was a historic occasion in the long life of the former frontier military post, and Williams went all out in promoting it.[16]

The chamber secretary, mindful of the historical significance of the event, arranged for Charles Windolph of Lead to be a guest of honor on the speaker's platform. Windolph, who had retired from the Seventh Cavalry at Fort Meade, was then ninety-four. He sat among the platform dignitaries and proudly wore the Medal of Honor he had earned at the Little Bighorn in 1876.

Congressman Case reviewed the military history of the fort and the events leading up to its transfer to the VA. He could speak with authority on both subjects. His father had pastored the Methodist church in Sturgis when the congressman was a teenager, and the family had lived on a relinquished homestead north of Bear Butte. So Case had firsthand knowledge of the fort's military period. And, of course, he had worked hard to persuade the army to regarrison the post when it had earlier been stripped of troops. He had also been an important intermediary in effecting the transfer of the facility from the War Department to the VA.[17]

The Army Day address was given by Colonel E. V. Allen of the Seventh Service Command's medical staff. He announced that Lieutenant Colonel Peter A. Peffer, U.S. Army Medical Corps, had been selected as the manager of the hospital. Colonel Carl A. Neeves formally accepted the facility on behalf of the VA. Erskine, the reverend who had originally proposed a

Sergeant Charles Windolph at the age of ninety-four. He is wearing the Purple Heart and the congressional Medal of Honor he earned at the Battle of the Little Bighorn when Lieutenant Colonel George Armstrong Custer (whose photograph he holds) led the Seventh Cavalry against the Sioux and Cheyenne in 1876. Windolph, who was in Captain Frederick Benteen's battalion, was a German immigrant who had joined the Seventh in 1871. He was discharged at Fort Meade in 1883, worked as a harness maker for the Homestake Gold Mine at Lead, S.D., until his retirement, and died 11 March 1950 at the age of ninety-nine. He is buried in the Black Hills National Cemetery on the old Fort Meade military reservation. (Courtesy of Old Fort Meade Museum Association.)

hospital role for Fort Meade, also participated in the dedication program. His plan for utilizing the fort's facilities had finally become reality. Another special guest was Davenport, who had been selected as "Man of the Year" in Sturgis for his work in promoting the conversion of the fort to a VA hospital.[18]

Hunn, the publisher of the *Tribune,* supplemented his report on the dedication with a nostalgic editorial headlined "The Curtain Comes Down."

While thousands of persons watched, and the band played The Star Spangled Banner, last Friday afternoon, Old Glory was run to the top of the flag pole at Fort Meade Hospital, ringing down the last chapter of Historic Fort Meade as a military post, home of some of the finest fighting units of the armed forces. Fort Meade has stood the test of time, but it took the advanced methods of training troops in large units to change the future of the fort.

No more will Fort Meade resound to the marching of many soldiers, or the galloping of the Black Horse cavalry, but the post will in the future serve even a greater need, that of restoring health and vigor to the sons of this area, who have every right to the best climate and facilities the nation has to offer. The Curtain Goes Down on Old Ft. Meade but it rises again to even greater glory![19]

Lieutenant Colonel Peffer arrived at Fort Meade late in April to assume the duties of hospital manager. The hospital received its first patients in May, when five men were transferred from Fort Snelling. They were soon followed by ninety-six more from St. Cloud, Minnesota.

On 23 May, with the war in Europe ended, the army contracted with the VA to reoccupy part of the former post for the purpose of establishing another German POW branch camp at the abandoned Camp Fechner. Additional prisoners were brought from the base camp at Fort Robinson at the request of the Western South Dakota Farm Labor Association. This organization, headquartered at Belle Fourche, had been unable to provide the labor needed to harvest the beet crop on the Belle Fourche Irrigation District. The War Manpower Commission was also unable to fill the need. So General Danielson in Omaha approved the use of more POWs until the end of the harvest in October.[20] Prisoners in the original camp at Fort Meade continued working on hospital projects: renovating wards, collecting garbage, and operating a laundry for the Rapid City Air Base as well as for themselves. Prisoners from the second camp were trucked from Fort Meade to the beet fields of the irrigation district. This proved to be a slow, costly procedure, however, and it was soon apparent that many of the beets would go unharvested unless additional labor was secured. So a subcamp of German POWs was established later in the summer at a former CCC camp at Orman Dam, east of Belle Fourche. It too was staffed with prisoners and guards from Fort Robinson. In addition to harvesting beets, some of the prisoners worked at gathering cucumbers for the pickle plant at Vale.[21]

In October, a month after World War II ended with V-J Day, the Seventh Service Command had 109 POWs at Camp No. 1 at Fort Meade, 240 at Camp No. 2 at the fort, and 214 at Belle Fourche. The subcamp was closed later that month, and Camp No. 2 at Fort Meade closed in November. The prisoners, except for those in Camp No. 1, were returned to Nebraska.[22] Meanwhile, former members of the "Fighting Fourth Cavalry," back from compiling an outstanding combat record in the European theater, held their first postwar reunion at the Fruth Hotel in Sturgis.

POW Camp No. 1 at Fort Meade was down to sixty-one prisoners by December. The prisoners participated in Christmas and New Year's programs at the hospital that winter, with hopes of soon being repatriated to Germany. They formed singing groups and performed at the Fort Meade chapel over the holidays. The special services also featured the girls' choir from Erskine's First Presbyterian Church in Sturgis. In addition to singing at the services, the girls went caroling through the hospital and outside the POW compound.[23]

Erskine, who had been conducting weekly worship services at the hospital since the first patients had arrived the previous summer, also ministered to the Germans. In appreciation, the prisoners selected an English-speaking spokesman to present Erskine with a gift one of them had made, a model ship inside a bottle ten inches long. Before being returned to Fort Robinson in January for shipment back to Germany, the prisoners had the same spokesman write a letter to the editor of the *Tribune* on their behalf. It stated, "No place have we ever lived where we found more hospitable and friendly people to us than are the people of Sturgis and the Black Hills."[24] Another of the prisoners, in letters written to his civilian work supervisor after being repatriated home, also expressed appreciation for the humane treatment received at Fort Meade.[25]

Hunn's earlier blunt reminder that the prisoners were "our enemies" was quickly forgotten during the jubilation over the war's end. Nevertheless, there were complaints by the civilian populace that the German POWs had been "pampered" in comparison with the treatment of American POWs in Nazi prison camps.[26] There is no evidence that the prisoners at Fort Meade were either pampered or harshly treated.

Congressman Case was back in Sturgis in January and spoke to the Rotary Club about the changes the war had wrought at the historic frontier military post. "If sometimes people here yearn for the Fourth Cavalry at Fort Meade," he said, "they should remember that the facility is now doing a good job in bringing back to health those who have given so much."[27] But memories of the fort's sixty-six years as an active military establishment would not soon fade away. There were just too many people still around, including a large number of the fort's former soldiers and civilian employees, determined to keep that from happening.

Fort Meade, the last of South Dakota's frontier posts, had gained a special place in the hearts of the people of the Black Hills—and appropriately so, for its turbulent history is also the story of the discovery, settlement, and progress of the region. In fact, during its sixty-six years as an active military installation, the fort played a significant role in bringing these developments to fruition.

EPILOGUE

The guards who escorted the last German POWs back to Fort Robinson in January 1946 were the last regular army soldiers to serve at Fort Meade. Their departure did not signal an end to the use of the old fort for military purposes, however, but merely a long hiatus.

The army closed the post cemetery when it turned Fort Meade over to the VA in 1944. The last burials had been made there the previous year. The cemetery came under the jurisdiction of the Bureau of Land Management in 1956 when the bureau acquired all of the old military reservation except for seven hundred acres retained by the VA for hospital purposes. The bureau developed wildlife habitat, livestock grazing, and recreation units on the acreage surrounding the cemetery.[1]

The Black Hills National Cemetery was created on the western edge of the old military reserve and opened in September 1948. It is situated in a picturesque valley fronted by a pass leading to the open prairies beyond the rocky outer rim of the Hills and backed by forested inner ridges. The beauty of the site gives the cemetery its sobriquet as "The Arlington of the West." Thirty-seven of the cemetery's 105 acres were developed for grave sites, and the remainder was retained for future expansion. In 1972, nearly thirty years after its closing, the old post cemetery was designated a national cemetery. It remained closed to new burials and was attached to the Black Hills National Cemetery for administrative and maintenance purposes.[2]

The VA used the converted Fort Meade barracks as hospital wards until completing an extensive modernization program in 1967. Three large, modern hospital buildings, completed in 1959, 1960, and 1966, were built behind the line of former barracks north of the parade grounds. Patients were gradually transferred until the barracks buildings were entirely vacated. In 1971, the VA declared the vacated buildings an economic burden because of maintenance costs. Several of the old buildings, including a stable and one of the two-story stone barracks, were torn down before action could be taken to prevent further demolition. The Old Fort Meade Museum and Historical Research Association, founded in 1964 to preserve the fort's rich historical heritage, intervened to stop the destruction.[3]

The association, organized as a South Dakota nonprofit corporation, was formed by area citizens interested in history. R. B. (Dick) Williams, the veteran Sturgis school principal and former chamber of commerce secretary, became its first president. Among active members were several former Fourth Cavalry soldiers who had become civilian employees at the VA hospital after the war. Operating on membership dues and donations, the group leased from the VA a former noncommissioned officers quarters building near the old main gate and converted it into a military museum. The group spearheaded a campaign to have Fort Meade placed on the National Registry of Historic Places and received the listing in 1971. This new status halted the VA's demolition program.[4]

The association's museum, featuring exhibits from the fort's military period, quickly outgrew its original building. A lease was negotiated with the VA to move the museum into the first floor and the basement of the old headquarters building fronting the parade grounds. The VA had retained the building because its second-floor assembly hall was useful for staff conferences and lectures.

In September 1973, the hospital became the Fort Meade Veterans Administration Medical Center. The name change reflected a change in mission from a strictly neuropsychiatric facility to a general medical and surgical installation serving veterans in the northern plains states. The transformation of the fort into a VA medical center had a far greater economic impact on Sturgis and the surrounding area than the old army post ever did. By 1990, for instance, the hospital's annual budget totaled twenty-five million dollars, including over eighteen million dollars in employee wages.[5]

Williams and other officers of the association were instrumental in promoting the beneficial use of the old army buildings at the fort by helping to find lessees for them. The state leased one of the buildings for storage of surplus equipment and for a time also operated the State Archeological Center there. The Sturgis School District acquired a tract of the old military reserve land north of the hospital and built a new high school, leasing one of the former barracks for vocational education classes. The National Guard, bringing a troop presence back to the fort, established the South Dakota Military Academy there in 1986 for training officers and noncommissioned officers and set up aviation and unit safety schools, specialized courses in winter survival, and nuclear, biological, and chemical defense training. "Expansion of programs will come as we continue to update facilities," South Dakota's adjutant general has reported. "We feel that Fort Meade will some day evolve into a National Guard Bureau Regional Training Center."[6]

In the summer of 1989 the South Dakota National Guard's 147th Army Band from Mitchell came to Fort Meade to play in the review of military academy graduates. A special attraction of the public ceremony, conducted in observance of the centennial of statehood for South and North Dakota, was the appearance of a mounted cavalry unit in the uniform of the frontier era.[7] As the band played "Garry Owen" and as the soldiers, mounted and afoot, marched by, those in attendance might have closed their eyes and been carried back in history to the post's earlier days, to the Seventh Cavalry band playing "Garry Owen" as the regiment marched in review . . . the sound of horses' hooves pounding across the parade grounds as the cavalrymen reined them through precision drills . . . the Black Horse troopers leaping their mounts through flaming hoops at exhibitions . . . Major Reno's ill-fated knock on the window to attract the attention of the lovely Ella . . . the guardhouse cell door closing on Plenty Horses . . . the beat of the drums as the "absentee Utes" performed the Bear Dance . . . the staccato of machine guns as Fort Meade soldiers zeroed in on the flaming Ku Klux Klan crosses above Sturgis . . . the shot that killed the soldier at Poker Alice's place . . . the roar of the motorcycles as horse troops of the Fourth Cavalry became mechanized . . . the singing of the Christmas carolers outside the German POW compound . . . the strains of "The Star-Spangled Banner" being played for the first time at a military retreat ceremony. These sounds might have conjured up visions of Fort Meade's long and colorful history. Much of that history is preserved

237

at the Old Fort Meade Museum, situated within the shadow of nearby Bear Butte, witness to Fort Meade's dramatic evolution from a frontier peace-keeping post to a modern medical center and training ground for space-age military units. Bear Butte still dominates the landscape as impressively as when Lieutenant Warren came down from the summit in 1857 and proposed the establishment of a post in the valley below.

APPENDIX: ROSTER OF POSTS

Roster of Posts in the Department of Dakota and the Units Stationed at the Posts at the Time of Fort Meade's Establishment in 1878.

ROSTER OF TROOPS
Independent Posts

Stations:

Fort Sisseton, Dak. (1864–89)
Lt. Col. C. C. Gilbert, Hqs., 7th Inf., cmdg.
Hqs., B, C, E, F, H, K, 7th Inf.

Fort Sisseton, Dak. (1864–89)
Capt. C. E. Bennett, F, 17th Inf., cmdg.
A, F, 17th Inf., two Indian scouts

Fort Totten, Dak. (1867–90)
Capt. Malcolm McArthur, C, 17th Inf., cmdg.
C, F, 7th Cav., C, 17th Inf.

Fort Pembina, Dak. (1870–95)
Capt. Ed. Collins, E, 17th Inf., cmdg.
E, K, 17th Inf.

Fort Buford, Dak. (1866–95)
Lt. Col. Daniel Huston, Jr., Hqs., 6th Inf., cmdg.
Hqs., C, D, E, F, G, I, 6th Inf., six Indian scouts

New post near Bear Butte, Dak. (Fort Meade, 1878–1944)
Maj. H. M. Lazelle, 1st Inf., cmdg.
E, M, 7th Cav., F, K, 1st Inf.

Middle District

Fort Abraham Lincoln, Dak. (1872–91)
Maj. R.E.A. Croften, 17th Inf., cmdg. post and Middle District.
Hqs., A, G, H, L, 7th Cav., B, 6th Inf., D, G, 17th Inf., four Indian scouts

Fort Rice, Dak. (1864–78)
Capt. John S. Poland, A, 6th Inf., cmdg.
A, 6th Inf., two Indian scouts

Fort Stevenson, Dak. (1867–83)
Maj. O. H. Moore, 6th Inf., cmdg.
H, K, 6th Inf., three Indian scouts

Standing Rock Agency, Dak. (Fort Yates, 1874–1903)
Capt. E. P. Pearson, B, 17th Inf., cmdg.
Hqs., B, H, I, 17th Inf., B, D, I, K, 7th Cav., one 11th Inf. officer attached, eight Indian scouts

Southern District

Cheyenne River Agency, Dak. (Fort Bennett, 1870–91)
Col. W. H. Wood, 11th Inf., cmdg. post and Southern District.
Hqs., A, D, E, G, I, K, 11th Inf., ten Indian scouts

Fort Randall, Dak. (1856–92)
Lt. Col. Pinkney Lugenbeel, 1st Inf., cmdg.
Hqs., A, C, E, I, 1st Inf.

Fort Sully, Dak. (1863–94)
Capt. T. M. Tolman, H, 1st Inf., cmdg.
D, H, 1st Inf., three Indian scouts

Lower Brulé Agency, Dak. (Fort Hale, 1870–84)
Capt. R. E. Johnson, B, 1st Inf., cmdg.
B, G, 1st Inf.

Red Cloud Agency, Dak.
Capt. Peter D. Vroom, Jr., L, 3rd Cav., cmdg.
E, L, 3rd Cav., fifteen Indian scouts

Spotted Tail Agency, Dak.
1st Lt. J. J. O'Connell, 1st Inf., attached, in charge of station.
H, M, 3rd Cav., one 1st Inf. officer attached, fifteen Indian scouts

District of Montana

Fort Shaw, Mont. (1867–91)
Lt. Col. John R. Brooke, 3rd Inf., cmdg. post and District of Montana.
Hqs, C, E, F, G, 3rd Inf., A, I, 7th Inf.

Fort Benton, Mont. (1869–81)
1st Lt. William Krause, A, 3rd Inf., cmdg.
A, 3rd Inf.

Fort Ellis, Mont. (1867–86)
Maj. J. S. Brisbin, 2nd Cav., cmdg.
F, H, K, L, 2nd Cav., G, 7th Inf.

Camp Baker, Mont. (subcamp of Fort Ellis, later renamed Fort Logan, 1869–80)
Maj. Guido Ilges, 7th Inf., cmdg.
D, 7th Inf., K, 3rd Inf.

Fort Missoula, Mont. (1877–1946)
Maj. Henry L. Chipman, 3rd Inf., cmdg.
B, D, H, I, 3rd Inf.

District of the Yellowstone

Fort Keogh, Mont. (1876–1908)
Col. N. A. Miles, 5th Inf., cmdg. District of the Yellowstone; Lt. Col. J.N.G. Whisler, Hqs., 5th Inf., cmdg. post.
Hqs., A, B, C, D, E, F, G, H, I, K, 5th Inf., A, B, E, I, 2nd Cav., twenty Indian scouts

Fort Custer, Mont. (1877–98)
Lt. Col. G. P. Buell, 11th Inf., cmdg.
B, C, F, H, 11th Inf., Hqs., C, D, G, M, 2nd Cav., ten Indian scouts

Source: *Index to the Executive Documents of the House of Representatives for the Third Session of the Forty-Fifth Congress 1878–79 in 18 Volumes, Volume II, 74–79: Report of the Secretary of War* (Washington, D.C., 1879)

NOTES

CHAPTER 1

1. Lieutenant Gouverneur Kemble Warren, *Preliminary Report of Explorations in Nebraska and Dakota in the Years 1855–56–57* (Washington, D.C., 1857), 51–54. Also see G. K. Warren, "Explorations in Nebraska and Dakota," *South Dakota Historical Collections* 11 (1922): 217.

2. Warren, *Preliminary Report,* 27–28.

3. George W. Kingsbury, *History of Dakota Territory,* 2 vols. (Chicago: S. J. Clarke Publishing Co., 1915), 1:452; Samuel E. Dicks, "A Territory with Many Flags," in *Dakota Panorama,* ed. J. Leonard Jennewein and Jane Boorman (Pierre, S.D.: Dakota Territory Centennial Commission, 1961), 73.

4. Kingsbury, *History of Dakota Territory* 1:452, 866.

5. Don C. Clowser, *Dakota Indian Treaties: From Nomad to Reservation* (Deadwood, S.D.: By the author, 1974), 133, 135–46.

6. U.S. Congress, Senate, Legislative Assembly of Dakota Territory, *Memorial Asking for a Scientific Exploration of That Territory,* 42d Cong., 3d sess., 1872–73, S. Misc. Doc. 45, 1–3; Watson Parker, *Gold in the Black Hills* (Norman: University of Oklahoma Press, 1966), 17, 23.

7. Paul Andrew Hutton, *Phil Sheridan and His Army* (Lincoln: University of Nebraska Press, 1986), 167; Kingsbury, *History of Dakota Territory* 1:874–75.

8. Kingsbury, *History of Dakota Territory* 1:875, 917–18.

9. "Report of Lieutenant General P. H. Sheridan," *Annual Report of the Secretary of War (1873),* 3 vols. (Washington, D.C., 1873), 1:39–42; Hutton, *Sheridan and His Army,* 150–51.

10. Lawrence A. Frost, ed., *With Custer in '74: James Calhoun's Diary of the Black Hills Expedition* (Provo, Utah: Brigham University Press, 1979), 103; Sheridan to Sherman, 1 May 1874, in Letters Received by the Office of the Adjutant General (main series), 1871–85 (hereafter cited as Letters Received), Records of the Adjutant General's Office, Record Group 94, National Archives, Washington, D.C. (hereafter cited as Records, RG 94).

11. U.S. Congress, Senate, *Report on the Reconnaissance to the Black Hills by Captain William Ludlow, Corps of Engineers, USA, with Troops under the Command of Lieutenant Colonel George A. Custer, 7th Cavalry, July and August 1874*, 43d Cong., 2d sess., 1875, S. Exec. Doc. 32, 60; "Dispatch of George A. Custer to Assistant Adjutant General, Department of Dakota, July 15, 1874," George A. Custer's Order and Dispatch Book, 29–30, ms. 128, Western Americana Collection, Yale University Library, New Haven, Conn.; Robert M. Utley, *Frontier Regulars: The United States Army and the Indian, 1866–1891* (New York: Macmillan Publishing Co., 1973), 244.

12. Lieutenant General Philip H. Sheridan, *Record of Engagements with Hostile Indians within the Military Division of the Missouri, from 1868 to 1882* (Washington, D.C., 1881), 38–39.

13. Sherman and Terry quoted in Frost, *With Custer in '74*, 117, 119; Kingsbury, *History of Dakota Territory* 1:915, quoting Red Cloud.

14. Annie Tallent, *The Black Hills; or, Last Hunting Ground of the Dakotahs* (1899; reprint, Sioux Falls, S.D.: Brevet Press, 1974), 38, 61. Mrs. David G. (Annie) Tallent was in the party evicted from the French Creek stockade in 1875 and became known as the first white woman to enter the Black Hills. She returned with her husband and son after the Hills were opened to lawful settlement and died at the home of her son in Sturgis in 1901.

15. *Message from the President of the United States Transmitting Information in Relation to the Black Hills Country*, 43d Cong., special sess., 15 Mar. 1875, S. Exec. Doc. 2, 13.

16. Kingsbury, *History of Dakota Territory* 1:784; Parker, *Gold in the Black Hills*, 66.

17. Henry Newton and Walter P. Jenney, *Report on the Geology and Resources of the Black Hills of Dakota, with Atlas* (Washington, D.C., 1880), 188; James D. McLaird and Lesta V. Turchen, "Exploring the Black Hills, 1855–1875: Reports of the Government Expeditions," *South Dakota History* 4, no. 4 (Fall 1974): 416–17.

Additional articles by McLaird and Turchen on the government expeditions to the Black Hills are contained in *South Dakota History* 3, no. 4 (Fall 1973), and 4, nos. 1 (Winter 1973), 2 (Spring 1974), and 3 (Summer 1974).

18. Parker, *Gold in the Black Hills,* 70–71; Kingsbury, *History of Dakota Territory* 1:907.

19. Hutton, *Sheridan and His Army,* 299; John S. Gray, *Centennial Campaign: The Sioux War of 1876* (Fort Collins, Colo.: Old Army Press, 1976), 24.

20. Kingsbury, *History of Dakota Territory* 1:897; Sheridan to Terry, 9 Nov. 1875, in "Military Division of the Missouri, Chicago: Letters Sent (1875)," Records of the United States Army, Record Group 393, National Archives, Washington, D.C.

21. Philip H. Sheridan and Michael V. Sheridan, *Personal Memoirs of Philip Henry Sheridan, General, United States Army, New and Enlarged Edition, with an Account of His Life from 1871 to His Death in 1888,* 2 vols. (New York: D. Appleton and Co., 1904), 2:531–32; *Annual Report of the Secretary of War (1874),* 2 vols. (Washington, D.C., 1874), 1:24.

22. Robert A. Murray, "The Camp at the Mouth of Red Canyon," *Council for Abandoned Military Posts (CAMP) Periodical* 1, no. 1 (Jan. 1967): 2–9. Agnes Wright Spring, *The Cheyenne and Black Hills Stage and Express Routes* (Lincoln: University of Nebraska Press, 1948), 124.

23. "The Famous Sherman Treaty of 1868," in Kingsbury, *History of Dakota Territory* 1:758; Utley, *Frontier Regulars,* 249–53, 255–56; Kingsbury, *History of Dakota Territory* 1:947; *Deadwood Pioneer,* 27 Sept. 1876.

24. Charles G. Du Bois, *The Custer Mystery* (El Segundo, Calif.: Upton and Sons, 1986), 24.

25. Ibid.; Utley, *Frontier Regulars,* 246.

26. Kingsbury, *History of Dakota Territory* 1:930; *Black Hills Pioneer,* 16 Sept. 1876.

27. *Black Hills Pioneer,* 27 Sept., 14 Oct. 1876; Hutton, *Sheridan and His Army,* 156.

28. Kingsbury, *History of Dakota Territory* 1:784–85.

29. Clowser, *Dakota Indian Treaties,* 218.

30. Kingsbury, *History of Dakota Territory* 1:948–54.

31. Clowser, *Dakota Indian Treaties,* 229.

32. Kingsbury, *History of Dakota Territory* 1:976–77.

33. Clowser, *Dakota Indian Treaties,* 228.

34. *Bismarck Tribune,* 28 Feb. 1877.

35. Second Lieutenant J. F. Cummings, Camp at Spearfish, D.T., to Headquarters, Military Department of the Platte, 26 Feb. 1877, in "Correspondence Relating to the Establishment of a Military Post in the Black Hills," in Letters Received (hereafter cited as "Correspondence").

36. *Bismarck Tribune,* 28 Feb. 1877.

37. Utley, *Frontier Regulars,* 281; *Bismarck Tribune,* 8 Aug. 1877.

38. *Bismarck Tribune,* 22 June 1877.

39. Kenneth C. Kellar, *Seth Bullock: Frontier Marshal* (Aberdeen, S.D.: North Plains Press, 1972), 99–100.

40. *Black Hills Daily Times,* 25 July 1877.

41. Ibid., 18, 26 July 1877; *Moorhead Advocate,* 28 July 1877; *Bismarck Tribune,* 1 Aug. 1877.

42. *Bismarck Tribune,* 1 Aug. 1877.

43. *Black Hills Daily Times,* 26 July 1877.

44. Ibid., 27 July, 1, 16, 24 Aug. 1877.

45. Sheridan to Crook, 3 Dec. 1877, in "Correspondence."

46. "Returns of the Seventh Cavalry, 1 Jan. 1873 to 1 Jan. 1878" (Aug., Sept., Oct., and Nov. 1877), Records, RG 94; *Bismarck Tribune,* 5 Dec. 1877.

47. *Black Hills Daily Times,* 28 Dec. 1877, reprint of undated *Yankton Press and Dakotian* article.

48. Ibid.

49. Ibid., 10, 19 Nov. 1877, reprinting Annual Report of P. H. Sheridan, Military Division of the Missouri, Chicago, dated 25 Oct. 1877; *Annual Report of the Secretary of War (1877)*, 2 vols. (Washington, D.C., 1877), 1:519; *Bismarck Tribune*, 2 Mar. 1878.

50. Major A. W. Evans, 3rd Cavalry, to Post Adjutant, Fort Laramie, Wy., from Camp on Spear-fish, 10 Jan. 1878, in "Correspondence."

51. Colonel George P. Buell, 11th Infantry, Headquarters, Fort Custer, Mont., to Assistant Adjutant General, Headquarters, Department of Dakota, 11 Jan. 1878, with endorsements, and Crook to Assistant Adjutant General, Military Division of the Missouri, 26 Feb. 1878, in "Correspondence."

52. General William T. Sherman to Secretary of War, 6 Mar. 1878, in "Correspondence."

53. Crook to Assistant Adjutant General, Headquarters, Military Division of the Missouri, 26 Feb. 1877, and Sheridan to Terry, 6 May 1878, Sheridan to Crook, 7 May 1878, in "Correspondence."

54. J. A. Hand, Crook City, D.T., to Hon. J. P. Kidder, Washington, D.C., 31 Jan. 1878, with endorsements; S. N. Wood, Deadwood, D.T., to Sen. J. B. Chaffee, Washington, D.C., 16, 26 Jan. 1878, with endorsements; Edwin Van Cise, Rapid City, D.T., to Secretary of War, 26 Feb. 1878, with endorsements, all in "Correspondence." Van Cise came to the Black Hills from Iowa in 1877. He opened a law office in Deadwood but moved his practice to Rapid City in January 1878 and became the first elected county attorney of Pennington County. See Tallent, *Black Hills,* 377.

55. Sheridan to Sherman, 30 Mar. 1878, and Terry to Headquarters, Military Division of the Missouri, 5th endorsement, 23 Mar. 1878, in "Correspondence."

56. *Secretary of War Annual Report, 1878–79,* 45th Cong., 3d sess., 1878–79, H. Exec. Doc., 18 vols., 2:4–5; Report of General Sherman, ibid., 2:33–39.

57. *Congressional Record,* 45th Cong., 2d sess., 1878, 7:2922; U.S. Congress, Senate, Committee on Military Affairs, Secretary of War George McCrary to Hon. George E. Spencer, Chairman, 6 Mar. 1878, Accompanying S. Bill 785, 45th Cong., 2d sess., 1878, S. Rept. 261.

58. *United States Statutes at Large* (Washington, D.C., 1878), 20:149; *Black Hills Daily Times,* 12 Aug. 1878.

59. Special Order No. 41, Headquarters, Military Division of the Missouri, Chicago, 18 May 1878, in "Correspondence."

CHAPTER 2

1. *Black Hills Weekly Times,* 1 June 1878.

2. M. V. Sheridan to General Phil Sheridan, 10 June 1878, in "Correspondence"; Tallent, *Black Hills,* 227; *Black Hills Journal,* 29 June 1878.

3. *Black Hills Journal,* 29 June 1878.

4. M. V. Sheridan to General Phil Sheridan, 10 June 1878, in "Correspondence."

5. Ibid.

6. J. M. Leedy and Sam Scott to Michael V. Sheridan, 31 May 1878, Quit Claim Deed Record Book, Vol. 1, 15, Pennington County Register of Deeds Office, Rapid City, S.D.

7. *Sturgis Weekly Record,* reprint of *Black Hills Journal* article, "Rapid City's Grievance," 7 Sept. 1888.

8. General Phil Sheridan's first endorsement of M. V. Sheridan Report on Reconnaissance of the Black Hills, 19 June 1878, in "Correspondence"; *Black Hills Daily Times,* 14 Sept. 1878.

9. General Alfred Terry to Colonel Samuel D. Sturgis, 15 June 1878, in "Correspondence."

10. First Infantry Returns, 20 May 1878, in "Returns from Regular Army Infantry Regiments, June 1821–Dec. 1916, First Infantry, January 1874–Dec. 1881," in Letters Received (hereafter cited as "Returns from Regular Army"); Captain Kenzie Bates to Assistant Adjutant General, Department of Dakota, St. Paul, Minn., from Camp at Bear Butte, 2 July 1878, in "Correspondence."

11. *Black Hills Daily Times,* 2 July 1878.

12. The quarterly publication of the Rapid City Genealogical Society, *Black Hills Nuggets* 21, no. 3 (Aug. 1988), reprints the letter from Sergeant Gustav Reider, Company I, First Infantry, from Camp at Bear Butte to his wife at Fort Randall, D.T., 11 July 1878. Sgt. Reider was discharged from the army at Camp J. G.

Sturgis, D.T., on 10 Sept. 1878 and homesteaded on the Fort Randall military reservation when the post there was abandoned in 1892. He is credited with being the first white settler in Gregory County.

13. *Black Hills Daily Times,* 15 July 1878.

14. Telegram, General Sheridan to General E. D. Townsend, Adjutant General, 5 July 1878; General Sherman to General Sheridan, 6 July 1878; General Sheridan to Sherman, 7 July 1878, all in "Correspondence."

15. Another Camp Sturgis, this one named for Colonel S. D. Sturgis, had been established at Yankton, D.T., in the spring of 1873 when the Seventh Cavalry had spent four weeks there during its transfer from the South to the Department of Dakota. Lieutenant Colonel Melbourne C. Chandler, *Of Garry Owen in Glory: The History of the Seventh U.S. Cavalry* (Annandale, Va.: Turnpike Press, 1960), 76; *Black Hills Daily Times,* 28 July, 12 Aug. 1878; *Bismarck Tribune,* 5 July 1878.

16. Chandler, *Of Garry Owen in Glory,* 76.

17. Francis B. Heitman, *Historical Register and Dictionary of the United States Army,* 2 vols. (1903; reprint, Urbana: University of Illinois Press, 1965), 1:881; Returns of the Seventh Cavalry, 1 Jan. 1873 to 1 Jan. 1878 (Dec. 1877), Records, RG 94.

18. *Black Hills Daily Times,* 26, 15, 22 July 1878.

19. Ibid., 27 July, 6 Sept. 1878.

20. Hugh L. Scott, *Some Memories of a Soldier* (New York: Century Co., 1928), 90–91; Herbert M. Hart, *Old Forts of the Northwest* (Seattle, Wash.: Superior Publishing Co., 1963), 162.

21. *Black Hills Daily Times,* 22 July 1878.

22. Scott, *Some Memories of a Soldier,* 90–91.

23. U.S. Congress, Senate, *Rebuilding and Enlarging Fort Meade, S.D., 18 May 1900,* 56th Cong., 1st sess., 1900, S. Rept. No. 1379; *Sturgis Tribune,* centennial edition, 25 Oct. 1978.

24. *Black Hills Daily Times,* 26, 27 July 1878.

25. Hutton, *Sheridan and His Army,* 171–73.

26. *Black Hills Daily Times,* 20 Aug. 1878.

27. Ibid., 13 Aug. 1878.

28. Thomas E. Odell, *Mato Paha: The Story of Bear Butte* (Ann Arbor, Mich.: Edwards Brothers, 1942), 93: Utley, *Frontier Regulars,* 294.

29. Peter J. Powell, *Sweet Medicine: The Continuing Role of the Sacred Arrows, the Sun Dance, and the Sacred Buffalo Hat in Northern Cheyenne History,* 2 vols. (Norman: University of Oklahoma Press, 1969), 1:418; Scott, *Some Memories of a Soldier,* 90.

30. Scott, *Some Memories of a Soldier,* 90.

31. Chandler, *Of Garry Owen in Glory,* 76.

32. *Black Hills Daily Times,* 2, 3, 16 Aug. 1878.

33. Ibid., 2, 19, 22, 23 Aug. 1878. Private Ned Alwell, Company F, Third Cavalry, was killed by Private Charles Clark, Company K, Third Cavalry, on 20 July 1878, during the altercation at Camp Devin. Clark was taken to Cheyenne for trial and was sentenced, on 29 May 1879, to six years in the territorial prison. Indictment papers are on file in the Wyoming State Archives, Cheyenne.

34. *Black Hills Daily Times,* 23, 24 Sept. 1878.

35. *Sturgis Tribune,* centennial edition, 25 Oct. 1978.

36. General Terry to Major Lazelle, 13 Aug. 1878, and Lieutenant George D. Ruggles, Acting Assistant Adjutant General, Department of Dakota, St. Paul, Minn., to Major H. M. Lazelle, 7 Sept. 1878, in Camp Ruhlen, D.T., Endorsement Book No. 1, both in "Correspondence." A parallelogram is a four-sided plane figure whose opposite sides are parallel.

37. *Black Hills Daily Times,* 23 Aug., 4 Sept. 1878.

38. Ibid., 4 Sept. 1878.

39. General Terry to Major Lazelle, 13 Aug. 1878, and Camp Ruhlen, Endorsement Book, 22 Sept. 1878, both in "Correspondence"; Heitman, *Historical Register* 1:851; Camp Hancock, located near Bismarck, was established in 1872, abandoned in 1874, reestablished in November 1875, and abandoned again in 1877.

CHAPTER 3

1. Special Order No. 19, Camp J. G. Sturgis, D.T., 26 Aug. 1878, in "Correspondence"; General Order No. 1, Camp Ruhlen, 12 Aug. 1878, in "Returns from Regular Army"; "Medical History of Posts, Fort Meade, August 1878–June 1913," Records, RG 94 (hereafter cited as "Medical History").

2. *Black Hills Daily Times,* 21, 30 Aug., 1 Sept. 1878.

3. Ibid., 21 Aug., 1, 9, 10, 11, 18, 25 Sept. 1878.

4. Ibid., 29 Aug., 8, 27 Sept., 1 Nov. 1878. Charlie Collins published the first newspaper in Sturgis City when he issued an election campaign paper in the fall of 1878. No copies of it are known to exist.

5. Ibid., 9 Sept. 1878. Dudley moved to Hot Springs in 1882 and started a sawmill. He became one of the incorporators of the Hot Springs Townsite Company in 1886.

6. *Sturgis Advertiser,* 8 May 1889, reprinted in *Sturgis Tribune,* centennial edition, 25 Oct. 1978. Wilcox published a newspaper in Omaha, Nebraska, after leaving the Black Hills.

7. Ibid.; *Sturgis Tribune,* 25 Oct. 1978; *Black Hills Daily Times,* 13 Nov. 1878; B. G. Caulfield to J. C. Wilcox, Book 26, Document 152127, Register of Deeds, Meade County, S.D., 2 Nov. 1878; Charley W. Waldman, *Early Day History of Sturgis and Fort Meade in the Beautiful Black Hills of South Dakota* (Sturgis, S.D.: By the author, 1964), 36.

8. *Sturgis Advertiser,* 8 May 1889; *Bismarck Tribune,* 10 Oct. 1878; *Black Hills Daily Times,* 6 Dec. 1878.

9. *Black Hills Press,* 5 Apr. 1934; *Sturgis Advertiser,* 25 Nov. 1879, 12 June 1880.

10. *Black Hills Daily Times,* 30 Oct. 1878. Today, the Sturgis High School boys' athletic teams are known as the Sturgis Scoopers and the girls' teams as the Scooperettes.

11. First Infantry Returns, Sept., Oct., Nov. 1878, in "Returns from Regular Army."

12. "Medical History," Oct. 1878. Louis Brechemin, a Pennsylvanian, was appointed assistant surgeon, U.S. Army, on 6 June 1878; Heitman, *Historical Register* 1:241. The 1880 federal census of Fort Meade lists Matilda McCarthy, thirty-

eight, as the wife of John McCarthy, thirty-four, a laborer at the fort, and as the mother of three children, ages nine, five, and two. "Records of Burials in Post Cemetery, Fort Meade, S.D.," rev. copy, 10 Mar. 1987, Black Hills National Cemetery, Sturgis, S.D.; Returns from U.S. Military Posts (main series), 1800–1916 (1878), Records, RG 94 (hereafter cited as Post Returns).

13. "Records of Burials in Post Cemetery, Fort Meade, S.D.," rev. copy, 10 Mar. 1987, Black Hills National Cemetery, Sturgis, S.D.; "Medical History," 89.

14. Chandler, *Of Garry Owen in Glory,* 77; First Infantry Returns, Oct. 1878, in "Returns from Regular Army"; Martin F. Schmitt and Dee Brown, *Fighting Indians of the West* (New York: Charles Scribner's Sons, 1948), 206–7.

15. *Black Hills Daily Times,* 30 Sept. 1878; Chandler, *Of Garry Owen in Glory,* 77; Heitman, *Historical Register* 1:961.

16. First Infantry Returns, Oct., Nov. 1878, in "Returns from Regular Army." Lt. James S. Pettit, an 1874 graduate of West Point, served in the First Infantry from 14 June 1878 to 20 May 1898. Heitman, *Historical Register* 1:787.

17. Schmitt and Brown, *Fighting Indians,* 207; Utley, *Frontier Regulars,* 284.

18. Chandler, *Of Garry Owen in Glory,* 78; Post Returns, Nov. 1878.

19. "Medical History," 14; Post Returns, Nov. 1878.

20. Post Returns, Nov. 1878.

21. Report of Judge Advocate, Department of Dakota, St. Paul, Minn., in *Annual Report of the Secretary of War (1878),* 2 vols. (Washington, D.C., 1878), 1:198–99. During the fiscal year ending 30 June 1878, there were 1,678 desertions from the U.S. Army. Of this number, the Seventh Cavalry led all other regiments with 136. The next highest regiment in terms of desertions was the Fifth Cavalry, with 98. D. Ray Wilson, *Fort Kearny on the Platte* (Dundee, Ill.: Crossroads Communications, 1980), 93; Post Returns, Sept. 1878.

22. "Records of U.S. Army Commands (Army Posts), Fort Meade," 1878, Records of the U.S. Army Continental Commands, 1821–1922, RG 93, National Archives, Washington, D.C.

23. Ibid. William S. Fanshawe is listed in the federal census of Fort Meade of 1880 as age thirty-two and born in New York. Others living with him at the fort were his

wife, Jessie, twenty-five, also born in New York, and four children, ages four, two, one, and four months, born in Connecticut, Minnesota, New York, and Dakota Territory, respectively, *Bismarck Tribune,* 3 Dec. 1878.

24. "Post Records, Fort Meade, South Dakota, Entry 4: Endorsements Sent, August 1878–December 1884," 12 vols., 1:64, in Records of the U.S. Army Continental Commands, 1821–1922, RG 93, National Archives, Washington, D.C.

25. "Medical History," 15; Post Returns, Dec. 1878.

26. Post Returns, Dec. 1878; "Medical History," 10.

27. "Medical History," 12; Post Returns, Dec. 1878.

28. "Medical History," 10, 71.

29. Ibid., 70.

30. U.S. Congress, House, "Report of the Commanding General of the Department of Dakota, Brvt. Maj. Gen. John Gibbon, Commanding," in *Secretary of War Annual Report, 1878–79,* 45th Cong., 3d sess., 1878–79, H. Exec. Doc., 18 vols., 2:33–35; Colonel John Gibbon, Headquarters, Department of Dakota, St. Paul, Minn., 4 Oct. 1878, to Army Headquarters, Washington, D.C., in "Annual Reports, 1871–86," in Letters Received.

31. "Report of the Commanding General of the Department of Dakota," 2:72–79.

32. "Annual Report of Major General P. H. Sheridan, Headquarters, Military Division of the Missouri, Chicago, Ill., 25 Oct. 1878, to Brigadier General E. D. Townsend, Adjutant General of the Army, Washington, D.C.," in Letters Received.

33. General Order No. 27, Department of Dakota, St. Paul, Minn., 31 Dec. 1878, in Post Returns, Dec. 1878; *Annual Report of the Secretary of War (1879),* 4 vols. (Washington, D.C., 1879), 1:51.

CHAPTER 4

1. *Black Hills Daily Times,* 15 Jan., 3 Feb. 1879; "Medical History," Jan. 1879.

2. Letter, Second Lieutenant James D. Mann, Seventh Cavalry, to his mother, 2 Mar. 1879, in Manuscript File H7826, 1878–91, South Dakota State Historical Society, Pierre; "Medical History," Jan. 1879.

3. Post Returns, Feb. 1879; *Black Hills Daily Times,* 23 Feb. 1879.

4. Letter, Second Lieutenant Mann to his mother, 2 Mar. 1879, in Manuscript File H7826; Post Returns, Feb. 1879.

5. *Black Hills Daily Times,* 14 Feb., 19 June 1879; *Black Hills Journal,* 22 Mar. 1879; "Medical History," Apr. 1879.

6. Post Returns, May 1879; "Court Martial Proceedings in the Case of Major Marcus A. Reno, St. Paul, Minn., 8–20 Mar. 1877, CC-QQ 1554," Records of the Judge Advocate General's Office, RG 153, National Archives, Washington, D.C.

7. Post Returns, Dec. 1878, Apr., June, July 1879; Heitman, *Historical Register* 1:437.

8. *Sentinel,* Fort Lincoln, D.T., vol. 1, no. 9, 27 Aug. 1881, facsimile copy in possession of author; Roster of Troops, Independent Posts, Department of Dakota, Oct. 1879, in Letters Received.

9. Chandler, *Of Garry Owen,* 420–21; *Black Hills Daily Times,* 17 July 1879; *Bismarck Tribune,* 10 May 1879.

10. "Medical History," Description of Post, 9; Post Returns, June, July 1879.

11. *Bismarck Tribune,* 9 Aug. 1879; *Black Hills Daily Times,* 9, 15, 16 Aug., 8, 15 Nov. 1879.

12. "Medical History," Aug. 1879.

13. *Black Hills Daily Times,* 12 Aug., 12, 23 Sept. 1879; Post Returns, Jan.–Dec. 1879; Tallent, *Black Hills,* 476.

14. *Black Hills Daily Times,* 26 Sept., 12 Aug., 12, 23 Sept. 1879.

15. *Bismarck Tribune,* 2 Aug., 16, 23 Dec. 1879. For more on Ella's stage activities, see Eleanor Lawler Pillsbury, with Virginia Huck, *My Family Story* (Minneapolis, Minn.: Southways, 1972), 52.

16. *Bismarck Tribune,* 9 Aug. 1879; *Black Hills Daily Times,* 4 Nov. 1879; Post Returns, Aug. 1879.

17. *Black Hills Journal,* 25 Oct. 1878.

18. "Proceedings of General Court Martial Convened at Fort Meade, Dakota, in the Case of Major Marcus A. Reno, Seventh Cavalry, 24 Nov.–8 Dec. 1879, QQ 1554," Records of the Judge Advocate General's Office, RG 153, National Archives, Washington, D.C.

19. Second Lieutenant Charles M. Carrow (Heitman, *Historical Register* 1:286) of Company I, who had joined the Seventh Cavalry fresh out of West Point the previous August, became enamored of Ella Sturgis. The love affair, however, did not meet the approval of Ella's parents. To discourage it, they sent Ella to visit her older married sister in St. Louis, where the family had lived when her father was stationed there. Carrow obtained a leave of absence, went to St. Louis, and risked court-martial by overstaying his leave while courting Ella. He reportedly "found himself confronted by a rival and motivated by jealousy," which led to his drinking and "criminations and recriminations between the lovers." On 19 May, in his hotel room in St. Louis, the lieutenant committed suicide by shooting himself in the head. Found beside his body were empty whiskey bottles and some letters from Ella. His desperate act was attributed to his "convivial habit" of drinking. See the *Bismarck Tribune* of 24 May 1879 for an account of his suicide.

20. "Proceedings of General Court Martial Convened at Fort Meade, Dakota, in the Case of Major Marcus A. Reno, Seventh Cavalry, 24 Nov.–8 Dec. 1879, QQ 1554," Records of the Judge Advocate General's Office, RG 153, National Archives, Washington, D.C.

21. *Black Hills Daily Times,* 8, 21 Nov. 1879.

22. Robert J. Casey, *The Black Hills and Their Incredible Characters* (Indianapolis: Bobbs-Merrill Co., 1949), 254–55.

23. *Black Hills Journal,* 8, 22 Sept. 1879.

24. Ibid.

25. *Annual Report of the Secretary of War (1879)* 1:45; Hutton, *Sheridan and His Army,* 331.

26. Post Returns, Dec. 1879.

CHAPTER 5

1. Except where otherwise indicated, all information in this chapter regarding Reno's two court-martials, court of inquiry, testimony of witnesses, and comments

of the reviewing authorities are taken from the following official sources: "Court Martial Proceedings in the Case of Major Marcus A. Reno, St. Paul, Minn., 8–20 Mar. 1877, CC-QQ 1554"; "Proceedings of a Court of Inquiry Convened at Chicago, Ill., Mar. 1879, in the Case of Major Marcus A. Reno, Seventh Cavalry"; "Proceedings of General Court Martial Convened at Fort Meade, Dakota, in the Case of Major Marcus A. Reno, Seventh Cavalry, 24 Nov.–8 Dec. 1879, QQ-1554," all in Records of the Judge Advocate General's Office, RG 153, National Archives, Washington, D.C. See also Col. William A. Graham, *The Reno Court of Inquiry: Abstract of the Official Record of Proceedings* (Harrisburg, Pa.: Stackpole Co., 1954), iv.

2. Kenneth Hammer, "Major Marcus A. Reno," *New York Posse Brand Book* 8, no. 3 (1961): 52–55; John Upton Terrell and Colonel George Walton, *Faint the Trumpet Sounds* (New York: David McKay Co., 1966), 237; Heitman, *Historical Register* 1:824, 1056.

3. Heitman, *Historical Register* 1:824; Hammer, "Marcus A. Reno," 54.

4. Hammer, "Marcus A. Reno," 55; Terrell and Walton, *Faint the Trumpet,* 40, 67, 77, 88–89; Heitman, *Historical Register* 1:824; "Returns from Regular Army Cavalry Regiments, 1833–1916, Seventh Cavalry, 1874–81," Records, RG 94.

5. Terrell and Walton, *Faint the Trumpet,* 89; Gene R. Boak, New Bloomfield, Pa., to author, citing Dauphin County Historical Records, Harrisburg, Pa., 27 Oct. 1989.

6. Colonel Sturgis's testimony about his previous rejection of late charges against Reno is included in the proceedings of Reno's court-martial at Fort Meade. Also see Terrell and Walton, *Faint the Trumpet,* 228.

7. Although a medical officer, Major Irwin had the distinction of earning the very first congressional Medal of Honor awarded by the army during the Indian campaigns. It was bestowed on him for voluntarily taking command of troops and defeating a party of Indians at Apache Pass, Arizona, in February 1861. Irwin was stationed at Fort Meade at the time of Reno's trial.

8. Post Order No. 124, 4 Dec. 1879, in Post Returns, Dec. 1879.

9. *Black Hills Journal,* 6 Dec. 1879; *Black Hills Daily Times,* 9, 28 Dec. 1879; "Returns from Regular Army Cavalry Regiments, 1833–1916, Seventh Cavalry, 1874–81," Oct., Nov. 1879, Records, RG 94; Terrell and Walton, *Faint the Trumpet,* 278.

10. *Black Hills Daily Times,* 23 Dec. 1879.

11. E. A. Grunwald, "General Sturgis and His Defeat at the Battle of Brice's Cross Roads, June 10, 1864" (Paper, Department of English, History, and Government, United States Naval Academy, Annapolis, Md., Mar. 1950).

12. Ibid.

13. General W. T. Sherman, *Memoirs of General W. T. Sherman,* 2 vols. (New York, 1892), 1:52.

14. *War of the Rebellion: Official Records of the Union and Confederate Armies* (Washington, D.C.: Government Printing Office, 1902), Series L, 70 vols., 1:340, 39:198; Philip H. Sheridan, *Personal Memoirs of P. H. Sheridan, General, United States Army,* 2 vols. (New York: 1888), 1:331–32; Terrell and Walton, *Faint the Trumpet,* 225–26.

15. Terrell and Walton, *Faint the Trumpet,* 306, 309–10; Hammer, "Marcus A. Reno," 52–55.

16. *New Bloomfield Dispatch* (Pa.), 9 Oct. 1888.

17. In 1966, Reno's great-nephew, Charles Reno, a New York bartender, petitioned the U.S. Army Board for the Correction of Military Records through the American Legion for a review of Major Reno's final court-martial. The board determined that Reno had been wrongfully treated and corrected his military records to show that he had been honorably discharged at Fort Meade in 1880. Secretary of the Army Stanley Resor, in commenting on the review, stated, "Life on the isolated frontier posts was not conducive to producing plaster saints" (*Sioux Falls Argus Leader,* 2 June 1967). Ironically, Resor has a family relationship to the Reno case. His wife is Ella Sturgis's granddaughter. Reno's remains were removed from the Glenwood Cemetery and reinterred with military honors at the Custer Battlefield National Cemetery on 9 Sept. 1967. See *Rapid City Journal,* 4 June 1967, *Sioux Falls Argus Leader,* 2 June 1967, *Billings Gazette,* 9 Sept. 1967, and *New York Times,* 4 May 1967.

CHAPTER 6

1. Post Returns.

2. "The 1880 Federal Census: Fort Meade, Lawrence County, Dakota Territory," National Archives, Washington, D.C., 1–16.

3. Ibid., 17; Heitman, *Historical Register* 1:934.

4. *Black Hills Journal,* 22 May 1880.

5. Post Returns, Aug. 1880; Heitman, *Historical Register* 1:124–25; John H. Nanki-vell, *The History of the Twenty-Fifth Regiment, U.S. Infantry* (Fort Collins, Colo.: Old Army Press, 1972), 36–37; Lieutenant George Andrews, "The Twenty-Fifth Regiment of Infantry," *The U.S. Army* (New York, 1896), 95–97, 274, 474–75, 525; Special Orders Nos. 73 and 103, Headquarters, Department of Dakota, St. Paul, Minn., 30 June, 30 Aug. 1880, in Post Returns, June and Aug. 1880.

6. Post Returns, Sept. 1880, Apr., June, Aug. 1881; *Sturgis Weekly Record,* 14 Oct. 1887; Chandler, *Of Garry Owen,* 78.

7. Post Returns, May–Nov. 1881; Chandler, *Of Garry Owen,* 78; "Medical History," Nov. 1881; *Black Hills Journal,* 28 Nov. 1881.

8. Presidential Executive Orders, 18 Apr. 1881, 16 Sept. 1889, 25 June 1925, in Engineering Office, Fort Meade VA Medical Center, Fort Meade, S.D.; Post Returns, Oct., Nov., Dec. 1881, July 1882; *Black Hills Pioneer,* 1 Jan. 1882; "Medical History," Feb. 1881, May, Aug., Sept., Oct. 1882.

9. "Medical History," Nov. 1882.

10. Scott, *Some Memories of a Soldier,* 111.

11. Ibid.; Vernon E. Holst, *A Study of the 1876 Bismarck to Deadwood Trail* (Belle Fourche, S.D.: Butte County Historical Society, 1983), 55.

12. *Black Hills Journal,* 19 Feb. 1881; "Medical History," Feb. 1881, Nov. 1882.

13. *Black Hills Journal,* 17 Nov. 1882.

14. Scott, *Some Memories of a Soldier,* 124.

15. "Medical History," Dec. 1881, Aug. 1883; *Black Hills Journal,* 12 Aug. 1883.

16. "Medical History," Apr., May, Aug. 1883; Andrews, "The Twenty-Fifth Regiment," 274; Exec. Doc. No. 54, 1887, in Letters Received.

17. First Lieutenant Q. O'M. Gillmore, Eighth Cavalry, Acting Assistant Quarter-master, Report of Barracks and Quarters and Other Public Structures, Fort Meade, D.T., 30 June 1889, in "Medical History," June 1889; Deed, William McMillan to U.S. Government, 2 Apr. 1888, in Engineering Office, Fort Meade VA Medical Center, Fort Meade, S.D.

18. "Medical History," Dec. 1881, Nov. 1882, Aug. 1883; *Black Hills Journal*, 12 Aug. 1883.

19. "Medical History," Aug., Sept. 1883; Andrews, "The Twenty-Fifth Regiment," 274.

20. "Medical History," Nov. 1883, Jan. 1884.

21. Post Returns, Apr., May, June, July, Aug. 1883.

22. Ibid., Apr., Sept., Nov. 1883; Heitman, *Historical Register* 1:409, 762, 881, 865, 961.

23. "Medical History," Apr. 1883; Bob Lee, *Gold, Gals, Guns, Guts: The Centennial History of Lawrence County* (Deadwood-Lead, S.D.: Lawrence County Centennial Committee, 1976), 136; Letters Received, 10 Oct. to 9 Dec. 1885; Heitman, *Historical Register* 1:409, 961; Special Order No. 94, AGO, Headquarters, Department of the Army, Washington, D.C., 12 May 1885, in Post Returns, May 1885; Hutton, *Sheridan and His Army*, 346–49; Gary Freedom, "Military Forts and Communications Network on the Northern Great Plains" (Paper presented at Dakota History Conference, Dakota State College, Madison, S.D., Apr. 1985), 307.

24. *Sturgis Weekly Record,* 27 July, 4 Aug., 12 Sept., 6 Dec. 1883.

25. Post Returns, June 1885; "Medical History," Oct. 1884.

26. *Sturgis Weekly Record,* 27 Aug. 1885; *Sturgis Tribune,* centennial edition, 25 Oct. 1978.

27. *Sturgis Weekly Record,* 27 Aug. 1885.

28. Ibid., 5 Sept. 1885.

29. Ibid., 20 June 1884.

30. Telegram, Colonel S. D. Sturgis, Fort Meade, D.T., to Adjutant General, Department of Dakota, St. Paul, Minn., 28 Oct. 1885, in "Report of Board of Officers Investigating Outrage upon the Citizens of Sturgis, D.T., by the Twenty-fifth Infantry," 1885, Records, RG 94 (hereafter cited as "Report of Officers").

31. Bernard J. Caulfield, Deadwood, D.T., 27 Sept. 1885, to President Grover Cleveland, in "Report of Officers."

32. Ibid.

33. Tallent, *Black Hills,* 473–74.

34. Letters Received, 1885; *Deadwood Pioneer,* 21 Sept. 1885.

35. "Report of Officers."

36. Terry to Adjutant General, Headquarters, Military Division of the Missouri, Chicago, Ill., 10 Nov. 1885, in "Report of Officers."

37. Ibid.

38. *Black Hills Daily Times,* 5 Oct. 1886; *Black Hills Pioneer,* 5 Oct. 1886; *Sturgis Weekly Record,* 8 Oct. 1886. Taylor died at the state penitentiary on 15 Feb. 1894; Letter, Vonna Marcus, Secretary, South Dakota State Penitentiary, Sioux Falls, S.D., to author, 16 June 1989.

39. Jerusha Wilcox Sturgis, unpublished biography of Colonel Samuel D. Sturgis, Minneapolis, Minn., 24 Feb. 1910; Pillsbury, with Huck, *My Family Story.* Mrs. Pillsbury is the daughter of Ella Sturgis. The Sturgis family moved to St. Paul when the colonel retired. Ella's husband was appointed Dakota Territorial Treasurer in 1887 and held the post until the two Dakotas were divided into separate states in 1889. The Sturgis's eldest daughter, Nina, married Louis Dousman, whose family had become wealthy in the fur-trading business and founded the famous Villa Louis at Prairie du Chien, Wis. Colonel Sturgis died on 28 Sept. 1889 in St. Paul and was buried with military honors at Arlington National Cemetery in Washington. Lawler died in 1896, leaving the widowed Ella with four children. She married Edmund Pennington, the president of the Soo Line Railroad, in 1906 and lived in Minneapolis until her death in 1925. Samuel Davis Sturgis, Jr., who had gone to West Point from Fort Meade, sired a son who would continue the family's military tradition. Samuel D. Sturgis III also graduated from the military academy and rose to the rank of major general, heading the Corps of Engineers, before his retirement.

40. *Black Hills Journal,* 15 May 1880.

41. Post Returns, July 1886.

42. Ibid., June 1886; "Reports of Persons and Articles Hired, Fort Meade, D.T.," Doc. 547, in Records of the Quartermaster General, 1886, RG 92, National Archives, Washington, D.C.

43. Scott, *Some Memories of a Soldier,* 125.

44. Post Returns, Oct. 1886, July 1887; *Sturgis Weekly Record,* 15 Nov. 1887; *Sturgis Advertiser,* 19 July 1887.

45. Post Returns, Aug. 1887; Letter, Abram Hill, Sturgis City, D.T., 18 Sept. 1887, to Secretary of War, in "Report of Officers"; Tilford to Assistant Adjutant General, Department of Dakota, St. Paul, Minn., 11 Oct. 1887, in Letters Received.

46. *Sturgis Advertiser,* 12 Oct. 1887; *Sturgis Weekly Record,* 16 Oct. 1887.

47. *Echoes thru the Valley: Southwestern Meade County* (Elk Creek, S.D.: Elk Creek Pioneer Society, 1968), 398; *Sturgis Weekly Record,* 2, 23 Dec. 1887.

48. *Sturgis Advertiser,* 7 Mar., 2, 27 July 1888; *Black Hills Journal,* 31 Mar. 1882.

49. *Sturgis Advertiser,* 7 Mar. 1888.

50. *Sturgis Weekly Record,* 25 May 1888; Post Returns, May 1888.

51. Post Returns, May, June 1888; *Sturgis Advertiser,* 30 May, 16 July 1888; *Sturgis Weekly Record,* 1 June 1888.

52. *Sturgis Weekly Record,* 1 June 1888. Comanche died at Fort Riley on 6 Nov. 1891, at the age of twenty-eight. His hide was stuffed and placed on exhibit at the University of Kansas Museum in Lawrence.

CHAPTER 7

1. Post Returns, May, Aug. 1888; Heitman, *Historical Register* 1:85.

2. Post Returns, May, July 1888.

3. Major W. G. Wilkinson, "Four Months in the Saddle: The Cross Country March of the Eighth Cavalry, 1888" (Manuscript, Old Fort Meade Museum and Historical Association, Fort Meade, S.D., n.d.). Wilkinson was a private in Troop G of the Eighth Cavalry at the time of the march. He wrote this report on the march while retired and living in Clearwater, Fla.

4. Ibid.; Post Returns, Aug., Sept. 1888.

5. Wilkinson, "Four Months."

6. Post Returns, Sept., Oct. 1888.

7. Ibid., Aug. 1888; Utley, *Frontier Regulars,* 294 n. 40, 400; General Order No. 62, AGO, Headquarters, Department of the Army, Washington, D.C., 14 Aug. 1888, in Post Returns, Aug. 1888; Heitman, *Historical Register* 1:708–9, 865, 881.

8. Utley, *Frontier Regulars,* 288; Post Returns, Sept., Oct. 1888.

9. "Medical History," Nov. 1888; "Records of Burials in Post Cemetery, Fort Meade, S.D.," rev. copy, 10 Mar. 1987, Black Hills National Cemetery, Sturgis, S.D.; Post Returns, Nov. 1888; *Sturgis Weekly Record,* 23 Nov. 1888.

10. *Sturgis Weekly Record,* 2 Dec. 1888; *Sturgis Advertiser,* 16 Jan. 1890; Post Returns, Apr. 1889.

11. *Sturgis Advertiser,* 16 Jan. 1890.

12. Special Order No. 255, AGO, Headquarters, Department of the Army, Washington, D.C., 1 Nov. 1888, in *Annual Report of the Secretary of War (1888),* 4 vols. (Washington, D.C., 1888), 1:236.

13. *Sturgis Tribune,* centennial edition, 25 Oct. 1978.

14. John Artichoker, *Indians of South Dakota,* Bulletin No. 67A, rev. (Pierre, S.D.: Department of Public Instruction, 1956), 22; Clowser, *Dakota Indian Treaties,* 244; Act of Congress, 2 Mar. 1889, 50th Cong., 2d sess., 1889; Robert M. Utley, *The Indian Frontier of the American West, 1846–1890* (Albuquerque, N.M.: University of New Mexico Press, 1984), 232; idem, *The Last Days of the Sioux Nation* (New Haven: Yale University Press, 1963), 53; Kingsbury, *History of Dakota* 2:1283–91.

15. Kingsbury, *History of Dakota* 2:1275.

16. "Records of Letters Sent, Fort Meade, 1881–1906," 31 May 1889 to 1 Mar. 1891, in Records of the U.S. Army Continental Commands, 1821–1922, RG 93, National Archives, Washington, D.C. (hereafter cited as Post Letters Sent).

17. *McMahon* vs. *Polk,* 10 S.D. 296, 73 N.W. (Northwest Reporting System) 77, 19 Nov. 1897.

18. First Lieutenant Q. O'M. Gillmore, Eighth Cavalry, Acting Assistant Quartermaster, Report of Barracks and Quarters and Other Public Structures, Fort Meade, D.T., 30 June 1889, in "Medical History," June 1889.

19. Post Returns, Aug., Sept. 1889; Heitman, *Historical Register* 1:293–94.

20. Otis to Adjutant General, Department of Dakota, St. Paul, Minn., 1 Nov. 1889, in Post Letters Sent.

21. Otis to Chaplain David Wilson, 8 Nov. 1889, in Post Letters Sent.

22. *Sturgis Advertiser,* 27 Feb. 1890; Post Returns, Apr., Oct., Nov., Dec. 1890, Jan. 1891; Heitman, *Historical Register* 1:985.

23. Post Returns, Apr., May, Nov. 1890; Heitman, *Historical Register* 1:936.

CHAPTER 8

1. James Mooney, *The Ghost Dance Religion and the Sioux Outbreak of 1890,* Bureau of American Ethnology, 14th Annual Report, Smithsonian Institution (Washington, D.C., 1896), chapter 5, "The Sioux Outbreak: Sitting Bull and Wounded Knee," 114–21, 138–40; Bob Lee, "Tragedy Ends an Empire," chapter 19 in *Dakota Panorama,* ed. Jennewein and Boorman.

2. Mooney, *Ghost Dance Religion,* 6, 14, 64, 88, 92, 93, 100; Utley, *Last Days,* 96.

3. Post Returns, Apr. 1890.

4. Ibid., Aug., Sept. 1890; General Order No. 84, Headquarters, Department of the Army, Washington, D.C., 1 Sept. 1890, in Post Returns, Sept. 1890.

5. Mooney, *Ghost Dance Religion,* 74–76.

6. Lee, "Tragedy Ends an Empire," 382; Utley, *Last Days,* 103, 123; Larry Pressler, *U.S. Senators from the Prairie* (Vermillion, S.D.: University of South Dakota Press, 1982), 26. Royer served two terms in the territorial legislature and also had drugstore, newspaper, and banking interests at Alpena, S.D.

7. Utley, *Last Days,* 105.

8. Mooney, *Ghost Dance Religion,* 93; Utley, *Last Days,* 104, 110–11; Julia B. McGillycuddy, *McGillycuddy, Agent* (Stanford: Stanford University Press, 1941), 261.

9. Rex Alan Smith, *Moon of Popping Trees* (New York: Reader's Digest Press, 1975), 125.

10. Post Returns, Oct., Nov. 1890; Utley, *Last Days*, 115–16, 118, 252; *Sturgis Weekly Record*, 14 Nov. 1890.

11. *Sturgis Weekly Record*, 14 Nov. 1890.

12. Ibid., 28 Nov. 1890; Post Returns, Nov. 1890; Mooney, *Ghost Dance Religion*, 145.

13. *Black Hills Journal*, 28 Dec. 1890; *Sturgis Weekly Record*, 5 Dec. 1890.

14. *Black Hills Journal*, 9 Dec. 1890; Utley, *Last Days*, 181–82; Post Returns, Nov. 1890.

15. Post Order No. 254, 29 Nov. 1890, in Post Returns, Nov. 1890.

16. Post Returns, Nov. 1890; Utley, *Last Days*, 136; *Black Hills Journal*, 9 Dec. 1890; Bert Hall, ed., *Roundup Years: Old Muddy to the Black Hills* (Pierre, S.D.: State Publishing Co., 1954), 274.

17. Post Returns, Nov. 1890; Mooney, *Ghost Dance Religion*, 113–14, 148–49; Utley, *Last Days*, 251–53.

18. Utley, *Last Days*, 121–22; *Sturgis Weekly Record*, 26 Dec. 1890.

19. *Black Hills Journal*, 25, 27 Dec. 1890.

20. Wright Tarbell, "History of the South Dakota National Guard," *South Dakota Historical Collections* 6 (1912): 427–28.

21. Ibid., 426, 428.

22. *Black Hills Journal*, 2, 7 Dec. 1890.

23. Tarbell, "South Dakota National Guard," 428–29.

24. *Black Hills Journal*, 24 Dec. 1890; Tarbell, "South Dakota National Guard," 431.

25. Mooney, *Ghost Dance Religion*, 109.

26. Ibid., 99–103; Louis L. Pfaller, *James McLaughlin: The Man with an Indian Heart* (New York: Vantage Press, 1978), 143.

27. Mooney, *Ghost Dance Religion*, 100, 145–46; Utley, *Last Days*, 123–25.

28. Utley, *Last Days*, 148; Mooney, *Ghost Dance Religion*, 102, 104.

29. Colonel E. G. Fechet, "The Capture of Sitting Bull," *South Dakota Historical Collections* 4 (1908): 185–93; Mooney, *Ghost Dance Religion*, 104–5.

30. Pfaller, *James McLaughlin*, 164; Mooney, *Ghost Dance Religion*, 338. In 1953, a group of South Dakotans representing three of Sitting Bull's granddaughters opened the Hunkpapa chieftain's grave at Fort Yates and spirited away his remains to a site west of Mobridge, S.D., for reburial. For further information on this incident, see Robb DeWall, *The Saga of Sitting Bull's Bones* (Custer, S.D.: Korczak's Heritage, 1984).

31. Fechet, "Capture of Sitting Bull," 193.

32. *Sturgis Weekly Record*, 19 Dec. 1890.

33. Exhibit H, Sumner to Assistant Adjutant General, Department of Dakota, St. Paul, Minn., 3 Feb. 1891, in *Annual Report of the Secretary of War (1891)*, 5 vols. (Washington, D.C., 1891), 1:226–29 (hereafter cited as Sumner Report).

34. *Annual Report of the Secretary of War (1891)* 1:225–26, 229, 232; Utley, *Last Days*, 181; Mooney, *Ghost Dance Religion*, 112.

35. Sumner Report 1:226.

36. *Sturgis Weekly Record*, 26 Dec. 1890.

37. *Annual Report of the Secretary of War (1891)* 1:208, 212, 227, 283; Utley, *Last Days*, 177, 185.

38. Utley, *Last Days*, 185.

39. *Annual Report of the Secretary of War (1891)* 1:212; Sumner Report 1:226–29; *Sturgis Weekly Record*, 3 Jan. 1891.

40. Sumner Report 1:121; *Annual Report of the Secretary of War (1891)* 1:212; *Sturgis Weekly Record*, 26 Dec. 1890.

41. *Sturgis Weekly Record*, 26 Dec. 1899, 3 Jan. 1891.

42. Sumner Report 1:121.

43. *Annual Report of the Secretary of War (1891)* 1:212, 235; *Sturgis Weekly Record,* 3 Jan. 1891.

44. *Sturgis Weekly Record,* 26 Dec. 1890.

45. Ibid.

46. Ibid., reprinting *Black Hills Journal,* 21 Dec. 1890.

47. *Black Hills Journal,* 2, 24 Dec. 1890.

48. Post Returns, Dec. 1890; *Annual Report of the Secretary of War (1891)* 1:150; Mooney, *Ghost Dance Religion,* 114–18; Utley, *Last Days,* 198.

49. Mooney, *Ghost Dance Religion,* 118–21; Utley, *Last Days,* 227–28.

50. Mooney, *Ghost Dance Religion,* 199; Utley, *Last Days,* 227–28.

51. Mooney, *Ghost Dance Religion,* 117–18; *Hot Springs Star,* 15 Jan. 1891; *Sturgis Weekly Record,* 22 Jan. 1891.

52. *Annual Report of the Secretary of War (1891)* 1:150, 154; Mooney, *Ghost Dance Religion,* 120–21, 123–31.

53. Mooney, *Ghost Dance Religion,* 121–26; Utley, *Last Days,* 239–40; *Annual Report of the Secretary of War (1891)* 1:223.

54. Mooney, *Ghost Dance Religion,* 135; Utley, *Last Days,* 254, 265; *Sioux Falls Argus Leader,* 7 Apr. 1891.

55. *Sioux Falls Argus Leader,* 28 Apr. 1891; Mooney, *Ghost Dance Religion,* 142; Utley, *Last Days,* 254, 257–58.

56. *Annual Report of the Secretary of War (1891)* 1:221–22; Utley, *Last Days,* 258.

57. Utley, *Last Days,* 246; "Report of Investigation into the Battle at Wounded Knee Creek, South Dakota, Fought December 29, 1890, Feb. 4, 1891," in U.S. Congress, Senate, *Wounded Knee Massacre: Hearings before the Committee on the Judiciary, United States Senate,* 94th Cong., 2d sess., 5–6 Feb. 1976, 113, 142 (hereafter cited as "Report of Investigation"); *Black Hills Journal,* 7 Jan. 1891.

58. Utley, *Last Days,* 246; "Report of Investigation," 113, 142, 395; Mooney, *Ghost Dance Religion,* 142.

59. *Sioux Falls Argus Leader,* 7 Apr. 1891.

60. Major General J. M. Schofield to Secretary of War Redfield Proctor, 1 Feb. 1891, 151, in "Report of Investigation."

61. U.S. Senate, Congress, *Medal of Honor Recipients: 1863–1963,* Prepared for the Subcommittee on Veterans Affairs of the Committee on Labor and Public Welfare, 88th Cong., 2d sess., 1964, Committee Print, Indian Campaigns, 621–80.

62. McGillycuddy, *McGillycuddy, Agent,* 273; *Custer County Chronicle,* 3 Feb. 1891.

63. Mooney, *Ghost Dance Religion,* 119.

64. Sumner Report 1:292–97.

65. *Sturgis Weekly Record,* reprint of *Hermosa Pilot* article, 23 Jan. 1891.

66. *Sturgis Advertiser,* 19 Feb. 1891.

CHAPTER 9

1. Mooney, *Ghost Dance Religion,* 143; Utley, *Last Days,* 261.

2. Mooney, *Ghost Dance Religion,* 143; Utley, *Last Days,* 262–64.

3. *Annual Report of the Secretary of War (1892),* 4 vols. (Washington, D.C., 1892), 1:222–23; *Sturgis Weekly Record,* 23 Jan. 1891.

4. *Annual Report of the Secretary of War (1892)* 1:222–23; *Sturgis Weekly Record,* 23 Jan. 1891.

5. *Annual Report of the Secretary of War (1892)* 1:222–23.

6. Clowser, *Dakota Indian Treaties,* 133–34; Utley, *Last Days,* 264.

7. Mooney, *Ghost Dance Religion,* 144.

8. *Sturgis Advertiser,* 19 Feb. 1891; Utley, *Last Days,* 265; President Harrison to Secretary of the Interior, 8 Jan. 1891, and General Order No. 2, Headquarters, Division of the Missouri, In the Field, Pine Ridge, S.D., 12 Jan. 1891, in Post Returns, Jan. 1891. Royer, failing to win reinstatement at Pine Ridge, moved to Orange, Calif., where he became mayor. On 19 Oct. 1927 he was found guilty of

unprofessional conduct under the provisions of the Medical Practices Act of California relating to the improper use of drugs. The charge was dismissed on the condition that he discontinue practicing medicine. Royer died at Orange on 29 Oct. 1929. Letter to author from Louis E. Jones, M.D., secretary-treasurer, Board of Medical Examiners, State of California, Department of Professional and Vocational Standards, Sacramento, 17 Oct. 1953.

9. *Annual Report of the Secretary of War (1892)* 1:153.

10. Mooney, *Ghost Dance Religion,* 146.

11. Ibid., 146–47; *Sturgis Weekly Record,* 13 Feb. 1891.

12. Post Returns, Jan. 1891.

13. *Sturgis Weekly Record,* 30 Jan., 1 May 1891; Post Returns, Feb., Mar., Apr., May, June 1981; "Journal of the Senate of the Second Session of the State Legislature, 1891, Pertaining to Joint Resolution No. 2 for Enlargement of Post and Garrison at Fort Meade," South Dakota State Historical Society, Pierre, S.D., 259; *Sturgis Advertiser,* 4 June 1891.

14. *Sturgis Weekly Record,* 20 Feb. 1891; *Sturgis Advertiser,* 19 Feb. 1891.

15. *Black Hills Daily Times,* 12 Mar., 21 Apr. 1891; *Sturgis Advertiser,* 26 Feb. 1891.

16. McGillycuddy, *McGillycuddy, Agent,* 272; *Sturgis Weekly Record,* 20 Feb. 1891.

17. *Black Hills Daily Times,* 12 Mar. 1891.

18. Ibid., 26 Mar., 18 Apr. 1891; *Sioux Falls Argus Leader,* 28 May 1891.

19. *Black Hills Journal,* 11 Mar. 1891; *Sioux Falls Argus Leader,* 28 May 1891.

20. *Sioux Falls Argus Leader,* 28 May 1891.

21. Ibid., 26 May 1891; Utley, *Last Days,* 265–66.

22. *Sioux Falls Argus Leader,* 27 Apr., 28 May 1891; *Black Hills Daily Times,* 8 Apr. 1891.

23. *Black Hills Daily Times,* 8, 19, 29 Apr. 1891; *Sturgis Advertiser,* 14 May 1891; *Sioux Falls Argus Leader,* 30 Apr. 1891.

24. *Sioux Falls Argus Leader,* 30 Apr. 1891.

25. Ibid.

26. *Black Hills Daily Times,* 12, 13 May 1891.

27. *Sturgis Weekly Record,* 27 Mar. 1891; *Sturgis Advertiser,* 14 May 1891.

28. *Black Hills Daily Times,* 27 May 1891.

29. *Sioux Falls Argus Leader,* 28 May 1891.

30. Ibid.

31. Ibid.; *Sturgis Weekly Record,* 5 June 1891.

32. *Sioux Falls Argus Leader,* 28, 29 May 1891.

33. Ibid., 29 May 1891; McGillycuddy, *McGillycuddy, Agent,* 272.

34. *Sioux Falls Argus Leader,* 30 May 1891.

35. Ibid., 2 June 1891.

36. *Black Hills Daily Times,* 6, 19 June 1891; *Sturgis Weekly Record,* 5 June 1891.

37. *Sturgis Weekly Record,* 9, 19 June 1891.

38. *Black Hills Daily Times,* 19 June 1891.

39. *Sturgis Weekly Record,* 26 June 1891; *Sturgis Advertiser,* 25 June 1891.

40. *Sturgis Advertiser,* 2 July 1891.

41. *Sturgis Weekly Record,* 26 June, 1891; *Black Hills Daily Times,* 2 July 1891; *Sioux Falls Argus Leader,* 1 July 1891.

42. *Sioux Falls Argus Leader,* 1 July 1891.

43. Ibid.

44. *Sturgis Advertiser,* 2 July 1891.

45. Post Returns, June 1891; *Sioux Falls Argus Leader*, 1 July 1891; *Black Hills Daily Times*, 2 July 1891; Post Order No. 86, 21 May 1891, in Post Returns, May 1891.

46. *Sturgis Weekly Record*, 26 June, 3 July 1891.

47. Ibid., 3 July 1891.

48. *Sturgis Advertiser*, 2 July 1891; *Black Hills Daily Times*, 4 July 1891.

49. McCall to Commissioner of Indian Affairs, 18 Mar. 1891, in Utley, *Last Days*, 267; *Sturgis Weekly Record*, 10 July 1891.

CHAPTER 10

1. *Annual Report of the Secretary of War (1892)* 1:82, 120.

2. Heitman, *Historical Register* 2:626; Eric Feaver, "Indian Soldiers, 1891–95: An Experiment on the Closing Frontier," *Prologue* (Summer 1975), 109–18.

3. General Order No. 28, AGO, Headquarters, Department of the Army, Washington, D.C., 9 Mar. 1891, in Post Returns, Mar. 1891.

4. *Annual Report of the Commissioner of Indian Affairs to the Secretary of the Interior for the Fiscal Year Ended June 30, 1890*, 2 vols. (Washington, D.C., 1891), 1:lvii–lviii; *Annual Report of the Commissioner of Indian Affairs to the Secretary of the Interior for the Fiscal Year Ended June 30, 1891*, 2 vols. (Washington, D.C., 1892), 1:78; *Annual Report of the Secretary of War (1891)* 1:81; *Annual Report of the Secretary of War (1892)* 1:82, 120. Richard Upton, ed., *The Indian As a Soldier at Fort Custer, Montana* (El Segundo, Calif.: Upton and Sons, 1983), 115–23; Maurice Frink and Casey Barthelmess, *Photographer on an Army Mule* (Norman: University of Oklahoma Press, 1965), 101, 121–22; *Sturgis Weekly Record*, 24 July 1903.

5. Feaver, "Indian Soldiers," 110; Ray Brandes, ed., *Troopers West: Military and Indian Affairs on the American Frontier* (San Diego: Frontier Heritage Press, 1970), 42–45; Byron Price, *The Utopian Experience: The Army and the Indian, 1890–1897* (Fort Collins, Colo.: Valor and Arms Press, 1975), 15–35; Upton, *The Indian As a Soldier*, 115–23.

6. Scott, *Some Memories of a Soldier*, 86, 168, 170; James A. Sawick, *Cavalry Regiments of the U.S. Army* (Dumfries, Va.: Wyvern Publications, 1985), 64; Upton, *The Indian As a Soldier*, 128.

7. Feaver, "Indian Soldiers," 109; Price, *Utopian Experience, 17.*

8. Upton, *The Indian As a Soldier,* 128; *Annual Report of the Secretary of War (1891)* 1:14; *Annual Report of the Secretary of War (1892)* 1:120; Letter, Dr. Elaine C. Everly, National Archives, to author, 4 May 1990.

9. Price, *Utopian Experience,* 21; Brandes, *Troopers West,* 55; Feaver, "Indian Soldiers," 111; Thomas R. Buecher, "Fort Niobrara, 1880–1906: Guardian of the Rosebud Sioux," *Nebraska History* 65, no. 3 (Fall 1984): 316.

10. Post Returns, Nov. 1891; *Sturgis Weekly Record,* 13 Nov. 1891; Price, *Utopian Experience,* 23.

11. *Sturgis Weekly Record,* 13 Nov. 1891; Upton, *The Indian As a Soldier,* 61, 128; Price, *Utopian Experience,* 18; Post Returns, Nov., Dec. 1891.

12. Feaver, "Indian Soldiers," 110.

13. First Lieutenant G. W. MacDonald to Post Adjutant, Fort Meade, 24 Nov. 1891, in "Register of Letters Sent, Troop L, Third Cavalry," Regular Army Mobile Units, RG 391, National Archives, Washington, D.C.; Post Returns, Dec. 1891; Price, *Utopian Experience,* 28.

14. Feaver, "Indian Soldiers," 112; Post Returns, Dec. 1891, Jan. 1892.

15. "Medical History," 1892, 263; Terri Howell, *St. Thomas Episcopal Parish* (Sturgis, S.D.: By the author, 1987), 7, 11, 16, 17; Post Returns, Oct. 1892.

16. *Sturgis Weekly Record,* 26 Feb. 1891.

17. Ibid., 8 Jan. 1892; Byron to Adjutant, Fort Meade, 29 Jan. 1892, in "Register of Letters Sent, Troop L, Third Cavalry," Regular Army Mobile Units, RG 391, National Archives, Washington, D.C.

18. Byron to Assistant Adjutant General, Department of Dakota, St. Paul, Minn., 14 Feb. 1892, in "Register of Letters Sent, Troop L, Third Cavalry," Regular Army Mobile Units, RG 391, National Archives, Washington, D.C.

19. Post Returns, Feb., Mar., Apr. 1892.

20. "Medical History," July 1892; Howell, *St. Thomas,* 7, 11, 16–17.

21. Brandes, *Troopers West,* 44.

22. Hare quoted in Howell, *St. Thomas,* 17, 21; "Medical History," Aug. 1892.

23. *Episcopal Church News,* Sioux Falls, S.D., Feb. 1893.

24. *Sturgis Weekly Record,* 29 Jan. 1892.

25. *Medal of Honor Recipients,* 88th Cong., 2d sess., 95, 649; *Sturgis Weekly Record,* 3 July 1891; *Black Hills Daily Times,* 27 Nov. 1891; Post Returns, June, Aug. 1891.

26. Post Returns, Jan. 1891; "Medical History," Feb. 1892; Price, *Utopian Experience,* 29.

27. Gregory J. W. Urwin, *The United States Cavalry: An Illustrated History* (Dorset, Eng.: Blandford Books, 1983), 164; Post Returns, Oct. 1892; Price, *Utopian Experience,* 29.

28. Schofield to Secretary of War, 8 Apr. 1893, in *Annual Report of the Secretary of War (1893),* 4 vols. (Washington, D.C., 1893), 1:168–69, 496–98.

29. James McLaughlin, Indian Agent, Standing Rock Agency, S.D., to Commissioner of Indian Affairs (hereafter CIA), 30 Jan. 1893, in "Correspondence Relating to the 1891–95 Experiment in Enlisting Indians in Companies of Regular Army Regiments," Records, RG 94; *Sturgis Weekly Record,* 10 June 1897; Price, *Utopian Experience,* 29; Feaver, "Indian Soldiers," 113–14, 116–18.

30. Sumner to Adjutant General, Army Headquarters, Washington, D.C., 12 Sept. 1894, in Post Letters Sent.

31. Carlton to Adjutant General, Department of Dakota, St. Paul, Minn., 3 Oct. 1894, and Carlton to Adjutant General, Army Headquarters, Washington, D.C., 15 Feb. 1895, in ibid.

32. *Annual Report of the Secretary of War (1892)* 1:120; Post Returns, Sept. 1893; Heitman, *Historical Register* 1:1039.

33. Carlton to Adjutant General, Army Headquarters, Washington, D.C., 15 Feb. 1895, in Post Letters Sent; Post Returns, Feb. 1893.

34. Feaver, "Indian Soldiers," 114–15.

35. Post Returns, Feb., May, Oct. 1894; Carlton to Adjutant General, Army Headquarters, Washington, D.C., 15 Feb. 1895, in Post Letters Sent.

36. Carlton to Adjutant General, Army Headquarters, Washington, D.C., 15 Feb. 1895, in Post Letters Sent.

37. Post Returns, Feb., Mar., Apr. 1895. It was also in February 1895 that a fire of undetermined origin destroyed the post hospital at Fort Meade.

38. Upton, *The Indian As a Soldier,* 23; Special Order No. 64, AGO, Headquarters, Department of the Army, Washington, D.C., 4 May 1895, in Post Returns, May 1895; *Annual Report of the Secretary of War (1897),* 5 vols. (Washington, D.C., 1897), 1:218.

39. *Annual Report of the Secretary of War (1897)* 1:218.

40. Scott, *Some Memories of a Soldier,* 170. Stephen B. Elkins was the secretary of war under President Harrison at the time the Indian experiment was started. He was replaced by Daniel S. Lamont of New York when Grover Cleveland returned to the presidency in 1893 after being out of office for four years.

41. Ibid., 168–69.

CHAPTER 11

1. Post Returns, Nov. 1897; Robert W. Frazer, *Forts of the West* (Norman: University of Oklahoma Press, 1965), 136–38; U.S. Congress, Senate, Report No. 64, Calendar No. 88, 53d Cong., 1st sess., 2 Nov. 1893.

2. Lt. Col. Sumner to J. J. Davenport, Sturgis, S.D., 9 Oct. 1893, and Davenport to Brig. Gen. Wesley Merritt, Department of Dakota, St. Paul, Minn., 28 Sept. 1893, in Davenport Papers, Leland D. Case Library for Western Historical Studies, Black Hills State College, Spearfish, S.D.

3. Sumner to Davenport, 9 Oct. 1893 in ibid.; U.S. Congress, Senate, Report No. 64, Calendar No. 88, 53d Cong., 1st sess., 2 Nov. 1893.

4. Annual Report of Brigadier General J. J. Coppinger, Department of the Platte, Omaha, Neb., 28 Aug. 1895, to Secretary of War, included in *Annual Report of the Secretary of War (1895),* 3 vols. (Washington, D.C., 1895), 1:163–67; Post Returns, June 1895; U.S. Congress, Senate, 55th Cong., 2d sess., S. Doc. 76, 20 Jan. 1898, 2–3. Fort Meade was assigned to the Department of the Platte by General Order No. 45, AGO, Headquarters, Department of the Army, Washington, D.C., 23 July 1895, and returned to the Department of Dakota and Lakes by General Order No. 7, AGO, 11 Mar. 1898, in Post Returns, July 1895 and Mar. 1898.

5. U.S. Congress, Senate, *Certain Correspondence Relating to the Matter of the Maintenance of Fort Meade, So. [cq.] Dak.,* 55th Cong., 2d sess., S. Ex. Doc. 76, second endorsement, Major D. D. Wheeler, Chief Quartermaster, Department of the Platte, Omaha, 20 Feb. 1897, to Commanding General, Department of the Platte, 2.

6. Ibid., third endorsement, Coppinger, Omaha, 16 Mar. 1897, to Secretary of War, 3–4, 9–10.

7. Ibid., ninth endorsement, Nelson A. Miles, Major General commanding, U.S. Army, Washington, D.C., 29 Mar. 1897, 5–7.

8. Ibid., fifteenth endorsement, Major General Nelson A. Miles, 20 Jan. 1898, 7; *Sturgis Weekly Record,* 14 Feb., 21 Sept. 1898.

9. U.S. Congress, Senate, *Certain Correspondence Relating to the Matter of the Maintenance of Fort Meade, So. [cq.] Dak.,* 55th Cong., 2d sess., S. Ex. Doc. 76, 4.

10. U.S. Congress, Senate, 56th Cong., 1st sess., S. Rept. 1379, 18 May 1900, 2; *Sturgis Weekly Record,* 14 Feb. 1898; Dale Morrison to author, 13 Aug. 1987, quoting Historical Data Sheet, Engineering Office, Fort Meade VA Medical Center.

11. "Site Report Concerning the Preservation of Fort Meade, S.D., July 1971," State Game, Fish, and Parks Department, South Dakota State Historical Society, Pierre, S.D.

12. Mabel Horner, "Colonel Caleb Carlton and 'The Star-Spangled Banner'" (Manuscript, Library of Congress, Washington, D.C., n.d.), copy in possession of author, also quoted in *Black Hills Press,* 8 May 197; Heitman, *Historical Register* 1:282.

13. Horner, "Colonel Caleb"; "National Anthem Honored First in South Dakota," *Middle Border Bulletin* 3, no. 4 (Spring 1944): 1–2; Gerald Weland, "Star Spangled Night," *Elks Magazine* 66, no. 4 (Oct. 1987): 26–36.

14. "National Anthem Honored," 1–2.

15. Ibid.

16. Horner, "Colonel Caleb"; "National Anthem Honored," 1–2; *World Almanac and Book of Facts* (New York: Newspaper Enterprise Association, 1982), 477–78; Historical Marker Dedication Program, 1976, Fort Meade VA Medical Center, Fort Meade, S.D., 4; *Sturgis Weekly Record,* 4 Dec. 1919. The governor of South Dakota

dedicated a marker on the grounds of old Fort Meade in 1976 that traces the history of "The Star-Spangled Banner" and proudly proclaims, "It Started Here."

17. Heitman, *Historical Register* 1:179; Post Returns, Aug. 1897, Apr. 1898.

18. *Sturgis Weekly Record,* 20 May 1898, 1 Sept. 1899; Post Returns, Apr., May, June, Aug. 1898.

19. Wright Tarbell, "History of Dakota Militia and the South Dakota National Guard," *South Dakota Historical Collections* 6 (1912): 471–72, 453–55.

20. Post Returns, May, June, July 1898; Heitman, *Historical Register* 1:272, 409, 461, 495. The four officers who obtained leave to serve in the volunteer regiments were Captains Edward A. Godwin and Andrew G. Hammond and First Lieutenants DeRosey C. Cabell and Elwood A. Evans.

21. Post Returns, May 1898; *Sturgis Weekly Record,* 6 May 1898.

22. Post Returns, May 1898; *Sturgis Weekly Record,* 29 June 1898.

23. *Sturgis Weekly Record,* 12 Aug. 1898; Bob Lee and Dick Williams, *Last Grass Frontier: The South Dakota Stock Grower Heritage* (Rapid City, S.D.: South Dakota Stock Growers Assn., 1964), 175.

24. *Sturgis Weekly Record,* 12 Aug. 1898, 12 Feb. 1899; Tarbell, "History of Dakota Militia," 472.

25. Post Returns, July, Aug., Sept., Oct. 1898; *Sturgis Weekly Record,* 8 Oct. 1898.

26. *Sturgis Weekly Record,* 20 May 1898; Post Returns, Oct. 1898; Heitman, *Historical Register* 1:65–66.

27. Post Returns, Oct. 1898, Jan. 1891; *Sturgis Weekly Record,* 8 Oct. 1898.

28. Post Returns, Oct. 1898, Jan. 1899; *Sturgis Weekly Record,* 20 May 1899.

29. *Sturgis Weekly Record,* 20 May 1899; Post Returns, May 1899.

30. Post Returns, Sept., Nov. 1898, Jan., Mar., Nov. 1899; General Order No. 69, AGO, Headquarters, Department of the Army, Washington, D.C., 12 Mar. 1899, in Post Returns, Mar. 1899.

31. Herbert S. Schell, *History of South Dakota* (Lincoln: University of Nebraska Press, 1961), 238.

CHAPTER 12

1. Fort Meade, "Buildings and Improvements, 1900–1907, 1907–1911," Engineering Office, Fort Meade VA Medical Center, Fort Meade, S.D.; *Sturgis Weekly Record,* 1 Feb. 1901.

2. *Sturgis Weekly Record,* 1 Feb., 4 May 1900.

3. Ibid., 21, 28 Sept., 12 Oct. 1900.

4. Ibid., 12 Oct., 21 Sept. 1900. The issue of 12 Oct. reprints and comments on the *Sioux Falls Argus Leader*'s defense of Pettigrew.

5. *Sturgis Weekly Record,* 9 Nov. 1900; *Sioux Falls Press,* 21 Sept. 1900; Pressler, *Senators from the Prairie,* 27–28.

6. *Sturgis Weekly Record,* 17 May, 15 Nov., 7 Dec. 1900; Heitman, *Historical Register* 1:626.

7. Post Returns, June 1899, July 1900, May, Oct. 1901.

8. Ibid., July 1900, May, Oct. 1901; *Sturgis Weekly Record,* 17 May 1901.

9. Post Returns, Feb. 1901–Jan. 1903; Heitman, *Historical Register* 1:515; *Sturgis Weekly Record,* 7 Dec. 1900, 5 Apr. 1901, 20 Mar. 1903.

10. *Sturgis Weekly Record,* 20 Mar. 1903, 8 Feb., 5 July 1901.

11. As a nine-year-old boy, Bob Tallent had been brought into the Black Hills by his parents, David and Annie Tallent, with the Gordon Party of 1874–75. His mother was living with him at Sturgis at the time of her death in 1901.

12. *Sturgis Weekly Record,* 14 June, 6 Sept. 1901, 6 Jan. 1903.

13. Ibid., 16 Apr. 1901.

14. Ibid., 5, 26 Apr., 19 July 1901.

15. Ibid., 21 June, reprinting undated *St. Paul Globe* article, and 6 Sept. 1901.

16. Ibid., 6, 13 Sept. 1901.

17. Ibid., 21 Nov. 1902, quoting undated article by Major S. L. Woodward, "Range Horses for Cavalry," in *Journal of the U.S. Cavalry Association.*

18. Ibid., 8 May 1903. Sir Robert Stephenson Baden-Powell was the founder of the Boy Scout and Girl Guide programs.

19. Ibid., 22 Apr. 1904.

20. Ibid., 21 Nov. 1902, 13 Dec. 1901, 4 July, 24 Oct. 1902.

21. Post Returns, May, Oct. 1902; *Sturgis Weekly Record,* 2 May 1902.

22. *Sturgis Weekly Record,* 10 Apr. 1903; Post Returns, Feb., Mar., Apr. 1903.

23. Post Returns, May, Sept., Oct. 1903; *Sturgis Weekly Record,* 27 Nov. 1903.

24. *Sturgis Weekly Record,* 4 Sept. 1903.

25. Ibid., 5 July 1905.

26. Ibid., 29 Sept., 6 Oct., 2 Mar. 1906.

27. Ibid., 28 Sept., 16 Mar., 5 Aug., 14 Sept. 1906; Post Returns, Apr. 1905, Mar., June, July 1906; Heitman, *Historical Register* 1:841.

CHAPTER 13

1. Post Returns, Oct. 1906; Floyd A. O'Neill, "An Anguished Odyssey: The Flight of the Utes, 1906–08," *Utah Historical Quarterly,* 36, no. 4 (Fall 1968): 315–27; "Selected Files Relating to the Ute Indian Trouble at Cheyenne River Agency," Central Classified Files, File 1455-07-121, Cheyenne River, 3 pts., Records of the Bureau of Indian Affairs, RG 75, National Archives, Washington, D.C., pt. 1, 56 (hereafter cites as "Selected Files"). Also see James McLaughlin, "The Unwhipped Utes," chapter 20 in *My Friend, the Indian* (Boston: Houghton Mifflin Co., 1910), 372–87; Stanley Vestal, *Warpath: The True Story of the Fighting Sioux Told in a Biography of Chief White Bull* (1948; reprint, Lincoln: University of Nebraska Press, 1984), 243; Pfaller, *James McLaughlin,* 248–61; and David D. Laudenschlager, "The Utes in South Dakota, 1906–1908," *South Dakota History* 9, no. 3 (Summer 1979): 236.

2. Commissioner of Indian Affairs to Secretary of the Interior, 2 Nov. 1907, in "Selected Files"; McLaughlin, *My Friend,* 379; Will G. Robinson, "Utes Invade South Dakota," *Wi-Iyohi* 7, no. 3 (1 June 1953): 1. In 1881, Adolphus Greely had led to the Arctic a U.S. expedition that made important discoveries in northwestern Greenland and on Ellesmere Island. Of the party of twenty-five, all but Greely and

six others perished during the winter of 1883 when relief supplies failed to reach them. The survivors were rescued in 1884, and Greely received the Founder's Medal of the National Geographic Society for his Arctic service.

3. *Annual Report of the Commissioner of Indian Affairs to the Secretary of the Interior for the Fiscal Year Ended June 30, 1907* (Washington, D.C.: Government Printing Office, 1907), 284, 783 (hereafter cited as CIA *Annual Report*); O'Neill, "An Anguished Odyssey," 323.

4. Rozella M. Bracewell, "Utes in Belle Fourche," *Cowboys and Sodbusters* (Sioux Falls, S.D.: Midwest-Beach, 1969), 218–19.

5. Ibid.; Post Returns, Nov., Dec. 1907, Jan. 1908; Bracewell, *Cowboys and Sodbusters*, 219; Heitman, *Historical Register* 1:271; *Sturgis Weekly Record*, 14 Dec. 1906.

6. *Sturgis Weekly Record*, 14 Dec. 1906; CIA to Capt. C. G. Hall, 2 Nov. 1907, in "Selected Files."

7. CIA to Capt. C. G. Hall, 2 Nov. 1907, in "Selected Files."

8. Laudenschlager, "The Utes in South Dakota," 241.

9. *Sturgis Weekly Record*, 25 Jan., 1 Feb. 1907.

10. Ibid., 1 Feb. 1907.

11. Ibid., 15 Feb., 8 Mar. 1907; CIA *Annual Report*, 127–31.

12. Post Returns, Feb.–June 1907; Laudenschlager, "The Utes in South Dakota," 240–41; Capt. Carter P. Johnson, Cheyenne Indian Reservation, to Adjutant General, Department of the Missouri, 15 July 1907, in "Selected Files."

13. Walter Baker, Thunder Butte, S.D., to CIA, 31 Jan. 1908, in "Selected Files."

14. *Sturgis Weekly Record*, 5 July 1907.

15. Captain Carter P. Johnson, Cheyenne River Agency, S.D., to Adjutant General, Department of Missouri, 15 July 1907, in "Selected Files."

16. *Sturgis Weekly Record*, 31 May, 5 July 1907.

17. Captain Carter P. Johnson, Cheyenne River Agency, S.D., to Adjutant General, Department of the Missouri, 15 July 1907, in "Selected Files."

18. Laudenschlager, "The Utes in South Dakota," 241; *Sturgis Weekly Record,* 5 July 1907; "Medical History," July 1907.

19. *Sturgis Weekly Record,* 21 June 1907.

20. Ibid.

21. Ibid.

22. Captain George L. Byram, Fort Meade, S.D., to Adjutant General, Department of the Missouri, 6 Sept. 1907, in "Selected Files"; *Sturgis Weekly Record,* 5 July, 6 Sept. 1907.

23. Thomas Downs, Cheyenne River Agency, S.D., to CIA, 17 Oct. 1907; Captain Carter P. Johnson, Thunder Butte, S.D., to Adjutant General, Army Headquarters, 30 Oct. 1907; and telegram, R. C. Craige, assistant clerk, Cheyenne River Agency, S.D., to CIA, 26 Oct. 1907, all in "Selected Files"; *Sturgis Weekly Record,* 5 July, 6 Sept. 1907.

24. Telegram, Adjutant General, Washington, D.C., to Commanding General, Department of Missouri, 24 Oct. 1907, and Thomas Downs to Charles W. Rastall, Cheyenne River Agency, S.D., forwarded to CIA, 24 Oct. 1907, both in "Selected Files."

25. Telegram, CIA to Thomas Downs, 4 Nov. 1907, in "Selected Files."

26. Captain Carter P. Johnson, Thunder Butte, S.D., to Adjutant General, Army Headquarters, 30 Oct. 1907, in "Selected Files."

27. CIA to Secretary of the Interior, 2 Nov. 1907, in "Selected Files."

28. CIA to the Secretary of the Interior, 2 Nov. 1907, 9, and Captain Carter P. Johnson, Thunder Butte, S.D., to Adjutant General, Army Headquarters, 30 Oct. 1907, in "Selected Files."

29. C. W. Rastall, Cheyenne River Agency, S.D., to CIA, 4, 7 Feb. 1908, in "Selected Files."

30. Captain James B. Hughes, Fort Meade, S.D., to Commanding General, Department of the Missouri, 31 Dec. 1907, in "Selected Files."

31. Vestal, *Warpath,* 248.

32. Frank Pierce, Assistant Secretary, Uintah Reservation, Utah, to CIA, 23 Oct. 1908, in "Selected Files."

CHAPTER 14

1. *Sturgis Weekly Record,* 31, 10, 24 Mar., 28 Apr. 1911; Post Returns, Mar. 1911.

2. *Sturgis Weekly Record,* 8 Dec. 1911.

3. Ibid.

4. Ibid., 1 Dec. 1911.

5. Ibid., 8 Dec. 1911.

6. Ibid., 22 Dec. 1911, reprint of *Sioux City Journal* article.

7. Ibid., 12 Jan. 1912; Post Returns, Jan., June 1912.

8. *Sturgis Weekly Record,* 18 Oct., 27 Sept. 1912; Post Returns, Sept., Oct. 1912.

9. Post Returns, Feb. 1913.

10. *Sturgis Weekly Record,* 18 July 1913. Poker Alice, as she was best known, is a mysterious figure in the history of Sturgis, especially as to her early life. There are so many contradictory stories about her, including many she told herself, that it is impossible to separate fact from fiction. For instance, she claimed to have been born in England, the daughter of a schoolmaster there, but she is listed on census returns as having been born in Virginia of parents who came to the United States from Ireland. It is known that she had three husbands. She is also credited with having up to seven children; if so, nobody in the Black Hills ever recalled seeing any of them. It is generally conceded, though, that Poker Alice was a well-known dealer in the gambling dens of Deadwood, Lead, and Rapid City before she settled in Sturgis sometime after the turn of the century. She admitted that she would rather play poker with experts than eat, summing up her philosophy as "easy come, easy go." After the death of her second husband in 1910 she became the operator of the thriving pleasure palace on Bear Butte Creek that catered to the Fort Meade soldier trade. She married for the third time in 1918, and her last husband died in 1924. She was frequently arrested for drunkenness and for keeping a disorderly house, but she paid her fines and continued her business as usual. She was extremely well liked in the community, even among the straitlaced. Many of the latter wrote to the governor urging leniency when she was finally sentenced to a

term in the state penitentiary for repeated convictions of operating a house of ill fame. The governor, noting that Poker Alice was seventy-five at the time, pardoned her. He explained that he wasn't going to send an old lady to prison when she obviously had so few years left. "Besides," the governor added in his letter of pardon, "Alice is not used to confinement." See Meade County Agricultural Census, Bureau of Vital Statistics, U.S. Commerce Department, Washington, D.C., 1925; Marriage License No. 66239, Meade County, S.D., 23 Dec. 1918, Meade County Clerk of Courts Office, Sturgis, S.D., and Governor's Book of Pardons, 27 Nov. 1928, 36, South Dakota State Archives, Pierre, S.D. Also see *Sturgis Weekly Record,* 5, 12 Dec. 1913.

11. Courtney Ryley Cooper, with Poker Alice Tubbs, "Easy Come, Easy Go," *Saturday Evening Post,* 3 Dec. 1927, 19–21, 108–10, 113–14; *Sturgis Weekly Record,* 19 Dec. 1913.

12. Post Returns, May, Oct., Nov. 1914; *Sturgis Weekly Record,* 1 May, 3 Oct. 1914, 17, 31 Mar., 15 Sept. 1916.

13. *Sturgis Weekly Record,* 17, 31 Mar. 1916.

14. Ibid., 22 Dec. 1916, 5, 19 Jan., 2 Feb. 1917; *Hot Springs Star,* 8 Dec. 1916; Richard Cropp, *The Coyotes: A History of the South Dakota National Guard* (Mitchell, S.D.: Educator Supply Co., 1962), 111.

15. *Sturgis Weekly Record,* 5, 19 Jan., 2 Feb. 1917; Cropp, *The Coyote,* 111.

16. *Sturgis Weekly Record,* 2 Feb. 1917; Cropp, *The Coyote,* 111.

17. *Sturgis Weekly Record,* 1 June 1917.

18. Ibid., 29 June 1917.

19. *Philip Weekly Review,* 3 Oct. 1918; *Sturgis Weekly Record,* 6 Sept. 1918; *Sioux Falls Argus Leader,* 27 Sept. 1918.

20. *Sturgis Weekly Record,* 19 July 1919; Heitman, *Historical Register* 1:1055; *Medal of Honor Recipients,* 88th Cong., 2d sess., 1964, 678; Post Returns, July 1917–Nov. 1918.

21. Post Returns, Jan.–Nov. 1917.

22. *Sturgis Weekly Record,* 19 July 1919; Heitman, *Historical Register* 1:1055; *Medal of Honor Recipients,* 88th Cong., 2d sess., 1964, 678.

23. *Sturgis Weekly Record,* 20 Mar. 1920; Alan L. Clem, *Prairie State Politics: Popular Democracy in South Dakota* (Washington, D.C.: Public Affairs Press, 1967), 60; Letter, Assistant Surgeon General W. G. Stimpson and Assistant Consulting Engineer Charles I. Stratton, Assistant Consulting Engineer to Surgeon General, U.S. Public Health Service, 7 Sept. 1920, in *Congressional Record,* 67th Cong., 2d sess., 31 Mar. 1922, 62:91.

24. *Sturgis Weekly Record,* 3, 17, 24 Feb., 12 May, 16, 30 June, 7 July 1921.

25. *Lead Daily Call,* 24 Feb. 1921.

26. *Sturgis Weekly Record,* 16 June, 7 July 1921.

27. Ibid., 7 July 1921.

28. Ibid., 1 Sept. 1921.

29. Ibid., 26 Jan. 1922.

30. *Newcastle News-Record,* 16 Mar. 1922.

31. *Sturgis Weekly Record,* 13 Apr. 1922.

32. Ibid., 22 June 1922.

33. Ibid., 15, 22 June 1922.

34. Ibid., reprint of *Aberdeen American-News* article, 29 June, 3, 6 July, 3 Aug. 1922, 22 Mar. 1923; Post Returns, Aug. 1922.

35. *Sturgis Weekly Record,* 29 Nov. 1923.

36. Ibid., 24 Oct. 1923.

37. Ibid., 27 Dec. 1923.

38. *Black Hills Press,* 17 Apr. 1924; *Sturgis Weekly Record,* 21 Feb., 13, 20, 26 Mar., 17 Apr. 1924; Post Returns, Feb. 1924.

39. *Sturgis Weekly Record,* 27 Dec. 1923.

40. Ibid., 8 May 1924.

41. Major K. S. Bradford, "A Short History of Fort Meade, South Dakota," in "Fort Meade D.T.S.D., 1878–1978: One Hundred Years of Service" (Mimeograph, Fort Meade Veterans Administration Medical Center, Fort Meade, S.D., 1978), 7–17; *Black Hills Press,* 8 May 1924; *Sturgis Weekly Record,* 12 July, 7 Aug., 9 Oct. 1924.

42. *Black Hills Press,* 15 May, 28 Aug. 1924; Charles Rambow, "The Ku Klux Klan in the 1920s: A Concentration in the Black Hills," *South Dakota History* 4, no. 1 (Winter 1973): 63–81; *Sturgis Weekly Record,* 25 Jan., 11 Sept. 1924.

43. Mrs. Douglas MacArthur, Waldorf Astoria, New York City, to R. B. Williams, Sturgis, S.D., 11 Feb. 1965, Old Fort Meade Museum and Historical Association, Fort Meade, S.D.

44. *Sturgis Weekly Record,* 23 June 1927; *Black Hills Press,* 30 June 1927.

CHAPTER 15

1. *Sturgis Tribune,* 30 June 1927; *Black Hills Press,* 9 June 1927; William Williamson, *William Williamson: An Autobiography* (Rapid City, S.D.: By the author, 1964), 192–93. Williamson was a U.S. congressman from South Dakota from 1921 to 1933.

2. Private Brokenleg's Letter of Commendation and Presidential Guard Medallion are owned by Dr. Kenneth O. Leonard of Keystone, S.D.

3. Williamson, *William Williamson,* 192; *Sturgis Tribune,* 17 Nov., 1, 8 Dec. 1927.

4. *Sturgis Tribune,* 15, 22 Dec. 1927; *Black Hills Press,* 10 Mar. 1990.

5. "2765th Company, SCS-6, Fort Meade, S.D.," *Official Annual, Civilian Conservation Corps, Nebraska-South Dakota District, Seventh Corps Area, August 1937* (Baton Rouge, La.: Direct Advertising Co., 1937), copy at the Old Fort Meade Museum and Historical Association, Fort Meade, S.D.; Bob Lee, "Camp Fechner Base for Hills CCC Camps," *Sturgis Tribune,* centennial edition, 25 Oct. 1978; author interviews on 12–13 Sept. 1978 with Francis Langin, the Sturgis mayor, and on 19 June 1978 with Ron Ringsrud, both of whom served at Camp Fechner.

6. *Sturgis Tribune,* 1 Jan. 1940; author interviews on 12–13 Sept. 1978 with Francis Langin and on 19 June 1978 with Ron Ringsrud.

7. Captain A. W. Stevens, "Exploring the Stratosphere," *National Geographic Magazine* 64, no. 4 (Oct. 1934): 397–434.

8. Ibid., 433–34.

9. Ibid., 434.

10. Ibid., 59–62, 65–69, 84–89; Captain A. W. Stevens, "Scientific Results of the World Record Stratosphere Flight," *National Geographic Magazine* 69, no. 5 (May 1936): 693–712; "Hubbard Medals Awarded to Stratosphere Explorers," ibid., 713–14; author interviews on 11 July 1978 with William Rudebeck, Arthur Piehl, and Henry Paulson, Sturgis, S.D., all of whom served with the Fourth Cavalry at the Stratocamp.

11. Colonel E. L. Nye, "Cavalry March" (Manuscript, n.d.), copy in possession of author.

12. Ibid.

13. *Sturgis Tribune,* 23 Nov. 1939, 8 Feb., 16 May 1940; "Peace-Time Routine at Post," *Sturgis Tribune,* centennial edition, 25 Oct. 1978.

14. Major General Neil D. Van Sickle, address at Fourth Cavalry Association Reunion, 20 Aug. 1966, Sturgis, S.D., copy in possession of author (hereafter cited as Van Sickle). Van Sickle came to Fort Meade as a second lieutenant just out of West Point. He transferred to the Air Corps when the Fourth Cavalry was mechanized and lost its horses. Both Van Sickle and Clarence (Pappy) Hoel, who was a civilian employee at Fort Meade when the Fourth Cavalry was mechanized, confirmed that the cavalry soldiers had trouble adjusting to motorcycles. Hoel founded the Black Hills Motor Classic, an annual event that attracts thousands of cyclists to Sturgis, in 1940.

15. *Sturgis Tribune,* 11 Apr., 2 May 1940.

16. Ibid., 2 May 1940.

17. Ibid., 29 Feb., 2 May 1940.

18. Ibid., 13 June 1940.

19. Ibid., 30 May, 6, 13 June, 4 July 1940.

20. Ibid., 6 June, 4 July 1940.

21. Ibid., 30 Oct. 1940.

22. Ibid., 26 Sept. 1940.

23. Ibid., 28 Nov., 5 Dec. 1940.

24. Ibid., 6 Mar. 1941.

25. *Black Hills Press,* 3 Apr. 1941; *Sturgis Tribune,* 27 Mar., 10 Apr., 10 July, 1941.

26. Ibid., 14 Aug. 1941.

27. Ibid., 27 Nov., 4 Dec. 1941.

28. Ibid., 12 Feb., 5 Mar. 1942; author interview on 25 June 1988 with Ronald Ringsrud.

29. *Sturgis Tribune,* 2, 16 Apr. 1942.

30. *Rapid City Daily Journal,* 25 June 1942.

31. Author interview on 6 Sept. 1978 with Vernon Allison, Sturgis, S.D., who served in Troop C, Fourth Cavalry, at Fort Meade and Camp Hale during this period; Jack Cannon, "Sabres of Fourth Have Flashed for 100 Years," *Rapid City Daily Journal,* 3 Aug. 1961; First Lieutenant John G. Keliher, "History of the Fourth United States Cavalry" (Manuscript, Old Fort Meade Museum and Historical Association, Fort Meade, S.D., n.d.), 19.

32. *Sturgis Tribune,* 21 May 1942.

33. Ibid., 28 Jan. 1943, 20 Aug., 10 Sept., 3 Dec. 1942.

34. Van Sickle; Bob Lee, "Fourth Cavalry Served at Fort Meade Longer Than Any Other Unit," *Sturgis Tribune,* centennial edition, 25 Oct. 1978.

CHAPTER 16

1. *Sturgis Tribune,* 22 Feb. 1943.

2. Ibid., 6 May, 10 June 1943.

3. Author interviews on 12 Sept. 1978 with Harold Kelley and George Welch, Sturgis, S.D., both of whom served in the Eighty-Eighth Glider Infantry Regiment during its tour at Fort Meade.

4. Confidential Orders, 19, 22 May, 31 July 1942, Secretary of War, in John M. Curran, "The Companies of the Damned," *Army Magazine* (Feb. 1982), 54–57; David Super, Public Affairs Office, War Department, the Pentagon, to author, 10 June 1985.

5. In addition to Curran's "The Companies of the Damned," information on these special organizations was gleaned from a series of four articles by E. J. Kahn, Jr., "Annals of Crime," which appeared in the *New Yorker* in the issues of 11, 18, 25 Mar. and 1 Apr. 1950.

6. *Sturgis Tribune,* 24 Feb., 9 Mar. 1944.

7. Ibid., 23 Mar. 1944.

8. Ibid., 10 Feb. 1944.

9. Ibid., 16 Mar. 1944.

10. Ibid.

11. Ibid., 9 Nov. 1944; Arnold Krammer, *Nazi Prisoners of War in America* (Briarcliff Manor, N.Y.: Stein and Day, 1979), 71; Secretary of War to Administrator, Veterans Administration, 11 Sept. 1944, in Engineering Office, Fort Meade VA Medical Center, Fort Meade, S.D.

12. Krammer, *Nazi Prisoners,* 72; *Sturgis Tribune,* 19 Oct. 1944.

13. *Sturgis Tribune,* 7 Dec. 1944.

14. Ibid.

15. Ibid., 4 Feb. 1945; author interview on 11 July 1978 with Arthur Piehl, Sturgis, S.D., who lived in Sturgis at the time the German POW camp was at Fort Meade. Piehl had formerly served with the Fourth Cavalry while it was stationed at Fort Meade.

16. *Sturgis Tribune,* 15 Feb., 12 Apr. 1945.

17. Ibid., 12 Apr. 1945; *Medal of Honor Recipients,* 88th Cong., 2d sess., 1964, 61, 677.

18. *Sturgis Tribune,* 12, 26 Apr. 1945.

19. Ibid., 12 Apr. 1945.

20. Secretary of War to Administrator, Veterans Administration, 23 May 1945, in Engineering Office, Fort Meade VA Medical Center, Fort Meade, S.D.; *Sturgis Tribune,* 14 June 1945.

21. Author interview on 11 July 1978 with Arthur Piehl, Sturgis, S.D.; Lieutenant Colonel Gordon N. Zelez, USA, Deputy, Congressional Correspondence Agency, Department of the Army, Washington, D.C., to U.S. Senator George McGovern, 28 June 1978, containing information on the Prisoner of War Camp at Fort Meade, showing strengths as of 1 June 1945, 1 Oct. 1945, 1 Dec. 1945, and 1 Jan. 1946, copies of which were supplied to author (hereafter cited as Zelez to McGovern, 28 June 1978).

22. Zelez to McGovern, 28 June 1978. The War Department's lease with the Veterans Administration for space at Fort Meade for the POW Camp was terminated on 1 Nov. 1945.

23. Ibid.; *Sturgis Tribune,* 28 Dec. 1944; author interview on 11 July 1978 with Arthur Piehl, Sturgis, S.D.

24. *Sturgis Tribune,* 3 Jan. 1945.

25. Author interview on 17 May 1978 with Mrs. Leonard Schryvers, whose husband was the foreman of the civilian carpentry crew at Fort Meade when the German POWs worked at converting the old army barracks into hospital wards.

26. Minta Ann Miller, "German Prisoners of War in the United States during World War II: Pampered?" (Senior thesis, Hollins College, Va., 1983), 11.

27. *Sturgis Tribune,* 31 Jan. 1946.

EPILOGUE

1. Author interview on 9 Oct. 1978 with Andrew Szilvasi, Superintendent, Black Hills National Cemetery, Sturgis, S.D.; *Black Hills Press,* 29 July 1987; "Fort Meade Planning Unit," South Dakota Area Office, Bureau of Land Management, Belle Fourche, S.D., 1.

2. "Fort Meade Planning Unit," South Dakota Area Office, Bureau of Land Management, Belle Fourche, S.D.

3. "Council Advises VA to Protect Barracks at Fort Meade: Demolition Would Denude Parade Grounds," *Preservation News* 11, no. 10 (October 1971): 3; Minutes, Old Fort Meade Museum and Historical Association, Fort Meade, S.D., 20 Apr. 1964.

4. Minutes, Old Fort Meade Museum and Historical Association, Fort Meade, S.D.

5. Ibid., 9 Nov. 1967, 19 Sept. 1971; "Hospital Admission Fact Sheet," Fort Meade VA Medical Center, Fort Meade, S.D.

6. Letter to author from Brigadier General Philip G. Killey, South Dakota Adjutant General, Camp Rapid, Rapid City, S.D., 13 Aug. 1967; "Site Report Concerning the Preservation of Fort Meade, S.D., July 1971," State Game, Fish, and Parks Department, South Dakota State Historical Society, Pierre, S.D. (July 1971), 8.

7. *Black Hills Press,* 29 July 1989.

BIBLIOGRAPHY

MANUSCRIPTS, PAPERS, AND THESES

Bradford, Major K. S. "A Short History of Fort Meade, South Dakota." In "Fort Meade D.T.S.D., 1878–1978: One Hundred Years of Service." Mimeograph. Fort Meade Veterans Administration Medical Center, Fort Meade, S.D., 1978.

Davenport, Jarvis. Fort Meade File. Sturgis Water Works Co., Sturgis, S.D.

"The 1880 Federal Census: Fort Meade, Lawrence County, Dakota Territory." Microfilm Series T9, Roll 113. National Archives, Washington, D.C.

Freedom, Gary. "Military Forts and Communications Network on the Northern Great Plains." Paper presented at Dakota History Conference, Dakota State College, Madison, S.D., April 1985.

Grunwald, E. A. "General Sturgis and His Defeat at the Battle of Brice's Cross Roads, June 10, 1864." Paper, Department of English, History, and Government, United States Naval Academy, Annapolis, Md., March 1950.

Horner, Mabel. "Colonel Caleb Carlton and 'The Star-Spangled Banner.'" Manuscript. Library of Congress, Washington, D.C., n.d. Copy in the possession of the author.

"Journal of the Senate of the Second Session of the State Legislature, 1891, Pertaining to Joint Resolution No. 2 for Enlargement of Post and Garrison at Fort Meade." South Dakota State Historical Society, Pierre, S.D.

Keliher, First Lieutenant John G. "History of the Fourth United States Cavalry." Manuscript. Old Fort Meade Museum and Historical Association, Fort Meade, S.D., n.d.

Krause, Randolph P. "History of Fort Meade." B.S. thesis, Black Hills State College, Spearfish, S.D., June 1949.

Laswell, Mrs. William S. Samuel D. Sturgis Family File. Dallas, Tex.

"A Memorial to the Secretary of War Praying for the Erection of a Military Post at the North Base of the Black Hills of Dakota." Laws, Memorials, and Resolutions of the Territory of Dakota Legislative Assembly. 5th sess., 1865–66. Chapter 50. South Dakota State Historical Society, Pierre, S.D.

Miller, Minta Ann. "German Prisoners of War in the United States during World War II: Pampered?" Senior thesis, Hollins College, Va., 1983.

Nye, Colonel E. L. "Cavalry March." Manuscript. N.d. Copy in the possession of the author.

Odell, Thomas E. "The Story of Bear Butte, Black Hills Landmark and Indian Shrine: Its Scenic, Historic, and Scientific Uniqueness." Paper, Department of Social Services (History), Black Hills State College, Spearfish, S.D., 1941.

Parker, Watson. "The Collins-Russell-Gordon Expedition to the Black Hills." Paper presented at Black Hills State College History Conference, Spearfish, S.D., 1973.

"Prisoner of War Camps, by Location and Types of Work, Army Service Forces, Office of the Provost Marshal General, June 1945–January 1946." South Dakota State Historical Society, Pierre, S.D.

Prisoner of War Operations. File. Office of the Chief of Military History, Department of the Army, Washington, D.C., 31 August 1945. Shelf Number 51427. Prisoner of War Division, Library of Congress, Washington, D.C.

"Records of Burials in Post Cemetery, Fort Meade, S.D." Black Hills National Cemetery, Sturgis, S.D., rev. copy, 10 March 1987.

Records of the Adjutant General's Office. Record Group 94. National Archives, Washington, D.C.

Letters Received by the Office of the Adjutant General (main series), 1871–85. Microfilm Publications MC 666.

"Medical History of Posts, Fort Meade, August 1878–June 1913." Microfilm Publications MC 402.

"Papers Relating to Military Operations in the Departments of the Platte and Dakota against the Sioux Indians." Sioux War Papers, 1876–96. Microfilm Publications MC 277, Roll 292.

"Report of Board of Officers Investigating Outrage upon the Citizens of Sturgis, D.T., by the Twenty-fifth Infantry." 1885. Microfilm Publications MC 689, Roll 393.

Returns from U.S. Military Posts (main series), 1800–1916. Microfilm Publications MC 617, Rolls 764, 765, 766.

"Returns of the Seventh Cavalry, 1 January 1873–1 January 1878." Microfilm Publications MC 136, Roll 2034.

Records of the Bureau of Indian Affairs. Record Group 75. "Selected Files Relating to the Ute Indian Trouble at Cheyenne River Agency." Selected Documents: Central Classified Files, Files 1455-07-121, Cheyenne River, Parts I, II, and III, 9757-08-121, and File 9410-08-121, Cheyenne River, 23190-08-124, Uintah. National Archives, Washington, D.C.

Records of the Judge Advocate General's Office. Record Group 153. "Court Martial Proceedings in the Case of Major Marcus A. Reno, St. Paul, Minn., 8–20 March 1877, CC-QQ 1554." Court Martial-QM 87. National Archives, Washington, D.C.

Records of the Provost Marshal General. Record Group 389. Prisoner of War Special Projects Division, Administrative Branch. Decimal File, 1943–46, Boxes 1593–1655. National Archives, Washington, D.C.

Records of the Quartermaster General. Record Group 92. "Reports of Persons and Articles Hired, Fort Meade, D.T." Doc. 547. National Archives, Washington, D.C.

Records of the U.S. Army Continental Commands, 1821–1922. Record Group 93. National Archives, Washington, D.C.

Regular Army Mobile Units. Record Group 391. "Register of Letters Sent, Troop L, Third Cavalry." National Archives, Washington, D.C.

"Site Report Concerning the Preservation of Fort Meade, S.D., July 1971." State Game, Fish, and Parks Department. South Dakota State Historical Society, Pierre, S.D.

Sturgis, Jerusha Wilcox. "Sturgis Family History." Manuscript. Minneapolis, Minn., 24 February 1910.

Van Sickle, Major General Neil D. Address at Fourth Cavalry Association Reunion, 20 August 1966, Sturgis, S.D. Copy in the possession of the author.

Wilkinson, Major W. G. "Four Months in the Saddle: The Cross Country March of the Eighth Cavalry, 1888." Manuscript. Old Fort Meade Museum and Historical Association, Fort Meade, S.D., n.d.

GOVERNMENT DOCUMENTS

Annual Reports of the Commissioner of Indian Affairs, 1890, 1891, 1907.

Annual Reports of the Secretary of War, 1873–97.

U.S. Congress. *Congressional Record.*
45th Cong., 2d sess., 1878.
67th Cong., 2d sess., 1922.
93d Cong., 2d sess., 1974.

U.S. Congress. House.

Annual Report of Captain William Ludlow, Corps of Engineers for the Fiscal Year Ending June 30, 1874. 43d Cong., 2d sess., 1874–75. H. Exec. Doc. 1.

Dakota Indian War of 1862: Memorial and Accompanying Papers of the Legislature of Dakota Territory. 42d Cong., 3d sess., 1872. H. Misc. Doc. 9.

Department of the Interior. *Survey of the Black Hills: Letter from the Secretary of the Interior Submitting Estimate of Appropriations for Expense of Geological Exploration and Report of Black Hills Country, 14 January 1876.* 44th Cong., 1st sess., 1875–76. H. Exec. Doc. 125.

Legislative Assembly of Dakota Territory. *Memorial in Reference to the Black Hills Country Serving as a Retreat for Hostile Indians.* 42d Cong., 3d sess. H. Misc. Doc. 65.

Letter from the Secretary of the Treasury Transmitting an Estimate from the Secretary of War of Appropriation for Purchase of Land Near Fort Meade, Dak., for the Purpose of Obtaining a Water Supply, 12 March 1888. 50th Cong., 1st sess., 1888. H. Exec. Doc. 211.

Report of a Reconnaissance of the Black Hills of Dakota Made in the Summer of 1874, by Captain William Ludlow, Corps of Engineers. 44th Cong., 1st sess., 1875–76. H. Exec. Doc. 1.

"Report of the Commanding General of the Department of Dakota, Brvt. Maj. Gen. John Gibbon, Commanding." *Secretary of War Annual Report, 1878.* 45th Cong., 3d sess., 1878–79. H. Exec. Doc. 18 vols.

U.S. Congress. Senate.

Certain Correspondence Relating to the Matter of the Maintenance of Fort Meade, So. [cq.] Dak. 55th Cong., 2d sess., 6 Dec. 1897 to 8 July 1898. S. Ex. Doc. 76.

Committee on Military Affairs. 45th Cong., 2d sess., 1878. S. Rept. 261, accompanying S. Bill 785, 16 April 1878.

Dakota Militia in the War of 1862. 58th Cong., 2d sess., 1904. S. Doc. 241.

Encounter between Sioux Indians of the Pine Ridge Agency, S. Dak., and a Sheriff's Posse of Wyoming. 58th Cong., 2d sess., 1904. S. Doc. 128.

End of Indian Wars Statement by Former Secretary of War in Relation to Distribution of the Army, 2 November 1893. 53d Cong., 1st sess., 1893. S. Cal. 88.

Explorations in Nebraska. 35th Cong., 2d sess., 1858–59. S. Doc. 1.

Legislative Assembly of Dakota Territory. *Memorial Asking for a Scientific Exploration of That Territory.* 42d Cong., 3d sess., 1872–73. S. Misc. Doc. 45.

Letter from the Secretary of the Treasury Transmitting Communication from the Acting Secretary of War Relative to an Appropriation for the Protection of Land near Fort Meade, Dakota, 27 January 1887. 49th Cong., 2d sess., 1887. S. Exec. Doc. 54.

Medal of Honor Recipients: 1863–1963. Prepared for the Subcommittee on Veterans Affairs of the Committee on Labor and Public Welfare. 88th Cong., 2d sess., 1964. Committee Print.

Message from the President of the United States Transmitting Information in Relation to the Black Hills Country. 43d Cong., special sess., 15 March 1875. S. Exec. Doc. 2.

The Mineral Wealth, Climate and Rainfall, and Natural Resources of the Black Hills of Dakota. 44th Cong., 1st sess., 1875–76. S. Exec. Doc. 51.

Rebuilding and Enlarging Fort Meade, S.D., 18 May 1900. 56th Cong., 1st sess., 1900. S. Rept. 1379.

Report of Brevet Brigadier General W. F. Raynolds on the Exploration of the Yellowstone and Missouri Rivers, 1859–1860. 40th Cong., 1st sess., 1867–68. S. Exec. Doc. 77.

Report of Lieutenant G. K. Warren to Brevet Brig. Gen. W. F. Harney, U.S. Army, Commanding Sioux Expedition. 34th Cong., 1st sess., 1855–56. S. Exec. Doc. 76.

Report of Lieut. G. K. Warren of His Explorations between the Missouri and Platte Rivers and the Rocky Mountains, 1855. 34th Cong., 1st sess., 1856. S. Exec. Doc. 76.

Report on the Reconnaissance to the Black Hills by Captain William Ludlow, Corps of Engineers, USA, with Troops under the Command Of Lieutenant Colonel George A. Custer, 7th Cavalry, July and August 1874. 43d Cong., 2d sess., 1875. S. Exec. Doc. 32.

Wounded Knee Massacre: Hearings before the Committee on the Judiciary. 94th Cong., 2d sess., 5–6 February 1976.

U.S. Department of the Army. *Unit Citation and Campaign Participation Credit Register.* Pamphlet 672-1. Washington, D.C.: Government Printing Office, July 1961.

U.S. Statutes at Large, vol. 20 (1878).

NEWSPAPERS

Army and Navy Journal (Washington, D.C.)

Belle Fourche Bee

Belle Fourche Weekly Post

Billings Gazette

Bismarck Tribune

Black Hills Daily Times (Deadwood)

Black Hills Journal (Rapid City)

Black Hills Press (Sturgis)

BIBLIOGRAPHY

Black Hills Weekly Times (Deadwood)

Chicago Tribune

Custer County Chronicle

Deadwood Pioneer

Fourth Cavalry Association News (Annandale, Minn.)

Hot Springs Star

Minneapolis Tribune

Moorhead Advocate

New York Times

Rapid City Daily Journal

St. Paul Pioneer Press

Sentinel (Seventh Cavalry newspaper published at Fort Lincoln, Dakota Territory)

Sioux Falls Argus Leader

Sioux Falls Press

Spearfish Mail

Sturgis Advertiser

Sturgis Tribune

Sturgis Weekly Record

Yankton Press and Dakotian

PUBLISHED SOURCES

Agnew, Brad. *Fort Gibson: Terminal on the Trail of Tears*. Norman: University of Oklahoma Press, 1980.

Alleger, C. N., ed. *History of District Headquarters Company, CCC, Fort Meade, S.D.* Rapid City, S.D.: Johnson and Bordewick Co., 1937.

Andrews, Lieutenant George. "The Twenty-Fifth Regiment of Infantry." In *The Army of the United States*, ed. Theodore F. Rodenbough and William L. Haskin. New York, 1896.

Artichoker, John. *Indians of South Dakota*. Bulletin No. 67A, rev. Pierre, S.D.: Department of Public Instruction, 1956.

Athearn, Robert G. *Forts of the Upper Missouri*. Englewood Cliffs, N.J.: Prentice-Hall, 1967.

Bailey, Dana R. *History of Minnehaha County*. Sioux Falls, S.D., 1899.

Bailey, John W. *Pacifying the Plains: General Alfred Terry and the Decline of the Sioux, 1866–1890*. Westport, Conn.: Greenwood Press, 1979.

Bearss, Edwin C., and A. M. Gibson. *Fort Smith: Little Gibralter on the Arkansas*. Norman: University of Oklahoma Press, 1969.

Bennett, Estelline. *Old Deadwood Days*. New York: Charles Scribner's Sons, 1935.

Blair, William M. "Little Bighorn Is Fought Anew in Pentagon: Relative Urges Army to Clear the Name of Major Reno." *New York Times*, 4 May 1967.

Bracewell, Rozella M. "Utes in Belle Fourche." In *Cowboys and Sodbusters*. Sioux Falls, S.D.: Midwest-Beach, 1969.

Brandes, Ray, ed. *Troopers West: Military and Indian Affairs on the American Frontier*. San Diego: Frontier Heritage Press, 1970.

Brice's Cross Roads, National Battlefield Site, Mississippi. Chicago: Gunthorp-Warren Printing Co., 1946.

Briggs, Harold E. "The Black Hills Gold Rush." *North Dakota Historical Quarterly* 5, no. 2 (January 1931).

———. "Early Freight and Stage Lines in Dakota." *North Dakota Historical Quarterly*, 3, no. 4 (July 1929).

Brown, Jesse, and A. M. Willard. *The Black Hills Trails: A History of the Struggles of the Pioneers*. Rapid City, S.D.: Rapid City Journal Co., 1924.

――――. "Early History of Fort Meade." *Black Hills Weekly,* 9 August 1908.

Buecher, Thomas R. "Fort Niobrara, 1880–1906: Guardian of the Rosebud Sioux." *Nebraska History* 65, no. 3 (Fall 1984).

Carroll, John. *A Bit of Seventh Cavalry History with All Its Warts.* Bryan, Tex.: By the author, 1987.

Carroll, John, and Byron Price. *Roll Call on the Little Big Horn, 28 June 1876.* Fort Collins, Colo: Old Army Press, 1974.

Carroll, John, and Lawrence Frost, eds. *Private Theodore Ewert's Diary of the Black Hills Expedition of 1874.* Piscataway, N.J.: Consultant Resources, 1976.

Casey, Robert J. *The Black Hills and Their Incredible Characters.* Indianapolis: Bobbs-Merrill Co., 1949.

Cassells, Steve E., with David B. Miller and Paul V. Miller. *Paha Sapa: A Cultural Resource Overview of the Black Hills National Forest, South Dakota and Wyoming.* Custer, S.D.: National Park Service, 1984.

Chandler, Lieutenant Colonel Melbourne C. *Of Garry Owen in Glory: The History of the Seventh U.S. Cavalry.* Annandale, Va.: Turnpike Press, 1960.

Clark, H. T. "Freighting to the Black Hills." *Nebraska State Historical Society Proceedings and Collections,* 2d ser., 5, no. 1 (October 1930).

Clem, Alan L. *Prairie State Politics: Popular Democracy in South Dakota.* Washington, D.C.: Public Affairs Press, 1967.

Clowser, Don C. *Dakota Indian Treaties: From Nomad to Reservation.* Deadwood, S.D.: By the author, 1974.

――――. *Deadwood: The Historic City.* Deadwood: Fenwynn Press, 1969.

Cooper, Courtney Ryley, with Poker Alice Tubbs. "Easy Come, Easy Go." *Saturday Evening Post,* 3 December 1927.

"Council Advises VA to Protect Barracks at Fort Meade, S.D." *Preservation News* 11, no. 10 (October 1971).

Cox, John E. "Soldiering in Dakota Territory in the Seventies." *North Dakota Historical Quarterly* 6, no. 1 (October 1931–July 1932).

Cropp, Richard. *The Coyotes: A History of the South Dakota National Guard.* Mitchell, S.D.: Educator Supply Co., 1962.

Curley, Edwin A. *Curley's Guide to the Black Hills.* Mitchell, S.D.: Dakota Wesleyan University Press, 1973.

Curran, John M. "The Companies of the Damned." *Army Magazine,* February 1982.

Dary, David. *Comanche.* Lawrence: University of Kansas Museum of Natural History, 1976.

DeWall, Robb. *The Saga of Sitting Bull's Bones.* Custer, S.D.: Korczak's Heritage, 1984.

Dicks, Samuel E. "A Territory with Many Flags." In *Dakota Panorama,* ed. J. Leonard Jennewein and Jane Boorman. Pierre, S.D.: Dakota Territory Centennial Commission, 1961.

Dodge, Richard Irving. *The Black Hills.* Minneapolis, Minn.: Ross and Haines, 1965.

Du Bois, Charles G. *A Casebook of the Custer Battle: Kick the Dead Lion.* Billings, Mont. By the author, 1954.

———. *The Custer Mystery.* El Segundo, Calif.: Upton and Sons, 1986.

Duratschek, Sister M. Claudia. *Crusading along Sioux Trails: A History of Catholic Indian Missions among the South Dakota Sioux, 1839–1945.* St. Meinrod, Ind.: Grail, 1947.

Dustin, Fred. *The Custer Tragedy: Events Leading Up to and Following the Little Big Horn Campaign of 1876.* Ann Arbor, Mich.: By the author, 1939.

Eastman, Elaine Goodale. *Sister to the Sioux: The Memoirs of Elaine Goodale Eastman, 1885–91.* Lincoln: University of Nebraska Press, 1978.

Elk Creek Pioneer Society. *Echoes thru the Valley.* Elk Creek, S.D.: Elk Creek Pioneer Society, 1968.

Ellison, Douglas W. *Sole Survivor: An Examination of the Frank Finkel Narrative.* Aberdeen, S.D.: Northern Plains Press, 1983.

Feaver, Eric. "Indian Soldiers, 1891–95: An Experiment on the Closing Frontier." *Prologue,* Summer 1975.

Fechet, Colonel E. G. "The Capture of Sitting Bull." *South Dakota Historical Collections* 4 (1908).

Fielder, Mildred. *Poker Alice*. Deadwood, S.D.: Centennial Distributors, 1978.

Finerty, John F. *War-Path and Bivouac; or, The Conquest of the Sioux*. Norman: University of Oklahoma Press, 1961.

Foner, Jack D. *The United States Soldier between Two Wars, 1865–1898: Army Life and Reforms*. New York: Humanities Press, 1970.

"The Forgotten Heroes." *VFW Magazine*, August 1985.

Fourth Cavalry, United States Army, 1855–1930. Fort Meade, S.D.: Old Fort Meade Museum and Historical Association, 1967.

Frazer, Robert W. *Forts of the West*. Norman: University of Oklahoma Press, 1965.

―――, ed. *Mansfield on the Condition of the Western Forts*. Norman: University of Oklahoma Press, 1963.

Frink, Maurice, and Casey Barthelmess. *Photographer on an Army Mule*. Norman: University of Oklahoma Press, 1965.

Frost, Lawrence A. *Custer Album*. Seattle: Superior Publishing Co., 1964.

―――. *Custer Legends*. Bowling Green, Ohio: Bowling Green University Popular Press, 1981.

―――. *Custer's Seventh Cavalry and the Campaign of 1873*. El Segundo, Calif.: Upton and Sons, 1986.

―――, ed. *With Custer in '74: James Calhoun's Diary of the Black Hills Expedition*. Provo, Utah: Brigham Young University Press, 1979.

Gerber, Max E. "The Custer Expedition of 1874: A New Look." *North Dakota History: Journal of the Northern Plains* 40, no. 1 (Winter 1973).

Graham, Colonel William A. *The Reno Court of Inquiry: Abstract of the Official Record of Proceedings*. Harrisburg, Pa..: Stackpole Co., 1954.

Grange, Robert T., Jr. "Fort Robinson: Outpost on the Plains." *Nebraska History* 39, no. 3 (September 1958).

Gray, John S. *Centennial Campaign: The Sioux War of 1876.* Fort Collins, Colo.: Old Army Press, 1976.

Hafen, LeRoy R., and Ann W. Hafen, eds. *Powder River Campaigns and Sawyers Expedition of 1865.* Glendale, Calif.: Arthur H. Clark Co., 1961.

Hall, Bert, ed. *Roundup Years: Old Muddy to the Black Hills.* Pierre, S.D.: State Publishing Co., 1954.

Hammer, Kenneth. *Little Big Horn Biographies.* Hardin, Mont.: Custer Battlefield Historical and Museum Association, 1964.

———. "Major Marcus A. Reno." *New York Posse Brand Book* 8, no. 3 (1961).

Hart, Herbert M. *Old Forts of the Northwest.* Seattle, Wash.: Superior Publishing Co., 1963.

———. *Tour Guide to Old Western Forts.* Boulder, Colo.: Pruett Publishing Co., 1980.

Hassrick, Royal B. *The Sioux: Life and Customs of a Warrior Society.* Norman: University of Oklahoma Press, 1964.

Hayden, Dr. F. V. *Geological Report of the Exploration of the Yellowstone and Missouri Rivers.* Washington, D.C., 1869.

Hedren, Paul L. *With Crook in the Black Hills: Stanley J. Morrow's 1876 Photography Legacy.* Boulder, Colo.: Pruett Publishing Co., 1985.

Heitman, Francis B. *Historical Register and Dictionary of the United States Army.* 2 vols. 1903. Reprint. Urbana: University of Illinois Press, 1965.

Herr, John K., and Edward S. Wallace. *The Story of the U.S. Cavalry, 1775–1942.* New York: Bonanza Books, 1984.

"History of the Fourth Cavalry." *Sturgis Tribune,* 1 June 1938.

"History of the Fourth United States Cavalry." *Army Information Digest,* February 1964.

Holst, Vernon E. *A Study of the 1876 Bismarck to Deadwood Trail.* Belle Fourche, S.D.: Butte County Historical Society, 1983.

BIBLIOGRAPHY

Horgan, Paul. *A Distant Trumpet*. New York: Farrar, Straus and Cudhay, 1951.

Howell, Terri. *St. Thomas Episcopal Parish*. Sturgis, S.D.: By the author, 1987.

"Hubbard Medals Awarded to Stratosphere Explorers." *National Geographic* 69, no. 5 (May 1936).

Hunt, Frazier, and Robert Hunt. *I Fought with Custer: The Story of Sergeant Windolph, Last Survivor of the Battle of the Little Big Horn*. New York: Charles Scribner's Sons, 1953.

Hutton, Paul Andrew. *Phil Sheridan and His Army*. Lincoln: University of Nebraska Press, 1986.

Hyde, George E. *Red Cloud's Folk*. Norman: University of Oklahoma Press, 1937.

———. *A Sioux Chronicle*. Norman: University of Oklahoma Press, 1956.

———. *Spotted Tail's Folk: A History of the Brule Sioux*. Norman: University of Oklahoma Press, 1961.

"It Started Here." *Crossed Sabers Newsletter: A Journal of the U.S. Horse Cavalry Association* 10, no. 1 (1 March 1986).

Jackson, Donald. *Custer's Gold: The United States Cavalry Expedition of 1874*. New Haven: Yale University Press, 1966.

Jennewein, J. Leonard, and Jane Boorman, eds. *Dakota Panorama*. Pierre, S.D.: Dakota Territory Centennial Commission, 1961.

Johnson, Barry C. *Case of Marcus A. Reno*. London: English Westerners Society, 1969.

Johnson, Lieutenant Colonel Leslie LeRoy. *Notes on the Cavalry, 1865–1890*. Little Rock, Ark.: Pioneer Press, 1960.

Johnson, Virginia W. *The Unregimented General: A Biography of Nelson A. Miles*. Boston: Houghton Mifflin Co., 1962.

Kahn, E. J., Jr. "Annals of Crime." *New Yorker*, 11, 18, 25 March, 1 April 1950.

Kellar, Kenneth C. *Seth Bullock: Frontier Marshal*. Aberdeen, S.D.: North Plains Press, 1972.

Kelley, William Fitch. *Pine Ridge 1890*. San Francisco, Calif.: Pierre Bovis, 1971.

King, James T. *War Eagle: A Life of General Eugene A. Carr*. Lincoln: University of Nebraska Press, 1963.

Kingsbury, George W. *History of Dakota Territory*. 2 vols. Chicago: S. J. Clarke Publishing Co., 1915.

Knight, Oliver. *Following the Indian Wars: The Story of the Newspaper Correspondents among the Indian Campaigners*. Norman: University of Oklahoma Press, 1960.

Kobbe, Gustav. "The Story of Our National Anthem." *Woman's World* 30, no. 9 (September 1914).

Krammer, Arnold. *Nazi Prisoners of War in America*. Briarcliff Manor, N.Y.: Stein and Day, 1979.

Krause, Herbert, and Gary D. Olson. *Custer's Prelude to Glory: A Newspaper Accounting of Custer's 1874 Expedition to the Black Hills*. Sioux Falls, S.D.: Brevet Press, 1974.

Lamar, Howard Roberts. *Dakota Territory, 1861–1889: A Study of Frontier Politics*. New Haven: Yale University Press, 1956.

Larsen, Arthur J., ed. "The Black Hills Gold Rush." *North Dakota Historical Quarterly*, 6, no. 3 (October 1931–July 1932).

Laudenschlager, David D. "The Utes in South Dakota, 1906–1908." *South Dakota History* 9, no. 3 (Summer 1979).

Lawrence County. *Some History of Lawrence County*. Pierre, S.D.: State Publishing Co., 1981.

Leckie, William H. *The Buffalo Soldiers: A Narrative of the Negro Cavalry in the West*. Norman: University of Oklahoma Press, 1967.

Lee, Bob. *Gold, Gals, Guns, Guts: The Centennial History of Lawrence County*. Deadwood-Lead, S.D.: Lawrence County Centennial Committee, 1976.

———. "Tragedy Ends an Empire: The Life Story of Sitting Bull." In *Dakota Panorama*, ed. J. Leonard Jennewein and Jane Boorman. Pierre, S.D.: Dakota Territory Centennial Commission, 1961.

————. "Valentine Scrip: The Saga of Land Locations in Southern Dakota Terri-tory." *South Dakota History* 2, no. 3 (Summer 1972).

Lee, Bob, and Dick Williams. *Last Grass Frontier: The South Dakota Stock Grower Heritage*. Rapid City, S.D.: South Dakota Stock Growers Assn., 1964.

McAuliffe, Eugene. *The Seventh United States Cavalry: Too Long Neglected*. Omaha, Nebr.: By the author, 1957.

McCarthy, Dan B. "P. O. W. Country." *VFW Magazine*, August 1966.

McClintock, John. *Pioneer Days in the Black Hills*. Deadwood, S.D.: By the author, 1939.

McGillycuddy, Julia B. *McGillycuddy, Agent*. Stanford: Stanford University Press, 1941.

McGregor, James H. *The Wounded Knee Massacre from the Viewpoint of the Sioux*. Minneapolis, Minn.: Lund Press, 1940.

McLaird, James D., and Lesta V. Turchen. *The Black Hills Expedition of 1875*. Freeman, S.D.: Pine Hill Press, 1975.

————. "Early Black Hills Expeditions." *South Dakota History* 3, no. 4 (Fall 1973), and 4, nos. 1 (Winter 1973), 2 (Spring 1974), 3 (Summer 1974).

————. "Exploring the Black Hills, 1855–1875: Reports of the Government Expedi-tions." *South Dakota History* 4, no. 4 (Fall 1974).

————. "Messages of the Territorial Governors, Chapter 50, General Laws, Memo-rials and Resolutions, Territory of Dakota, 1865–66." *South Dakota Historical Collections* 38 (1976).

McLaughlin, James. *My Friend, the Indian*. Boston: Houghton Mifflin Co., 1910.

Mandat-Grancey, Edmond. *Cow-Boys and Colonels: Narrative of a Journey across the Prairie and over the Black Hills of Dakota*. New York: J. B. Lippincott Co., 1963.

Mattes, Merrill J. *Indians, Infants, and Infantry: Andrew and Elizabeth Burt on the Frontier*. Denver, Colo.: Old West Publishing Co., 1960.

Mattison, Ray H. *The Army Post on the Northern Plains, 1865–1885*. Gering, Nebr.: Oregon Trail Museum Association, 1960.

Milligan, Edward A. *Dakota Twilight: The Standing Rock Sioux, 1874–1890.* Hillsview, N.Y.: Exposition Press, 1976.

Mooney, James. *The Ghost Dance Religion and the Sioux Outbreak of 1890.* Smithsonian Institution, Bureau of American Ethnology, 14th Annual Report. Washington, D.C., 1896.

Murray, Robert A. "The Camp at the Mouth of Red Canyon." *Council for Abandoned Military Posts (CAMP) Periodical* 1, no. 1 (January 1967).

————. *Military Posts in the Powder River Country of Wyoming, 1865–1894.* Lincoln: University of Nebraska Press, 1968.

————. *Military Posts of Wyoming.* Fort Collins, Colo.: Old Army Press, 1974.

Nankivell, John H. *The History of the Twenty-Fifth Regiment, U.S. Infantry.* Fort Collins, Colo.: Old Army Press, 1972.

"National Anthem Honored First in South Dakota." *Middle Border Bulletin* 3, no. 4 (Spring 1944).

Newton, Henry, and Walter P. Jenney. *Report on the Geology and Resources of the Black Hills of Dakota, with Atlas.* Washington, D.C., 1880.

Odell, Thomas E. *Mato Paha: The Story of Bear Butte.* Ann Arbor, Mich.: Edwards Brothers, 1942.

O'Neill, Floyd A. "An Anguished Odyssey: The Flight of the Utes, 1906–08." *Utah Historical Quarterly* 36, no. 4 (Fall 1968).

Palais, Dr. Hyman. "General Crook in Deadwood in 1876." *Black Hills Engineer* 18, no. 1 (January 1930).

————. "A Survey of Early Black Hills History." *Black Hills Engineer* 27, no. 1 (April 1941).

Parker, Watson. *Gold in the Black Hills.* Norman: University of Oklahoma Press, 1966.

————. "Report of the Reverend Samuel D. Hinman of an Expedition to the Black Hills during August, 1874." *Bits and Pieces* 5, no. 11 (1969).

Pfaller, Louis L. *James McLaughlin: The Man with an Indian Heart.* New York: Vantage Press, 1978.

Pillsbury, Eleanor Lawler, with Virginia Huck. *My Family Story.* Minneapolis, Minn.: Southways, 1972.

Potomac Corral of The Westerners, Publications Committee. *Great Western Indian Fights.* Lincoln: University of Nebraska Press, 1960.

Powell, Peter J. *Sweet Medicine: The Continuing Role of the Sacred Arrows, the Sun Dance, and the Sacred Buffalo Hat in Northern Cheyenne History.* 2 vols. Norman: University of Oklahoma Press, 1969.

Pressler, Larry. *U.S. Senators from the Prairie.* Vermillion: University of South Dakota Press, 1982.

Price, Byron. *The Utopian Experience: The Army and the Indian, 1890–1897.* Fort Collins, Colo.: Valor and Arms Press, 1975.

Prucha, Francis Paul. *Broadaxe and Bayonet: The Role of the United States Army in the Development of the Northwest, 1815–1860.* Lincoln: University of Nebraska Press, 1967.

———. *Documents of United States Indian Policy.* Lincoln: University of Nebraska Press, 1975.

Rambow, Charles. "The Ku Klux Klan in the 1920s: A Concentration in the Black Hills." *South Dakota History* 4, no. 1 (Winter 1973).

Rickey, Don, Jr. *Forty Miles a Day on Beans and Hay: The Enlisted Soldier Fighting the Indian Wars.* Norman: University of Oklahoma Press, 1963.

———. *$10 Horse, $40 Saddle: Cowboy Clothing, Arms, Tools and Horse Gear in the 1880's.* Fort Collins, Colo.: Old Army Press, 1976.

Robinson, Doane. *A History of the Dakota or Sioux Indians.* Minneapolis, Minn.: Ross and Haines, 1956.

———. "History of the Sioux Indians." *South Dakota Historical Collections* 2 (1904).

———. "Treaties with Indians Opening Dakota Soil to Settlement." *South Dakota Historical Collections* 1 (1902).

Robinson, Will G. "Utes Invade South Dakota." *Wi-Iyohi* 7, no. 3 (1 June 1953).

Rodenbough, Theodore F., and William L. Haskin, eds. *The Army of the United States.* New York, 1896.

Rosen, Rev. Peter. *Pa-Ha-Sa-Pah; or, The Black Hills of South Dakota.* St. Louis, Mo., 1895.

Ruby, Robert H. *The Oglala Sioux.* New York: Vantage Press, 1955.

Sawick, James A. *Cavalry Regiments of the U.S. Army.* Dumfries, Va.: Wyvern Publications, 1985.

Schell, Herbert S. "Dakota Territory during the Eighteen Sixties." *University of South Dakota Governmental Research Bureau,* Report No. 30, August 1954.

————. *History of South Dakota.* Lincoln: University of Nebraska Press, 1961.

Schmitt, Martin F. *General George Crook: His Autobiography.* Norman: University of Oklahoma Press, 1946.

Schmitt, Martin F., and Dee Brown. *Fighting Indians of the West.* New York: Charles Scribner's Sons, 1948.

Scott, Hugh L. *Some Memories of a Soldier.* New York: Century Co., 1928.

Scudder, Ralph E. *Custer Country.* Portland, Oreg.: Binfords and Mort Publishers, 1963.

"The Seventh U.S. Cavalry Memorial Association Commemorating the Battle of the Little Big Horn, June 25–26, 1876." *Seventh U.S. Cavalry Memorial Association,* 11 November 1957.

Severn, Bill. *William Howard Taft: The President Who Became Chief Justice.* New York: David McKay Co., 1970.

Sheridan, Lieutenant General Philip H. *Outline Descriptions of the Posts in the Military Division of the Missouri.* Facsimile ed. Fort Collins, Colo.: Old Army Press, 1969.

————. *Personal Memoirs of P. H. Sheridan, General, United States Army.* 2 vols. New York, 1888.

————. *Record of Engagements with Hostile Indians within the Military Division of the Missouri, from 1868 to 1882.* Washington, D.C., 1881.

Sheridan, Philip H., and Michael V. Sheridan. *Personal Memoirs of Philip Henry Sheridan, General, United States Army, New and Enlarged Edition, with an Account of His Life from 1871 to His Death in 1888.* 2 vols. New York: D. Appleton and Co., 1904.

Sherman, Gen. W. T. *Memoirs of General W. T. Sherman.* 2 vols. New York, 1892.

Shiflet, Kenneth. *The Convenient Coward.* Harrisburg, Pa.: Stackpole Co., 1961.

Smith, George Martin. *South Dakota: Its History and Its People.* 3 vols. Chicago: S. J. Clarke Publishing Co., 1915.

Smith, Helen Huntington. *The War on Powder River: The History of an Insurrection.* Lincoln: University of Nebraska Press, 1966.

Smith, Rex Alan. *Moon of Popping Trees.* New York: Reader's Digest Press, 1975.

Spring, Agnes Wright. *The Cheyenne and Black Hills Stage and Express Routes.* Lincoln: University of Nebraska Press, 1948.

Standing Bear, Luther. *Land of the Spotted Eagle.* Lincoln: University of Nebraska Press, 1933.

Stevens, Captain A. W. "Exploring the Stratosphere." *National Geographic Magazine* 64, no. 4 (October 1934).

———. "Man's Farthest Aloft." *National Geographic Magazine* 69, no. 1 (January 1936).

———. "National Geographic Society-United States Army Air Corps Stratosphere Flight of 1935 in Balloon Explorer II: Contributed Technical Papers Stratosphere Series No. 2." *National Geographic Magazine* 71, no. 3 (March 1937).

———. "Scientific Results of the World Record Stratosphere Flight." *National Geographic Magazine* 69, no. 5 (May 1936).

Sullivan, Charles J. *Army Posts and Towns: The Baedeker of the Army.* Los Angeles: Haynes Corporation, Publishers, 1942.

Sully, Langdon. *No Tears for the General: The Life of Alfred Sully, 1821–1879.* Palo Alto, Calif.: American West Publishing Co., 1974.

Sundstrom, Jessie Y., ed. *Custer County History to 1976.* Custer, S.D.: Custer County Historical Society, 1977.

Tallent, Annie. *The Black Hills; or, Last Hunting Grounds of the Dakotahs*. 1899. Reprint. Sioux Falls, S.D.: Brevet Press, 1974.

Tarbell, Wright. "History of Dakota Militia and the South Dakota National Guard." *South Dakota Historical Collections* 6 (1912).

Terrell, John Upton, and Colonel George Walton. *Faint the Trumpet Sounds*. New York: David McKay Co., 1966.

"2765th Company, SCS-6, Fort Meade, S.D." *Official Annual, Civilian Conservation Corps, Nebraska-South Dakota District, August 1937*. Baton Rouge, La.: Direct Advertising Co., 1937.

Upton, Richard, ed. *Fort Custer on the Big Horn, 1877–1898*. Glendale, Calif.: Arthur H. Clark Co., 1973.

———. *The Indian As a Soldier at Fort Custer, Montana*. El Segundo, Calif.: Upton and Sons, 1983.

Urwin, Gregory J. W. *The United States Cavalry: An Illustrated History*. Dorset, Eng.: Blandford Books, 1983.

Utley, Robert M. *Cavalier in Buckskin: George Armstrong Custer and the Western Military Frontier*. Norman: University of Oklahoma Press, 1988.

———. *Frontier Regulars: The United States Army and the Indian, 1866–1891*. New York: Macmillan Publishing Co., 1973.

———. *Frontiersmen in Blue: The United States Army and the Indian, 1848–1865*. New York: Macmillan, 1967.

———. *The Indian Frontier of the American West, 1846–1890*. Albuquerque: University of New Mexico Press, 1984.

———. *The Last Days of the Sioux Nation*. New Haven: Yale University Press, 1963.

———. "War Houses in the Sioux Country." *Montana, the Magazine of Western History*, Autumn 1985.

Vestal, Stanley. *New Sources of Indian History, 1850–1891*. Norman: University of Oklahoma Press, 1934.

――――. *Warpath and Council Fire*. New York: Random House, 1948.

――――. *Warpath: The True Story of the Fighting Sioux Told in a Biography of Chief White Bull*. 1948. Reprint. Lincoln: University of Nebraska Press, 1984.

Waldman, Charley W. *Early Day History of Sturgis and Fort Meade in the Beautiful Black Hills of South Dakota*. Sturgis, S.D.: By the author, 1964.

――――. *Sturgis and Fort Meade, 1874–1910*. Sturgis, S.D.: By the author, 1964.

Ware, Captain Eugene F. *The Indian War of 1864*. Lincoln: University of Nebraska Press, 1960.

War of the Rebellion: Official Records of the Union and Confederate Armies. Series L, 70 vols. Washington, D.C.: Government Printing Office, 1902.

Warren, Gouverneur Kemble. "Explorations in Nebraska and Dakota," *South Dakota Historical Collections* 11 (1922).

――――. *Preliminary Report of Explorations in Nebraska and Dakota in the Years 1855–56–57*. Washington, D.C., 1857.

Weland, Gerald. "Star Spangled Night." *Elks Magazine* 66, no. 4 (October 1987).

Wemett, W. M. "Custer's Expedition to the Black Hills in 1874." *North Dakota Historical Quarterly* 6, no. 3 (October 1931–July 1932).

Whitman, S. E. *The Troopers: An Informal History of the Plains Cavalry, 1865–1890*. New York: Hastings House Publishers, 1962.

Wike, John W. "Our Regimental Heritage: The Soldier's Link with Tradition." *Army Information Digest*, February 1944.

Williamson, John P. *A Brother to the Sioux*. Clements, Minn.: Sunnycrest Publishing, 1980.

Williamson, William. *William Williamson: An Autobiography*. Rapid City, S.D.: By the author, 1964.

Wilson, D. Ray. *Fort Kearny on the Platte*. Dundee, Ill.: Crossroads Communications, 1980.

INDEX